JOBS UNDONE

JOBS UNDONE

Reshaping the Role of Governments toward Markets and Workers in the Middle East and North Africa

Asif M. Islam, Dalal Moosa, and Federica Saliola

WORLD BANK GROUP

Contents

BOXES

FIGURES

TABLES

Foreword

There is no more important agenda for the Middle East and North Africa (MENA) region today than the creation of more and better jobs, especially for young people. More than half the population—nearly 250 million people across the region—are under the age of 30. They are increasingly educated and ambitious, looking outward to their peers around the world and demanding decent lives and better government services.

Yet, a decade since one of the most significant movements in the region, the frustrations that ignited what came to be called the "Arab Spring" still dominate MENA's economies. Many young people continue to be idle; others suffer from unemployment and underemployment, including among the better educated; women remain excluded from economic activity; and informal, and hence unprotected, employment still prevails. People in the region feel these economic pressures. Nearly three-quarters of respondents to the Arab Barometer wave of 2018, especially among younger generations, viewed their economic circumstances to be bad or very bad and clearly worsening over time.

These preexisting conditions are now amplified by the repercussions of the coronavirus (COVID-19) pandemic. The pandemic has shattered businesses and slashed jobs. It is pushing millions of people into poverty in the region, and its impact on vulnerable workers and women is worrying. All this is threatening to set back years of reforms.

This report argues that the main reason behind this unmet jobs challenge in the MENA region is a lack of market contestability. New evidence generated for this report shows that the governments of MENA countries are visibly active in many economic sectors through state-owned enterprises (SOEs), much more than in other middle- and high-income countries. And while the presence of SOEs alone may not be a major issue if the playing field is leveled, SOEs in the region receive favorable treatment and are exempt from competition laws that regulate private enterprises.

The presence of the state is also evident in other ways. This report shows that formal manufacturing firms in the region are much more likely to be politically connected than in countries with similar income levels. At the macro level, the contribution of the public sector to capital accumulation is still significant in many countries. At the same time, labor regulations instituted by the state remain relatively restrictive, hindering the movement of workers into better jobs, while also providing insufficient protection to these workers. And despite improvements on the legal front for women, much more can be done to unleash their untapped potential.

Governments in the MENA region can avoid another lost decade for current and future generations. And there is no time like the present. The COVID-19 pandemic, as difficult as it has been, is also an opportunity to support a resilient and inclusive recovery that can generate better jobs while addressing both the immediate devastation wrought by COVID-19 and longer-term challenges. In fact, many MENA governments have shown innovative resilience in the face of this crisis, instituting some of the most rapid initiatives of the past decade. Emergency cash transfers were swiftly deployed for the poor and vulnerable in the Arab Republic of Egypt, Jordan, Morocco, Tunisia, and West Bank and Gaza. This action speaks multitudes to the adage, "Where there is a will, there is a way." MENA is no different.

Reimagining a new recovery requires both brave and politically feasible reforms, and it all starts with a new social contract. This report argues that governments must reshape their relationships toward the private sector, toward workers, and, equally important, toward women. The new social contract must replace state involvement with fair regulation and transparent enforcement. Instead of being active in economic sectors, the state must unleash a well-regulated competitive private sector. Instead of controlling worker transitions through a labor code designed for the nineteenth century, the state must rethink its social protection and labor market programs. And instead of guarding the legacy of some historical and social norms, the states in the MENA region must be the faithful guardians of gender equity.

The fact is that the youth of this vibrant region are already blazing trails. Not only do they continue to force their hopes and sheer will on MENA governments, but they are also innovating and taking risks in the market. This report showcases seven entrepreneurial young men and women from the Mediterranean to the Gulf who have built businesses and created jobs—especially in the digital space—despite difficult circumstances. We hear the voices of a young Jordanian creator of an online platform promoting quality education, a food processing entrepreneur who advocates for women empowerment in West Bank, an innovative Tunisian beverage manufacturer, the founder of a safe carpool system to share trip costs in Morocco, a passionate Egyptian developer of a pharmaceutical delivery platform, a Lebanese entrepreneur whose platform is improving the profitability and dining experience of restaurants around the world, and a young Saudi creator of an application to help women and other customers run errands.

Young people in MENA are waiting for no one.

Ferid Belhaj
Regional Vice President
Middle East and North Africa
The World Bank

Acknowledgments

The 2022 Middle East and North Africa (MENA) flagship report, *Jobs Undone: Reshaping the Role of Governments toward Markets and Workers in the Middle East and North Africa*, is a product of the Office of the Chief Economist of the MENA region and the Social Protection and Jobs Global Practice (SPJ) of the World Bank. The report was initiated under the leadership of Rabah Arezki (former Chief Economist for the MENA region) and completed under the overall guidance of Roberta Gatti (current Chief Economist for the MENA region) and Ian Walker (Manager, Jobs Group). The report was coauthored by Asif M. Islam, Dalal Moosa, and Federica Saliola.

The team thanks Maho Hatayama for her work on labor regulation (see the working paper for this volume, "Revisiting Labor Market Regulations in the Middle East and North Africa" [Hatayama 2021]) and her assistance throughout the production of the report. The team also thanks collaborators from the competition team in the Finance, Competitiveness, and Innovation Global Practice, including Seidu Dauda, Graciela Miralles Murciego, Georgiana Pop, and Azza Raslan, for collecting and analyzing the product market regulation data (see the background paper, "Restrictive Regulation as a Challenge for Competition, Productivity, and Jobs in the MENA Region: Closing the Gap" [Dauda et al., forthcoming]) and for their help in conceptualizing the links between market contestability, competition, and jobs outcomes. The team is grateful to Mariana Viollaz and Hernan Winkler for their work on the skill content of jobs and for their work in conceptualizing the flagship program through the concept review and initiation of the research work. The team thanks Hisham Jabi for his work on the seven case studies, and the young entrepreneurs who shared their stories and inputs from across the MENA region: the Arab Republic of Egypt, Jordan, Lebanon, Morocco, Saudi Arabia, Tunisia, and West Bank. The team thanks Giuseppe Bertola for his help with the conceptualization of the political economy in the flagship. The team also thanks the Women, Business and the Law Group for their support with the analysis of gender laws. Finally, the team thanks Shaimaa Yassin for her work on the analysis of the labor market.

The team is also grateful for the input, comments, and feedback during the concept and later review stages from Angela Elzir Assy, Andrea Barone, Kathleen G. Beegle, Anush Bezhanyan, Dorothée Boccanfuso, Kamel Braham, Hana Brixi, Leila Dagher, Andreas Eberhard, Ahmed Galal, Dorina Peteva Georgieva, Alvaro Gonzalez, Caren Grown, Arvo Kuddo, Prakash Loungani, Mohamed Ali Marouani, Denis Medvedev, Dino Merotto, Mustapha Nabli, Cristobal Ridao-Cano, Bob Rijkers, Javier Sanchez-Reaza, Tea Trumbic, Hulya Ulku, and Michael Weber. The team is also grateful for the further input and support from Daniel Lederman and from the MENA Country Directors Issam A. Abousleiman, Jesko S. Hentschel, Saroj Kumar Jha, and Marina Wes.

Helpful guidance and comments were provided by Ferid Belhaj (Regional Vice President) and Michal Rutkowski (Global Director, SPJ). The team thanks discussants and other participants at the May 2021 authors' workshop for their valuable feedback. The team thanks the World Bank Jobs Group for the extensive consultation. The team also thanks the participants of the virtual consultative workshop organized by the Center for Mediterranean Integration and the Policy Center for the New South in June 2021, and the organizers, Giulia Marchesini and Blanca Moreno-Dodson.

Last, but certainly not least, the team thanks the publishing production team for bringing this report to its final stage—namely, Steve Pazdan for managing the production of the report and Nancy Morrison for editing the manuscript, as well as Jihane El Khoury Roederer and Christel El Saneh for designing the report's look and generating the creative illustrations. Administrative support was provided by Harifera Raobelison and Swati Raychaudhuri.

REFERENCES

Dauda, Seidu, Graciela Miralles Murciego, Georgiana Pop, and Azza Raslan. Forthcoming. "Restrictive Regulation as a Challenge for Competition, Productivity, and Jobs in the MENA Region: Closing the Gap." Background paper for *Jobs Undone: Reshaping the Role of Governments toward Markets and Workers in the Middle East and North Africa*. World Bank, Washington, DC.

Hatayama, Maho. 2021. "Revisiting Labor Market Regulations in the Middle East and North Africa." Jobs Working Paper 64, World Bank, Washington, DC. https://openknowledge.worldbank.org/handle/10986/36887.

About the Authors

Asif M. Islam is a senior economist in the Office of the Chief Economist for the Middle East and North Africa region. He has written on a wide range of issues related to economic development, with a focus on the private sector. He has published in peer-reviewed journals on entrepreneurship, technology, informality, and gender. He has coauthored several reports, including the *World Development Report 2019: The Changing Nature of Work* and *What's Holding Back the Private Sector in MENA? Lessons from the Enterprise Survey*. He holds a PhD in applied economics from the University of Maryland at College Park.

Dalal Moosa is an economist with the Social Protection and Jobs Global Practice at the World Bank, focusing on the Middle East and North Africa region. She has worked on operations in several countries in the region and Sub-Saharan Africa, focusing on areas related to social protection, the labor market, and productive inclusion. She has launched several surveys to capture labor demand and skills in the private sector, as well as the impact of COVID-19 on firms. She joined the World Bank as a Young Professional and holds a PhD in economics from the University of Paris 1–Panthéon-Sorbonne in France and the Catholic University of Louvain in Belgium.

Federica Saliola is a lead economist with the Social Protection and Jobs Global Practice at the World Bank. She was the codirector of the *World Development Report 2019: The Changing Nature of Work*. Under her intellectual leadership, several World Bank global reports have been published, including reports in the *Enabling the Business of Agriculture* and *Benchmarking Public Procurement* series. She has published in peer-reviewed journals, including studies on firm productivity, global value chains, and the impact of regulation on growth and competition. She has also contributed to several World Bank reports, including *The Environment for Women's Entrepreneurship in the Middle East and North Africa* and *Golden Growth: Restoring the Lustre of the European Economic Model*. She holds a PhD in economics and a laurea in political science from the University of Rome, la Sapienza.

Executive Summary

A decade after the first spark of the Arab Spring, large shares of healthy and capable working-age populations remain excluded from the labor force and employment altogether in the Middle East and North Africa (MENA) region. This is most evident for youth and women. Nearly 1 in 3 youth (32 percent) aged 15 to 24 in MENA are not engaged in employment, education, or training (NEET). The youth unemployment rate in MENA is the highest in the world—estimated at around 26 percent (as of 2019)—and has been persistently so for the past two decades. The share of employment that is informal (defined as lacking social security contributions, whether for pensions, disability, sickness, or other risks) varies within the region but remains notably high. The share of informal employment is estimated to be as high as 77 percent of total employment in Morocco, 69 percent in the Arab Republic of Egypt, and 64 percent in West Bank and Gaza, and as low as about 16 percent in Bahrain. Restrictions on women in the labor market also persist. Female labor force participation, averaging about 20 percent, is still the lowest in the world. Finally, the jobs available are emphatically not the jobs of the future. This report analyzes the task content of jobs and finds that workers in those countries in the region where data are available, including Egypt, Jordan, and Tunisia, perform significantly fewer tasks that require nonroutine interpersonal and analytical skills—the jobs of the future in both the public and private sectors.

These preexisting conditions are now amplified by the repercussions of the coronavirus (COVID-19) pandemic. The pandemic has shattered businesses and slashed jobs. It is pushing millions of people into poverty in the region, and its impact on young workers and women is worrying. All this is threatening to set back years of reforms.

Despite the daunting challenges, the youth of this vibrant region are not discouraged and are already blazing trails. Not only do they continue to force their hopes and sheer will on MENA governments, but they are also innovating and taking risks in the market. This report showcases seven entrepreneurial young men and women from the Mediterranean to the Gulf who have built businesses and created jobs, especially in the digital space, despite difficult circumstances. The entrepreneurs in the case studies range from a young Jordanian creator of a quality education platform, to a food processing entrepreneur who advocates for women empowerment in the West Bank, to an innovative Tunisian beverage manufacturer, to the founder of a safe carpool system in Morocco, to a passionate Egyptian developer of a platform to deliver pharmaceuticals, to a Lebanese entrepreneur finding ways to improve the dining experience of restaurants around the world, to a young Saudi creator of an application to help women and others run errands safely.

Governments in the region must avoid another lost decade for current and future generations. It is time to attain the economic potential of a growing, competent, and ambitious labor force. *If not now, then when?*

This report takes a step back and asks: Why has the jobs challenge remained unmet? To answer this question, the report uses a comprehensive framework of looking at jobs in the region, with a particular focus on labor demand and the creation of more and productive jobs. To do so, the report draws on several new data sources. In addition to this in-depth analysis of the region's labor market and macroeconomic performance, the report makes three key contributions.

First, the report's conceptual framework provides an approach to explain how the region's product market influences labor market outcomes. This approach suggests that the number and quality of jobs depend on the ease of entry, growth, and exit of firms in the economy—so-called market contestability. Most of the region's economies lack market contestability. The report argues that the lack of market contestability makes it hard for new firms to start up and expand—so employment cannot grow fast enough to keep up with the growth of the working-age population.

Second, this report offers a new glimpse into the evolution of the private sector over the years, using two rounds of the World Bank Enterprise Surveys (WBES) available for the first time for several economies in the region. The report shows that limited market dynamism and stunted job creation continue to depress MENA's sclerotic private sector. In 2019, only 6 percent of firms surveyed across the MENA economies were young firms (at most five years old), and this share on average fell between 2012 and 2019. In addition, a low share of private sector firms in the MENA region invest in physical capital (fixed assets) or in their workforce. Only 1 in 4 firms on average invested in physical capital as of 2019. Research and development spending is also low and declining in the region. And, using a measure of political connection available for the first time in the WBES, this report shows that about 8 percent of firms in MENA, on average, affirmed that the owner, chief executive officer, or top manager (or any of the board members of the firm) has been elected or appointed to a political position in the country. Shares vary among countries, with the highest share reaching 28 percent of firms in Tunisia. Finally, MENA's private sector continues to pose barriers for women. Several of the MENA region's shortcomings are also reflected in the region's macroeconomic performance. Little of the region's recent growth has come from growth in labor productivity, and little has come from structural change (workers moving toward more productive sectors).

Third, the report highlights the importance of understanding the policies and regulations that can hinder market contestability. Product market regulations (PMRs) are particularly relevant in this context because they affect the costs that firms face when they enter the market, and the degree of competition among firms already operating in the market. The rigidity or flexibility of these regulations directly affect the number of firms that operate, their growth, and their ability to create jobs. This report presents new evidence on PMRs in Egypt, Jordan, Kuwait, Morocco, Saudi Arabia, Tunisia, the United Arab Emirates, and West Bank and Gaza. For the first time, the data collected on PMRs permit comparisons against two sets of comparators: 37 high-income countries and 14 upper-middle-income countries.

The PMR analysis reveals three aspects that weaken the private sector and reduce market contestability for most countries in the MENA region. First, state presence through state-owned enterprises (SOEs) is still significant, even in sectors where the economic rationale for it is unclear and the sector could benefit from private sector involvement, such as manufacturing, accommodation and food and beverage services, trade, and construction.

Second, there is little competitive neutrality that would level the playing field between these SOEs and their private sector peers. The closeness of these SOEs to governments results in favoritism and exemptions. The fact that many MENA countries have agencies that act as both regulators and operators weakens competitive neutrality. Tax exceptions remain in place that favor SOEs. Furthermore, the advantages that SOEs reap from being close to the government also result in preferential access to finance and subsidies.

Third, price controls are still prevalent. All the MENA economies analyzed control the price of staples (such as milk and bread) and liquefied petroleum gas (LPG). Almost all of them control prices for gasoline and medicine. This is far higher than the share of countries that do so among upper-middle-income countries (40 percent) and high-income countries (10 percent). Often viewed as a pillar of the welfare state, such controls reduce incentives for greater productivity and efficiency. Meanwhile, mechanisms to assess the negative impact of regulations remain limited.

This report scrutinizes the regulatory role of the state through two additional dimensions: labor regulations and taxes, and "gendered" laws that differentiate between men and women. The analysis shows that in some MENA economies, labor regulations—including relatively high severance pay—limit companies from firing existing workers or hiring new ones, while the lack of unemployment benefits hurts those who lose their jobs. Labor taxes are high and comprise a significant share of the tax obligations of firms and workers; fixed-term contracts, which would open up opportunities for other workers, are not common; and coverage and enforcement of the minimum wage is limited. When it comes to gender-differentiated laws, despite reforms enacted over the past few years, women in MENA continue to face unfair laws that disempower them economically. In practice, women face multiple layers of legal restrictions and inequality in entering and participating in the labor market.

Reimagining a new recovery requires both brave and politically feasible reforms—and it all starts with a new social contract. This report argues that the road to contestability and better jobs in the MENA region should be implemented through a multipronged approach in three key reform areas: (1) leveling the playing field in product markets, given the high presence of the state (product market regulations); (2) reshaping the relationship between the government and workers (labor market regulations and social protection systems); and (3) fostering women's inclusion in all economic spheres (gendered laws). Interventions on these three fronts are essential to forging a new social contract in MENA (figure ES.1).

Figure ES.1 Toward a new social contract through contestable markets

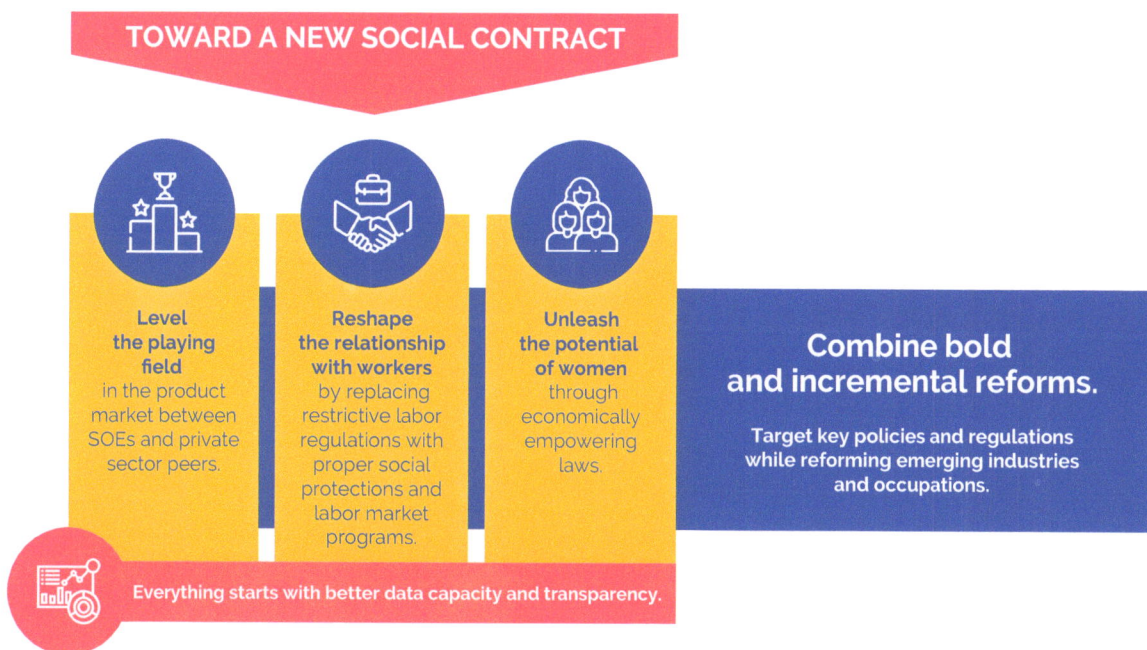

TOWARD A NEW SOCIAL CONTRACT

Level the playing field in the product market between SOEs and private sector peers.

Reshape the relationship with workers by replacing restrictive labor regulations with proper social protections and labor market programs.

Unleash the potential of women through economically empowering laws.

Combine bold and incremental reforms. Target key policies and regulations while reforming emerging industries and occupations.

Everything starts with better data capacity and transparency.

Source: Flagship team elaboration.
Note: SOEs = state-owned enterprises.

At the same time, given the challenging political economy of undertaking and instituting reforms in MENA, the report argues that it is important to carefully sequence reforms to promote greater market contestability and sometimes to adopt an incremental approach. Another possible approach to finding a politically feasible path to reform is to focus first on emerging sectors where there are few incumbents and where interest groups have less power, so there is less disruption to current workers and vested interests. This focus can facilitate the emergence of new occupations—and the new activities can even be complementary to existing jobs, rather than replacing them. The digital economy and the green economy are good examples of rapidly emerging new sectors where incremental reforms might set in motion structural transformations. Last, but certainly not least, the road to contestability needs better data and transparency, which are lacking in most MENA economies, constraining both evidence-based policy making and effective implementation.

Abbreviations

ALMPs	active labor market policies
CEO	chief executive officer
COVID-19	coronavirus disease 2019 (SARS-CoV-2)
GCC	Gulf Cooperation Council
GDP	gross domestic product
ILO	International Labour Organization
ILOSTAT	International Labour Organization Labour Statistics
IT	information technology
MENA	Middle East and North Africa
NEET	not in employment, education, or training
OECD	Organisation for Economic Co-operation and Development
PMRs	product market regulations
R&D	research and development
RIA	Regulatory Impact Assessment
SOE	state-owned enterprise
TPA	third-party access
VAT	value added tax
WBES	World Bank Enterprise Surveys
WBL	Women, Business and the Law (World Bank)

CHAPTER 1

Introduction: Meeting the Jobs Challenge in the Middle East and North Africa

INTRODUCTION

It has been a decade since the first spark of the Arab Spring, when large waves of increasingly well-educated and ambitious youth took to the streets in the Middle East and North Africa (MENA) region in search of better lives and better services. Yet, despite the optimism and hope that brimmed at the time, the past decade has not been one of notable prosperity. Turmoil has continued in many countries, and new conflicts and fragility have emerged in others. The growth of real GDP per capita has been limited compared to income peers, and even negative for some high-income Gulf Cooperation Council countries. Then came the coronavirus (COVID-19) pandemic, increasing vulnerability and poverty, slashing economic activity and employment, and putting tremendous pressure on the region's already tight fiscal space.

The result has been a continuously disappointing jobs reality for MENA's sizeable and healthy working-age population (see chapter 2). Over the past two decades, the MENA region has seen a large rise in 20- to 34-year-olds as a share of the population compared to other regions around the world. This share peaked in 2010, to constitute almost 30 percent of the population and continues to be high today, second only to the South Asia region.

> *Any society that does not succeed in tapping into the energy and creativity of its youth will be left behind.*
>
> *—Kofi Annan*

Yet, many youths continue to be unemployed. Youth unemployment rates in MENA have been persistently the highest in the world over the past few decades. Moreover, the share of youth that are not in employment, education, or training also remains high, even among the high-income countries of the region. Meanwhile, women continue to be underrepresented in the workforce. Female labor force participation, averaging about 20 percent, is the lowest in the world. And for those who cannot afford to be idle or unemployed, informality awaits. In fact, for younger and more educated cohorts across several countries in the region, the probability of being informally employed, without social insurance, has increased over time—especially as public sector hiring has declined. Evidence from some countries in the region shows that informality is not necessarily a stepping-stone into something better. Wage differentials exist, and transitions from informality to formality are generally limited.

At the same time, the jobs of the MENA region are emphatically not the jobs of the future. In 2018, only one-quarter of the region's employed workers were in high-skill occupations, while almost half were in medium-skill occupations that are prone to automation. The share of high-skill occupations is even lower when looking at the private sector alone. New analysis on the task content of jobs, done for this report, shows that workers typically perform fewer tasks that require nonroutine interpersonal and analytical skills—the jobs of the future. Compared to countries like Chile and Turkey, both public and private sector workers in MENA undertake fewer nonroutine tasks; and those in the private sector perform the least. Even among higher-skilled occupations, nonroutine tasks, especially analytical ones, are more limited than in comparator countries.

During the pandemic, these outcomes undoubtedly worsened, affecting not only people's livelihoods, but also the health of workers and their families. Initial evidence from various phone surveys conducted during 2020 shows that shortly after the outbreak, many workers were unable to work altogether. This loss of work was even higher among private sector workers as governments deferred laying off their staff. It was also more pronounced among self-employed workers. While some signs of recovery emerged in 2021, informal workers and female workers appear to still bear the brunt of the pandemic and its ensuing economic downturn.

This report takes a step back and asks: Why has the jobs challenge remained unmet over the past couple of decades?

To answer this question, the report uses a comprehensive framework of looking at jobs in the region, with a particular focus on labor demand and the creation of more and productive jobs (see chapter 3). While there may be many reasons behind limited quantity and quality job creation, the report argues the main culprit is a lack of market contestability, which is the ease of entry, growth, and exit of firms in the economy. This lack of contestability makes it hard for new firms to start up and expand—so employment cannot grow fast enough to keep up with the growth of the working-age population (see chapter 4).

The region has seen notable improvements in access to education over the past decades, with one of the highest rates of intergenerational education mobility in the world. It has also maintained a relatively open relationship to the rest of the world in terms of trade. However, the one constant over time has been limited competition and market contestability that has prohibited a thriving and productive private sector, which is the cornerstone of good jobs. Meanwhile, the state continues to play an important role in both employment and market activity. As a result, often, private firms that are "outsiders" lack a "level playing field" on which to operate, much less thrive.

The result is that for too long, limited market dynamism and stunted job creation have been evident in MENA's sclerotic private sector. Findings from two rounds of the World Bank Enterprise Surveys, available for the first time in the region and analyzed for this report, show that few new formal firms enter the market, few grow, and those that exit are not necessarily the less productive ones. Moreover, firms in MENA do not invest much in physical capital, in their workers, or in innovation. This has led to both meager job creation and low productivity gains—with the situation deteriorating over time. Much of MENA's anemic private sector is also still intertwined with the state. Data available for the first time across many countries show that the share of firms that are politically connected is much higher in MENA than in other regions and countries with similar levels of income ("peers").

These shortcomings are also reflected in the region's macroeconomic performance. Little of the region's recent growth has come from growth in labor productivity, and little has come from structural change (workers moving toward more productive sectors). The low level of productivity growth, however, is not due to low levels of capital per capita. Most MENA countries have levels of capital per capita comparable to their income peers and exceed their income peers in terms of capital per worker. However, a considerable legacy of public capital accumulation has led to much higher shares of public capital than peers. This raises issues of crowding out the private sector as well as inefficiency in capital allocation. Moreover, other countries around the world are clearly catching up to MENA. The growth rate of the accumulation of capital per capita has slowed in the region over the past two decades.

This sclerosis of the labor market and the private sector, and the implications for the whole economy, cannot continue to be a feature of the MENA region in the future. The region's growing population in the face of its tightening fiscal space and a slow road to COVID-19 recovery necessitate action. To advance this urgent agenda, MENA governments will need a clearer understanding of the policies and regulations that can hinder market contestability in the region.

Product market regulations (PMRs) are particularly relevant because they affect the costs that firms face when they enter the market for goods and services, and the degree of competition between the firms that already exist in this market. New evidence on PMRs in eight economies generated for this report shows that MENA has a much higher prevalence of state-owned enterprises (SOEs) than in comparable middle- and high-income countries. SOEs operate not only in sectors with a natural monopoly or other intractable market failures, but also in sectors where private firms could generate better outcomes (subject, as appropriate, to adequate regulation). MENA's SOEs typically benefit from exemptions from competition and extensive state support. And in many countries, government agencies act as both regulators and operators, flouting the basic principles of separation of functions and undermining competitive neutrality. At the same time, instead of providing targeted assistance to the poor and vulnerable, governments continue to control retail prices for some products that are regarded as important to the cost of living, subsidizing the nonpoor while potentially undermining firms and jobs in these activities (see chapter 4).

Moreover, the report analyzes two other important regulatory dimensions: labor regulations and taxes; and "gendered" laws that differentiate between men and women. The analysis shows that some MENA economies have somewhat restrictive labor regulations, including relatively high severance pay, while lacking unemployment benefits. Some economies also feature a significant share of labor taxes in the tax obligations of firms and workers; limited use of fixed-term contracts; and limited coverage and enforcement of the minimum wage. When it comes to gender-differentiated laws, despite reforms over the past few years, women in MENA face unfair laws that disempower them economically. In fact, women face multiple layers of legal restrictions and inequality in entering and participating in the labor markets.

The good news is that many MENA governments already recognize the importance of increasing market contestability. All but four countries in the region today have antitrust legislation, and almost all of them have established competition authorities to enforce their laws. However, much more is needed.

Interventions in these three dimensions would be essential pillars for a new social contract in MENA (see chapter 5). Yet, viable reform strategies will vary across countries. In some places, simultaneous, large-scale reforms may be feasible, including altering the role of the state in both product and labor markets in favor of more quality private sector participation and better social protection. In others, a more cautious and incremental approach might be more politically viable, favoring a path that does not immediately threaten incumbents, such as fostering the growth of new sectors currently unburdened by the distortions that prevail in established sectors. Here, digital transformation as well as the green economy and green jobs can play a key role. Policy makers might identify the new (or complementary) sectors and occupations with high jobs potential—which can then become the pilots for modern regulatory arrangements.

Finally, the report emphasizes that the road to contestability depends on better access to and transparency of data, which are lacking in most MENA countries. This is constraining evidence-based policy making and effective policy implementation. The preparation of this report has been hampered by the lack of access to detailed, up-to-date data.

VOICES OF YOUNG ENTREPRENEURS IN THE MENA REGION

The report includes seven case studies (Voices) that provide inspiring entrepreneurial stories by young men and women in seven MENA economies: the Arab Republic of Egypt, Jordan, Lebanon, Morocco, Saudi Arabia, Tunisia, and West Bank. These entrepreneurs have found creative ways to challenge the status quo, create successful businesses to meet real needs, and create jobs. These Voices capture the entrepreneurs' own personal stories, describe the main feature of the businesses they have built, and present some of the challenges they have faced and their recommendations to other fellow entrepreneurs in the MENA region. Each Voice also highlights policy topics that have implications for the success of entrepreneurs, including leveraging technology; accessing finance; finding the right talent; expanding into domestic and international markets; dealing with laws, regulations, and reforms; and navigating challenges related to the political economy.

The entrepreneurs have been selected through a nomination process based on factors such as demographics; setting (rural/urban); sector (formal/informal); and industry (agriculture, manufacturing, or services). They each have operated the business for at least two years; have at least 10 full-time employees; and have seen at least 15 percent growth in revenue, in the number of formal employees with wages and social insurance, and in exports to regional markets (if applicable) over the last three years.

COUNTRY TABLES

The report concludes with a series of country tables that present detailed data related to the analysis of regulations. Appendix A explores product market regulations. Appendix B examines labor market regulations. Appendix C presents information on gendered laws.

CHAPTER 2

The Lost Promise of More and Better Jobs

INTRODUCTION

To demographers, sociologists, and economists, the uprisings of the Arab Spring should not have come as a surprise. The magnitude of the protests since 2010 in the Middle East and North Africa (MENA) has been driven not only by the aspirations and sheer will of young people in the region, but also by their outsize share of the population. In 2011, the share of 20- to 34-year-olds, the catalysts of the Arab Spring, was almost 30 percent of the population—the highest in the world, and the highest share that any region had seen over the previous 50 years (figure 2.1). Even today, the share of 20- to 34-year-olds is around 27 percent, second to South Asia, and only by a small margin. This is also an increasingly educated generation. The MENA region has had the highest rates of intergenerational education mobility in the world over the past few decades (Narayan et al. 2018).

Yet the grim reality is that when these young people have entered the labor market in search of better jobs and better lives, many of them have not been able to prosper. Unlike intergenerational mobility in education, mobility in terms of income has been particularly low in the region, and even more so among its middle-income countries (Narayan et al. 2018).

Deep structural problems in the job market are largely at fault. Formal jobs with good paths of advancement are scarce, especially for youth. The working-age population in the MENA region face exclusion from employment altogether, or relegation to low-quality, informal jobs when they can find them. With the retrenchment of public sector hiring over the past two decades, it has become clear that the formal private sector is not going to be the main job creator for the region, and that informal and low-wage jobs are the reality for many.

Figure 2.1 The share of 20- to 34-year-olds in the total population in the Middle East and North Africa is among the highest in the world

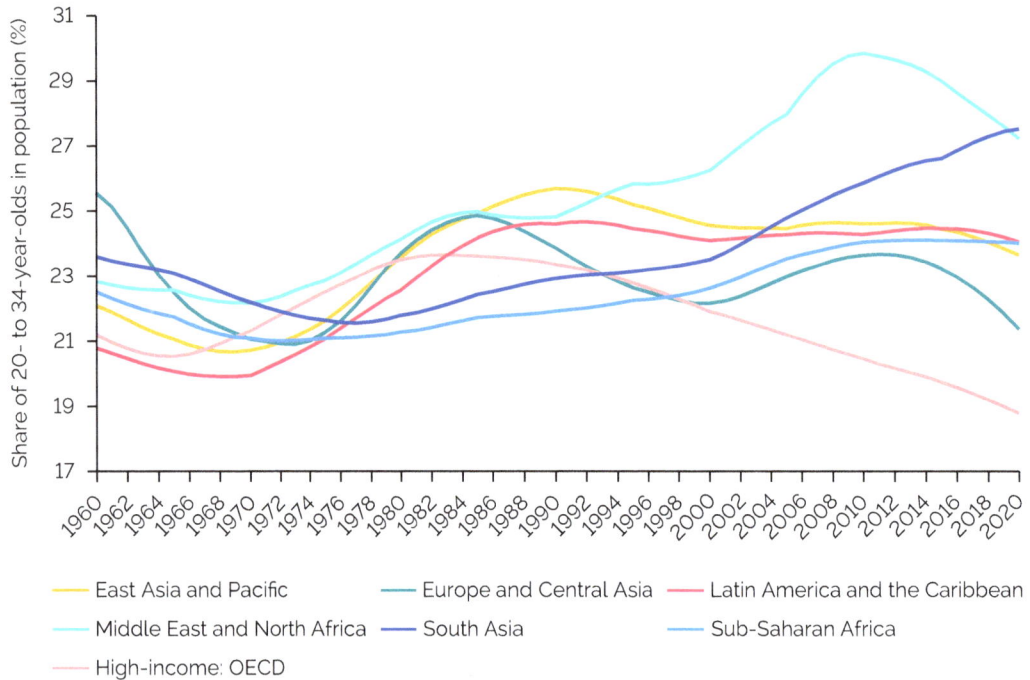

Source: United Nations, World Population Prospects 2019.
Note: OECD = Organisation for Economic Co-operation and Development.

EXCLUSION AND INFORMALITY

One of the most striking and persistent patterns of the labor market in the MENA region today is the large share of healthy and capable working-age populations that are excluded from the labor force and employment altogether. This is most evident for youth and women.

Of particular concern is the persistently high share of youth aged 15 to 24 years who are not in employment, education, or training (NEET). This large segment of idle youth is clear lost potential, in terms of both learning and income-generating activities. As of 2019, nearly 1 in 3 youth (32 percent) in MENA fell into this group,[1] ranging from a low of 8 percent in Malta to a high of 44 percent in Iraq and the Republic of Yemen. This share of idle youth is considerably higher than the world average of 22 percent, and higher than the average for Sub-Saharan Africa (21 percent) and South Asia (30 percent).[2] Even among the high-income countries of the region, the estimated share of NEETs is around 20 percent. And these shares have been on the rise. For a country like the Arab Republic of Egypt, for instance, the estimated share of NEETs increased from around 28 percent in 1998 to 31 percent in 2012, before dropping to 27 percent in 2018, around the same level as 20 years earlier.[3] The rate is higher among 20- to 24-year-olds than among 15- to 19-year-olds. And while some of these NEETs search for work, the majority remain out of the labor force altogether (Amer and Atallah 2019).

The influence of education levels on the likelihood of being a NEET varies across countries. Whereas the higher the education level, the lower the likelihood of being a NEET in Jordan and Morocco (Alfani et al. 2020), the pattern is the opposite in Egypt. Evidence from other economies, like

Iraq and West Bank and Gaza, shows that both primary- and tertiary-educated youths are more likely to be NEETs compared to youths with intermediate levels of education (Gatti et al. 2013). These trends do not seem to have changed much over time. Evidence from Morocco also shows persistence in the status as a NEET. Those who were NEETs in 2010 were 70 percent to 90 percent more likely to remain NEET after a decade; youth become stuck in a rut (Alfani et al. 2020).

While many of the region's promising youth remain idle, there are many others who want to work but cannot find any employment. The youth unemployment rate in MENA is the highest in the world, estimated at around 26 percent in 2019,[4] and has been persistently so for the past two decades (figure 2.2).

The unemployment rate in the MENA region is driven to a large extent by unemployment among youth—the new entrants into the labor market—with the exception of three higher-income and oil-reliant members of the Gulf Cooperation Council (GCC): Bahrain, Qatar, and the United Arab Emirates. Even in Saudi Arabia, youth who are 15 to 24 years old represented 20 percent of the unemployed in the fourth quarter of 2019, and those who were 25 to 29 years old—which captures the cohorts that finished tertiary education—represented 40 percent of the unemployed.[5] This raises issues regarding labor market insertion in the region, where young and less experienced youth, even if they are better qualified in terms of education, fail to find employment. Youth in the region also represent a large share of the long-term unemployed (Assaad and Krafft 2016).

Yet, for many who find jobs, informality awaits. The share of employment that is informal, defined as lacking social security contributions (whether for pensions, disability, sickness, or other risks), varies within the region but remains notably high (figure 2.3, panel a). The share of informal employment is estimated to be as high as 77 percent of total employment in Morocco (as of 2019), 69 percent in Egypt, and 64 percent in West Bank and Gaza, and as low as about 16 percent in Bahrain. For GCC countries—namely, Bahrain and Saudi Arabia—the exclusion of social insurance is concentrated among domestic workers, who often come from abroad and work within households as cleaners, personal drivers, housekeepers, and nannies. Their work visa is issued under a household head (their employer) who is not obligated to register them in the social insurance system.

Figure 2.2 MENA has had the world's highest youth unemployment rate for 15- to 24-year-olds for two decades

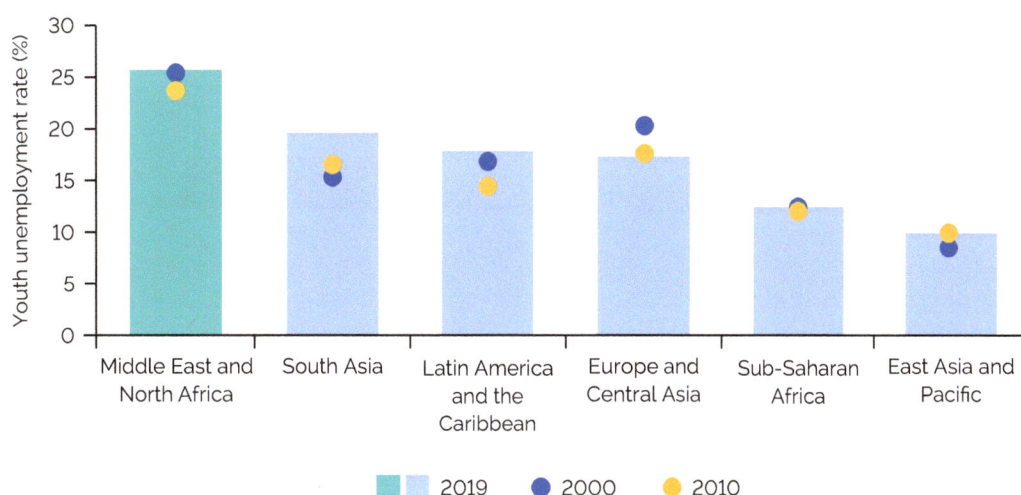

Source: International Labour Organization (ILO) ILOSTAT database.
Note: Data for Europe and Central Asia exclude high-income countries.

Figure 2.3 The share of informal employment is higher when looking at the private sector only, considering that many private sector jobs lack pensions and other types of social insurance

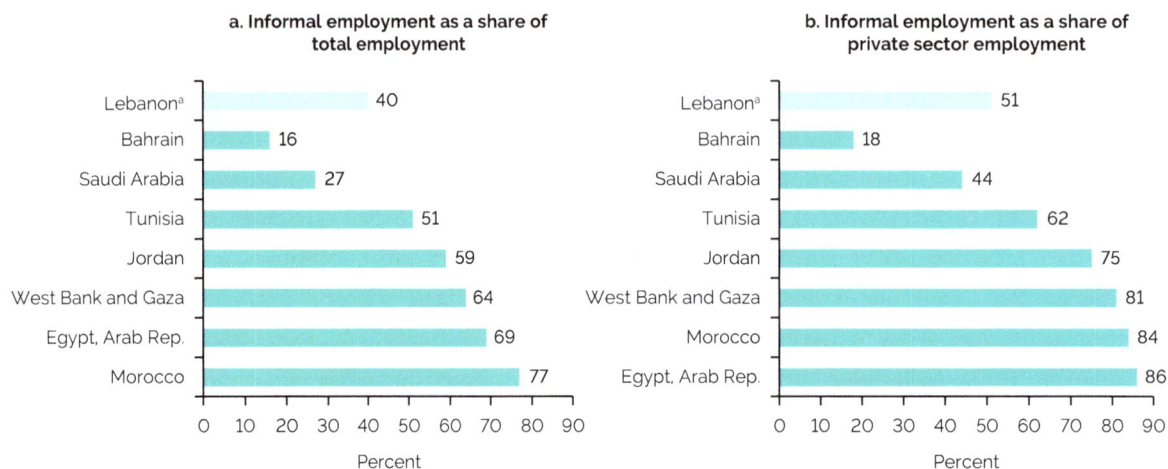

a. Informal employment as a share of total employment

Country	Percent
Lebanon[a]	40
Bahrain	16
Saudi Arabia	27
Tunisia	51
Jordan	59
West Bank and Gaza	64
Egypt, Arab Rep.	69
Morocco	77

b. Informal employment as a share of private sector employment

Country	Percent
Lebanon[a]	51
Bahrain	18
Saudi Arabia	44
Tunisia	62
Jordan	75
West Bank and Gaza	81
Morocco	84
Egypt, Arab Rep.	86

Sources: Microdata from the Egypt Labor Market Panel Survey (2018); Jordan Labor Market Panel Survey (2016); Tunisia Labor Market Panel Survey (2014); and West Bank and Gaza Labor Force Survey (2018). Aggregate statistics from Bahrain Labor Market Regulatory Authority (Q4: 2019); Lebanon Labour Force and Household Living Conditions Survey (2018–19); and the Saudi Arabia Labor Force Survey (Q4: 2019). For Morocco for 2019, Lopez-Acevedo et al. 2021.
Note: These calculations typically exclude military personnel, who are often not part of these surveys. The data focus on civil employment.
a. For Lebanon, data are available only for the share of the employed who have health insurance coverage.

What is important to note, however, is the high share of informal jobs when public sector employment is excluded from the calculation. Public sector employment is a legacy of the region going back many decades. Public sector jobs made up nearly half (47 percent) of total employment in Iraq in 2012–13; and more than one-fifth of employment in Jordan, Egypt, Tunisia, West Bank and Gaza, and Kuwait. The rest of the economies in the region have much lower shares (figure 2.4). For economies where data are available, this share has been decreasing, particularly in Egypt, West Bank and Gaza, and Iraq. When excluding public sector employment and focusing on the private sector only, the share of informal employment becomes much higher. Informal employment is estimated to be around 86 percent of all private sector employment in Egypt, 75 percent in Jordan, and 44 percent in Saudi Arabia (figure 2.3, panel b).

The type and coverage of social insurance also varies greatly, increasing the extent of informality. In Lebanon, more than half of private sector workers do not have health insurance. Lebanon and West Bank and Gaza also lack a social insurance system that covers retirement for private sector workers. For expatriate workers in the GCC countries who are not domestic workers, injury insurance is often available, but not retirement benefits. And for the majority of workers who are self-employed, who make up a significant share of workers in many middle-income countries, social insurance for old-age and retirement is either limited or nonexistent. If social insurance is restricted to pensions, the share of informality would be much higher than illustrated, leaving the majority of workers vulnerable and exposed to shocks when they can no longer work.

At the same time, informality has not spared the better educated, especially men, and particularly with the retrenchment of public sector hiring. Between 1970 and 2015, the probability of a young university-educated labor market entrant being employed in the public sector decreased in several countries in the region, including Algeria, Egypt, Jordan, and Tunisia (Assaad and Barsoum 2019). This retrenchment has been driven by a number of factors, most notably fiscal constraints, forcing governments to reconsider

Figure 2.4 **The share of public sector employment is high in several MENA economies**

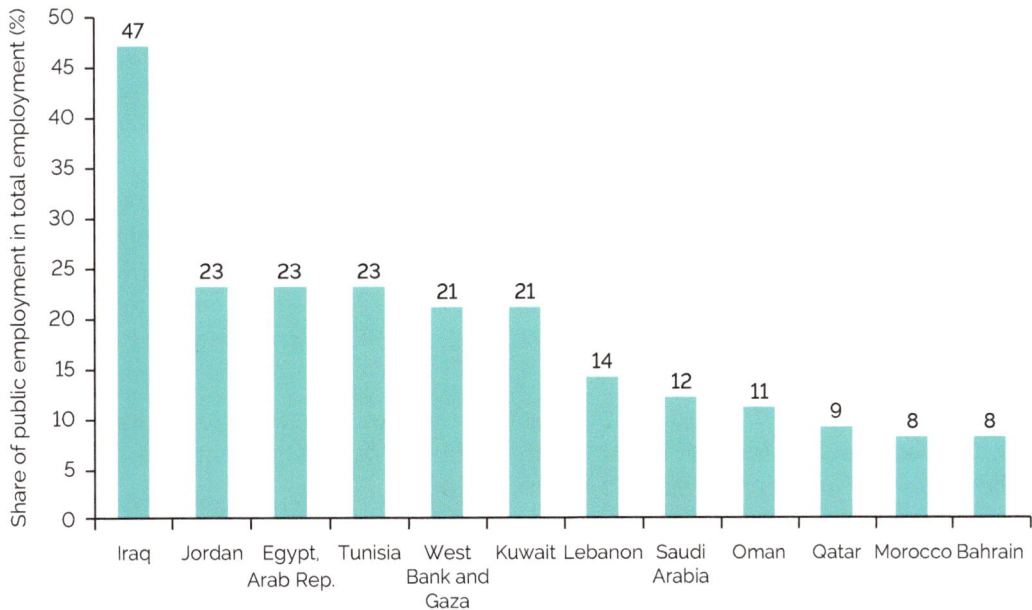

Sources: Microdata from the Egypt Labor Market Panel Survey (2018); Iraq Household Socio-Economic Survey (2012–13); Jordan Labor Market Panel Survey (2016); Tunisia Labor Force Survey (2013); and the West Bank and Gaza Labor Force Survey (2018). Aggregate statistics from the Bahrain Labor Market Regulatory Authority (Q4, 2019); Kuwait Labor Force Survey (2015); Lebanon Labour Force and Household Living Conditions Survey (2018–19); Morocco National Labor Force Survey (2019); Oman National Centre for Statistics and Information (2019); Qatar Labor Force Survey (2019); and Saudi Arabia Labor Force Survey (Q4, 2019).

their employment programs as a pillar of their social contract with the populations. Such constraints are now further exacerbated by the coronavirus (COVID-19) pandemic.

This retrenchment, along with weak growth of private formal employment, has resulted in a notable increase in informal employment—especially for people who could not afford to be out of work. Simulated probabilities that account for demographic changes for Egypt, Tunisia, and West Bank and Gaza show that the probability of a 25-year-old university-educated male landing a job in the public sector has decreased over the past few decades, while the probabilities of informal wage employment and non-wage employment (which include self-employment) have increased (figure 2.5).[6]

At the same time, in all three economies, the probability of being unemployed has increased. This is in line with evidence on the increasing rate of unemployment among university graduates (Gatti et al. 2013). The rise in unemployment is far more evident in Jordan, where the probability of landing a job in the public sector, or wage and nonwage private sector, all decreased between 2000 and 2016. In Iraq, however, between 2007 and 2013, the probability of tertiary-educated males entering the public sector increased, while it decreased for other types of employment, and unemployment. This highlights the importance of public sector employment in a country such as Iraq, whose oil resources and political economy have expanded government employment, especially given that the private sector remains weak.

The data show that irregular work constitutes a large portion of informality. This irregular work often relies on seasonality, or casual type of employment, as opposed to a sustained relationship with an employer over a long period of time. Irregularity can still be in the form of wage work, but it is less stable than typical wage work. At the same time, various forms of nonwage work, such as own-account workers and employers (the self-employed) as well as unpaid family workers, are significant in the region.

The shares of nonwage work increase with age in Egypt, Jordan, and Tunisia, but it appears to decrease with age in West Bank and Gaza, for instance.

Overall, informal work often comes with an income penalty for many people. In Egypt, evidence shows that there is a 27 percent raw average wage gap (meaning not accounting for factors such as age, education, and hours worked) between formal and informal wage workers. When accounting for both observable and unobservable characteristics, taking advantage of panel data, this wage gap decreases to 15 percent, which is still considerable (Tansel, Keskin, and Ozdemir 2020). At the same time, while there is some heterogeneity between informal workers in terms of remuneration, the majority of workers in Jordan, for instance, who are in the lowest quintiles of wealth work informally (Rother et al., forthcoming). Earlier evidence has also confirmed this pattern for Lebanon, the Syrian Arab Republic, and the Republic of Yemen (Angel-Urdinola and Tanabe 2012). When accounting for self-employment, some evidence from Morocco shows that poorer households are more likely to rely on self-employed work, and more so in rural areas (Lopez-Acevedo et al. 2021). Average income generated by household

Figure 2.5 **The probability of a 25-year-old male with tertiary education working in the public sector has decreased in favor of informal employment (wage and nonwage) in the Arab Republic of Egypt, Tunisia, and West Bank and Gaza**

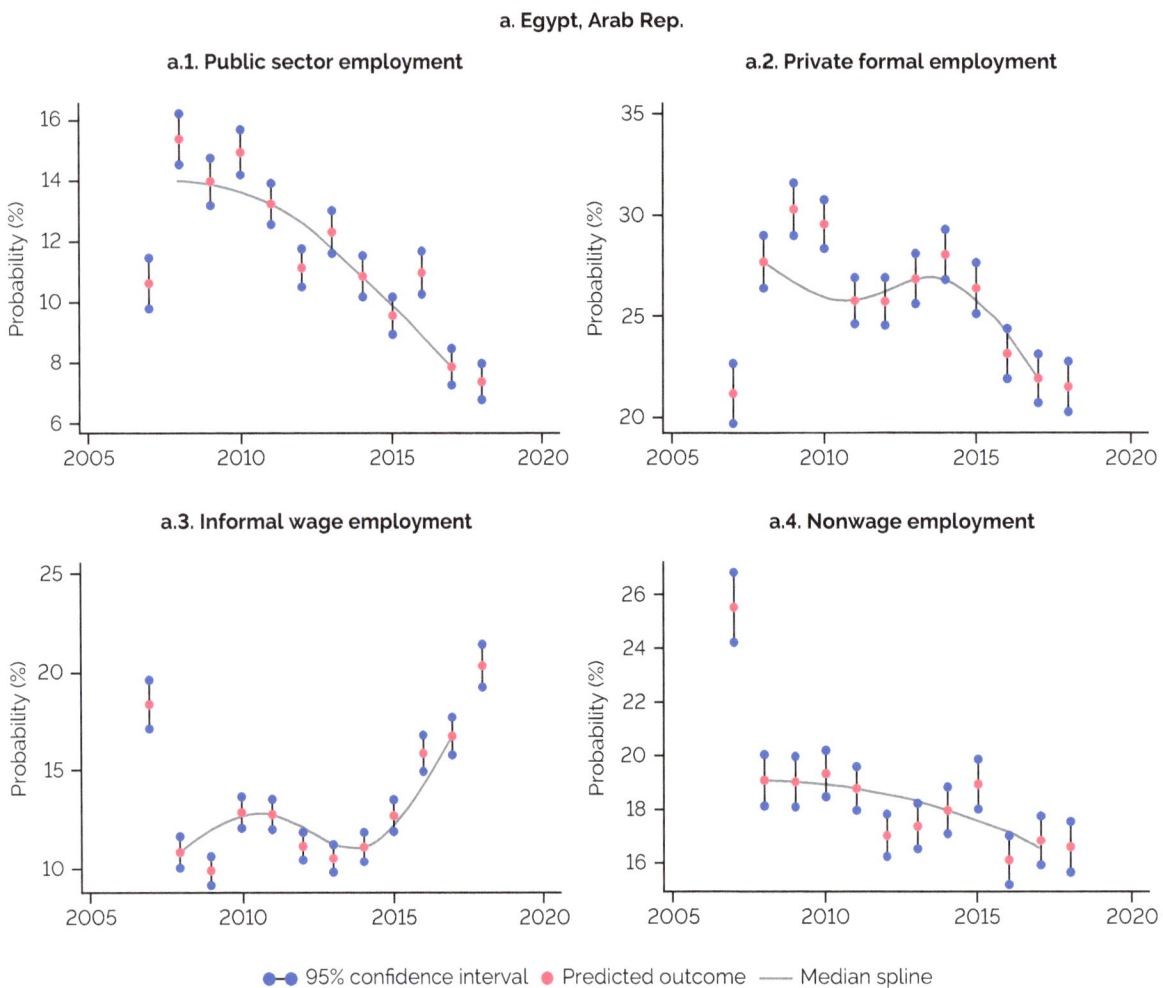

a. Egypt, Arab Rep.

a.1. Public sector employment

a.2. Private formal employment

a.3. Informal wage employment

a.4. Nonwage employment

● 95% confidence interval   ● Predicted outcome   —— Median spline

(figure continues on next page)

Figure 2.5 The probability of a 25-year-old male with tertiary education working in the public sector has decreased in favor of informal employment (wage and nonwage) in the Arab Republic of Egypt, Tunisia, and West Bank and Gaza *(continued)*

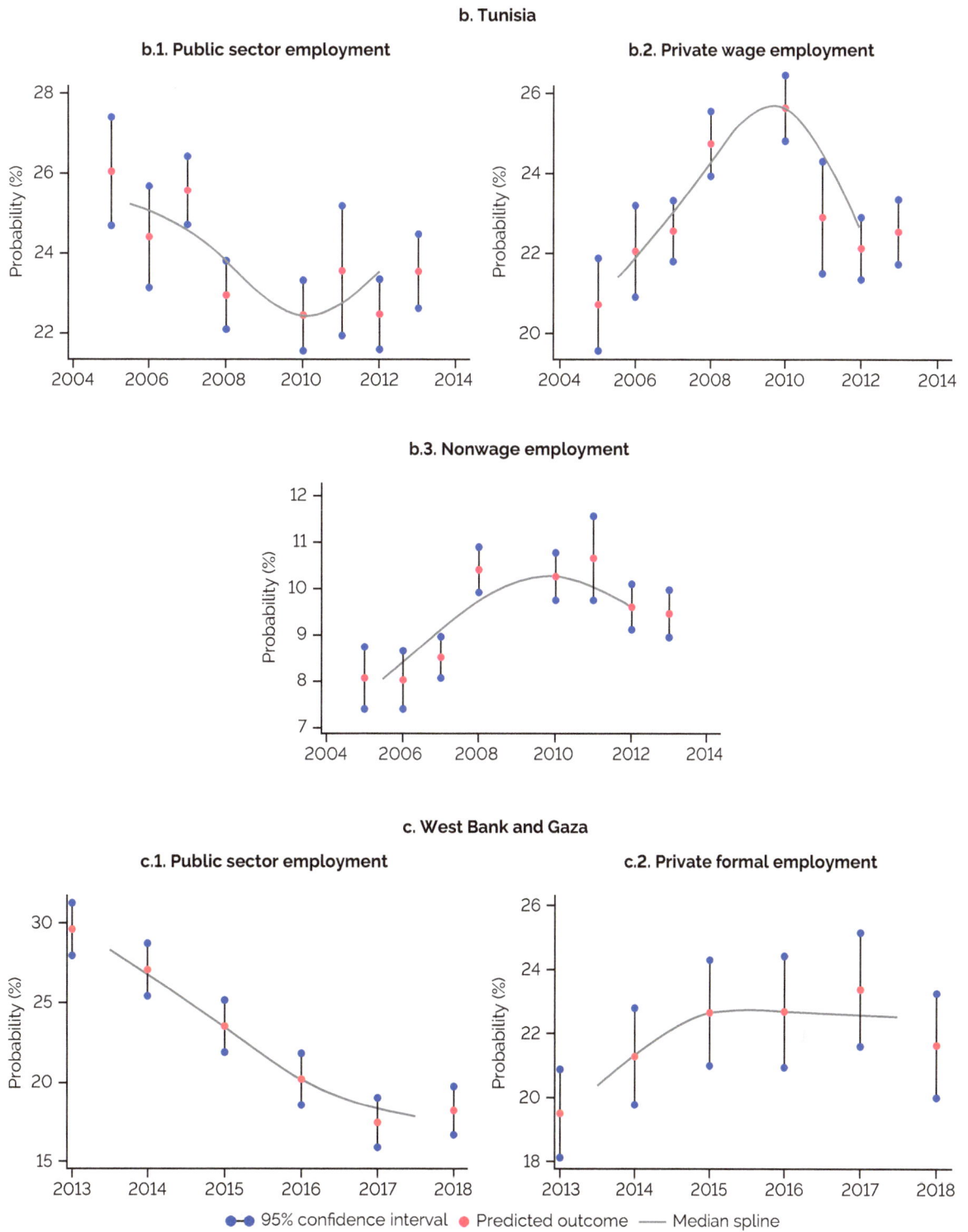

b. Tunisia

b.1. Public sector employment   **b.2. Private wage employment**

b.3. Nonwage employment

c. West Bank and Gaza

c.1. Public sector employment   **c.2. Private formal employment**

● 95% confidence interval   ● Predicted outcome   — Median spline

(figure continues on next page)

Figure 2.5 **The probability of a 25-year-old male with tertiary education working in the public sector has decreased in favor of informal employment (wage and nonwage) in the Arab Republic of Egypt, Tunisia, and West Bank and Gaza** *(continued)*

c. West Bank and Gaza *(continued)*

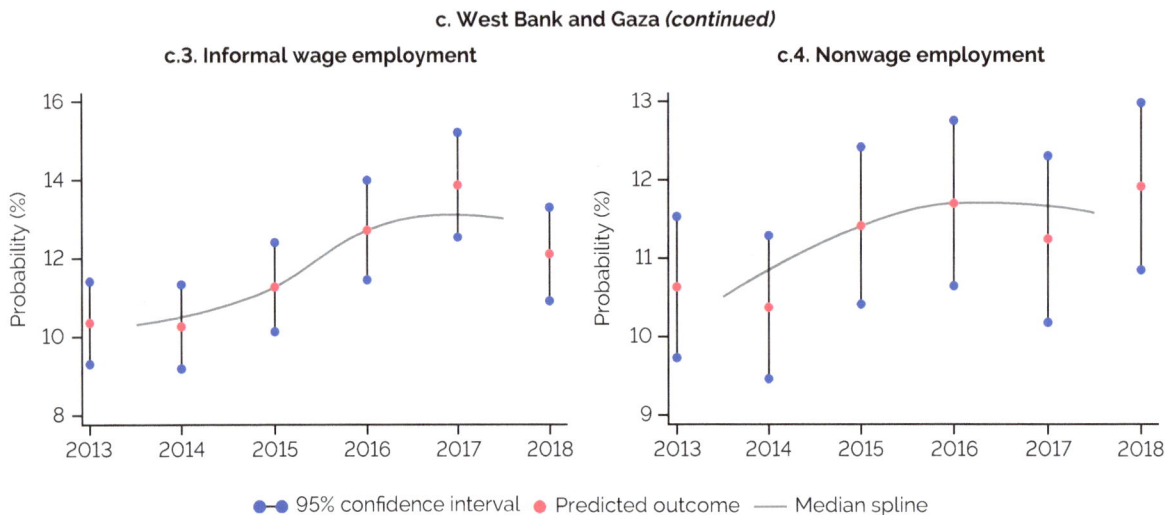

c.3. Informal wage employment

c.4. Nonwage employment

● 95% confidence interval   ● Predicted outcome   —— Median spline

Sources: Labor Force Surveys for Egypt, Tunisia, and West Bank and Gaza.

enterprises run by household entrepreneurs and the self-employed is also significantly lower in Iraq than wage work in the private sector, especially in rural areas.

At the same time, the probability of transitioning from the informal to formal sector is relatively limited, although more likely for well-educated males than for others (Wahba 2009). For a male wage worker in Egypt, the probability of moving up from informal to formal work was 12 percent between 2006 and 2012. This is lower than the probability of dropping back into informality, estimated at 16 percent (Tansel and Ozdemir 2014). Transitions from informal to formal were also low in Jordan between 2010 and 2016 (Rother et al., forthcoming).

Lastly, it is also worth noting that the wage gap between GCC nationals (who are typically formal wage workers) and nonnationals (who are more likely to be informal) is significant. In Saudi Arabia, the average monthly wage of a national was 2.7 times higher than that of a nonnational in the last quarter of 2019 (Saudi Arabia Labor Force Survey 2019). In Bahrain in 2011, the average basic wage of a national was more than three times that of a nonnational, and the difference between a national's wage and a domestic worker's (all of whom are informal) was more than 10 times (Labour Market Regulatory Authority, Open Data).

These labor market outcomes emphasize the exclusion of many people in the labor market from good income opportunities in many countries in the region, regardless of the country's income level or context.

THE PLIGHT OF FEMALE WORKERS

The lack of inclusivity in the labor market in the Middle East and North Africa is most apparent in the plight, and lost potential, of women. One of the mainstays of the MENA region in terms of labor market outcomes is the lack of tangible and notable changes to the situation of its women. Female labor force participation, averaging about 20 percent, is still the lowest in the world.

However, younger, and better-educated, cohorts of women are increasingly more likely to want to enter the labor market (Arezki et al. 2020). In Saudi Arabia, the female labor force participation of a

Figure 2.6 More-educated Saudi women have higher labor force participation rates

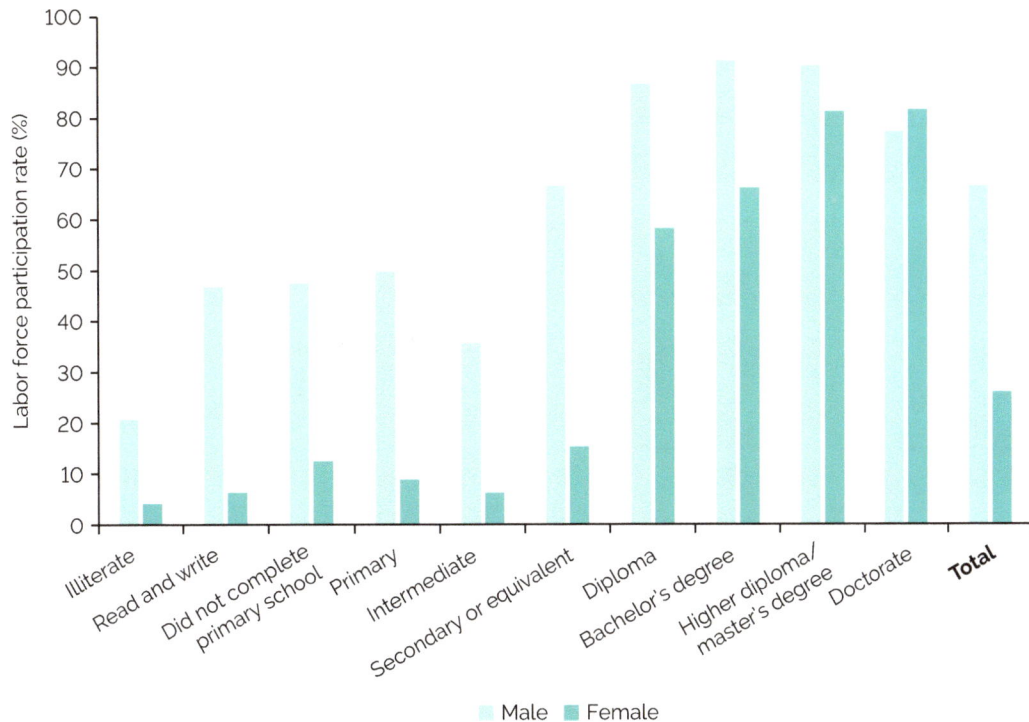

Source: Government of Saudi Arabia, General Authority for Statistics (GASTAT) 2019.

Saudi woman with a bachelor's degree or above is three to four times the national average (figure 2.6). This trend is similar in many other economies in the region, including Egypt, Iraq, Jordan, Tunisia, and West Bank and Gaza.

Yet, as these women enter the market, unemployment awaits. Women in the region have persistently high unemployment rates that have not changed much over time (Gatti et al. 2014). One of the features of the region is that as women get better educated, they enter the labor force and face the challenge of joblessness.

The increase in the probability of being unemployed has also come at a time when employment in the public sector has become less viable for women (and men, as discussed). Historically, public employment offered favorable benefits for women in terms of working hours and amenities such as maternity leave. It was also perceived as a safer and more socially acceptable environment for female workers. However, the increase in female labor force participation among younger cohorts has coincided with the decreasing probability of being employed in the public sector.[7] This decline has translated into an increase in the probability of being unemployed—and not necessarily the probability of being employed in the private sector (whether formal or informal), as is the case with some male peers. Simulated probabilities of the labor market show that for 25-year-old university-educated women in Iraq, Jordan, and Tunisia, there is a clear decline in the probability of being employed by the public sector over time, mirrored by an increase in the probability of being unemployed (figure 2.7). In the case of Iraq and Jordan, there is also an increase in the probability of dropping out of the labor force altogether. On the other hand, women in Egypt have been more likely to join the informal sector as wage workers.

Being unemployed reaps little benefits. While unemployment insurance exists for some countries in the region, it is typically limited in both eligibility and duration, as well as benefits. For many young new

Figure 2.7 **The probability of a 25-year-old woman with a tertiary education working in the public sector has decreased in the Arab Republic of Egypt, Iraq, Jordan, and Tunisia in favor of unemployment and dropping out of the labor force**

a. Egypt, Arab Rep.

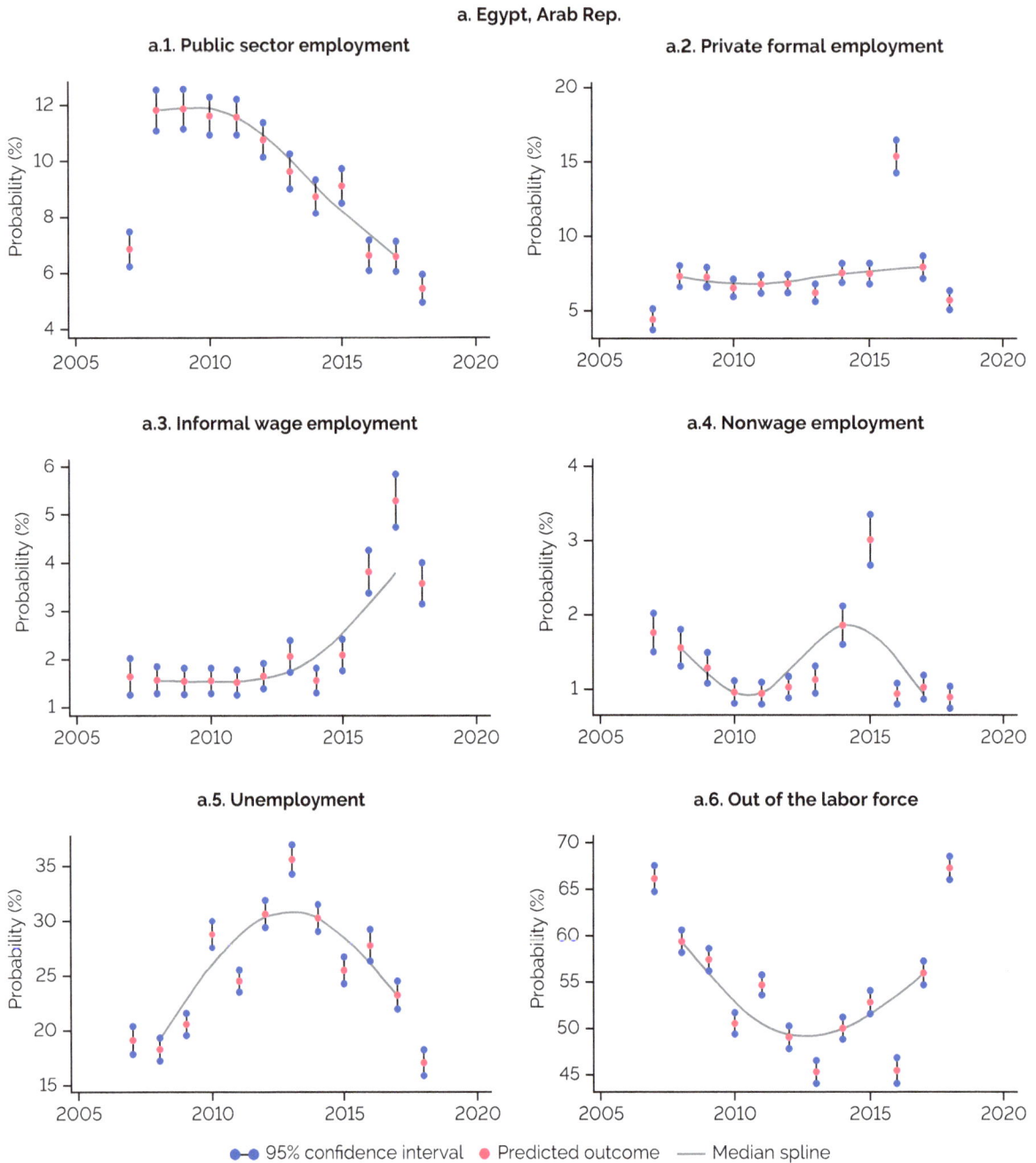

a.1. Public sector employment

a.2. Private formal employment

a.3. Informal wage employment

a.4. Nonwage employment

a.5. Unemployment

a.6. Out of the labor force

● 95% confidence interval　● Predicted outcome　— Median spline

(figure continues on next page)

Figure 2.7 The probability of a 25-year-old woman with a tertiary education working in the public sector has decreased in the Arab Republic of Egypt, Iraq, Jordan, and Tunisia in favor of unemployment and dropping out of the labor force *(continued)*

b. Iraq

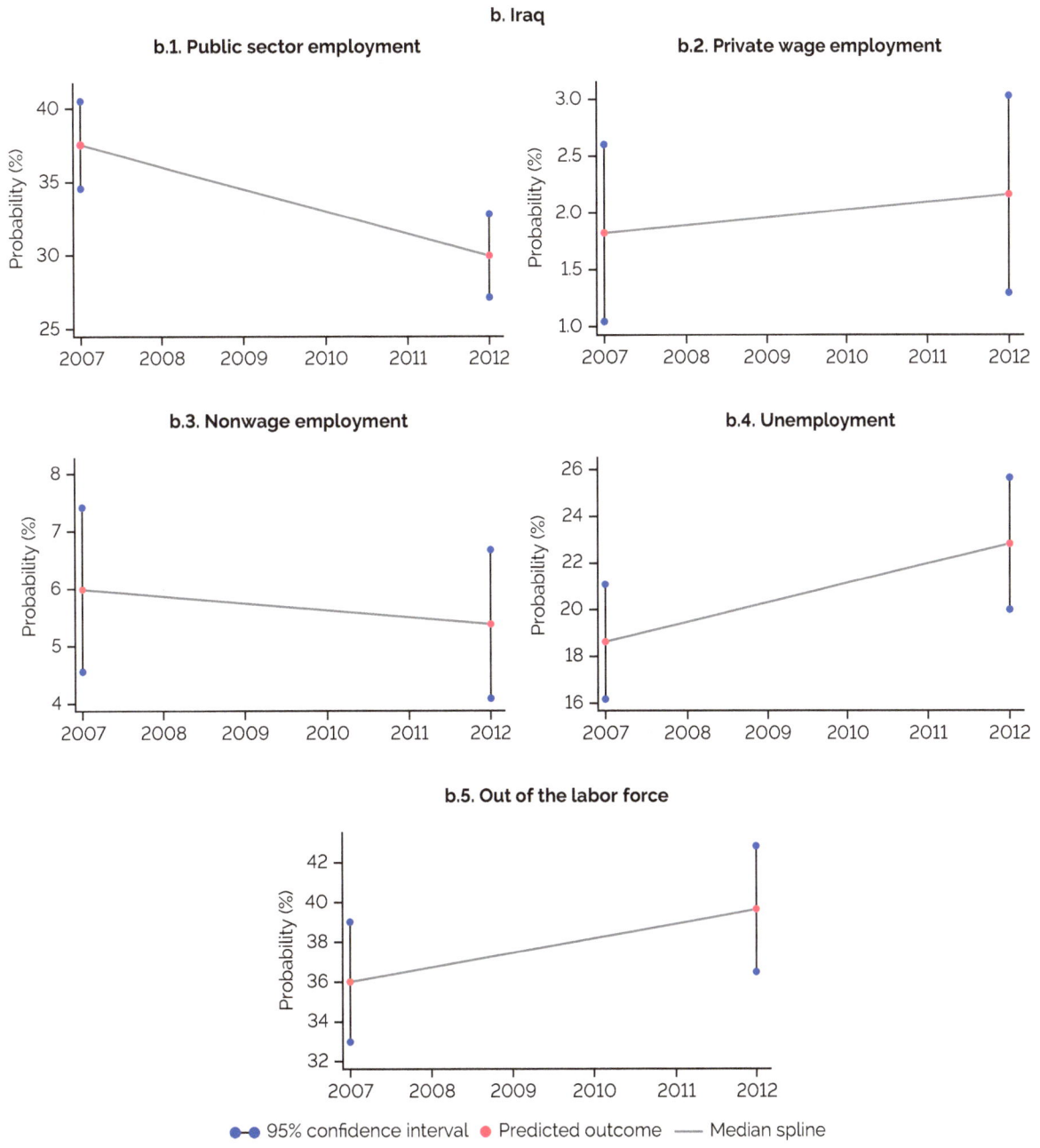

b.1. Public sector employment

b.2. Private wage employment

b.3. Nonwage employment

b.4. Unemployment

b.5. Out of the labor force

95% confidence interval • Predicted outcome — Median spline

(figure continues on next page)

Figure 2.7 The probability of a 25-year-old woman with a tertiary education working in the public sector has decreased in the Arab Republic of Egypt, Iraq, Jordan, and Tunisia in favor of unemployment and dropping out of the labor force *(continued)*

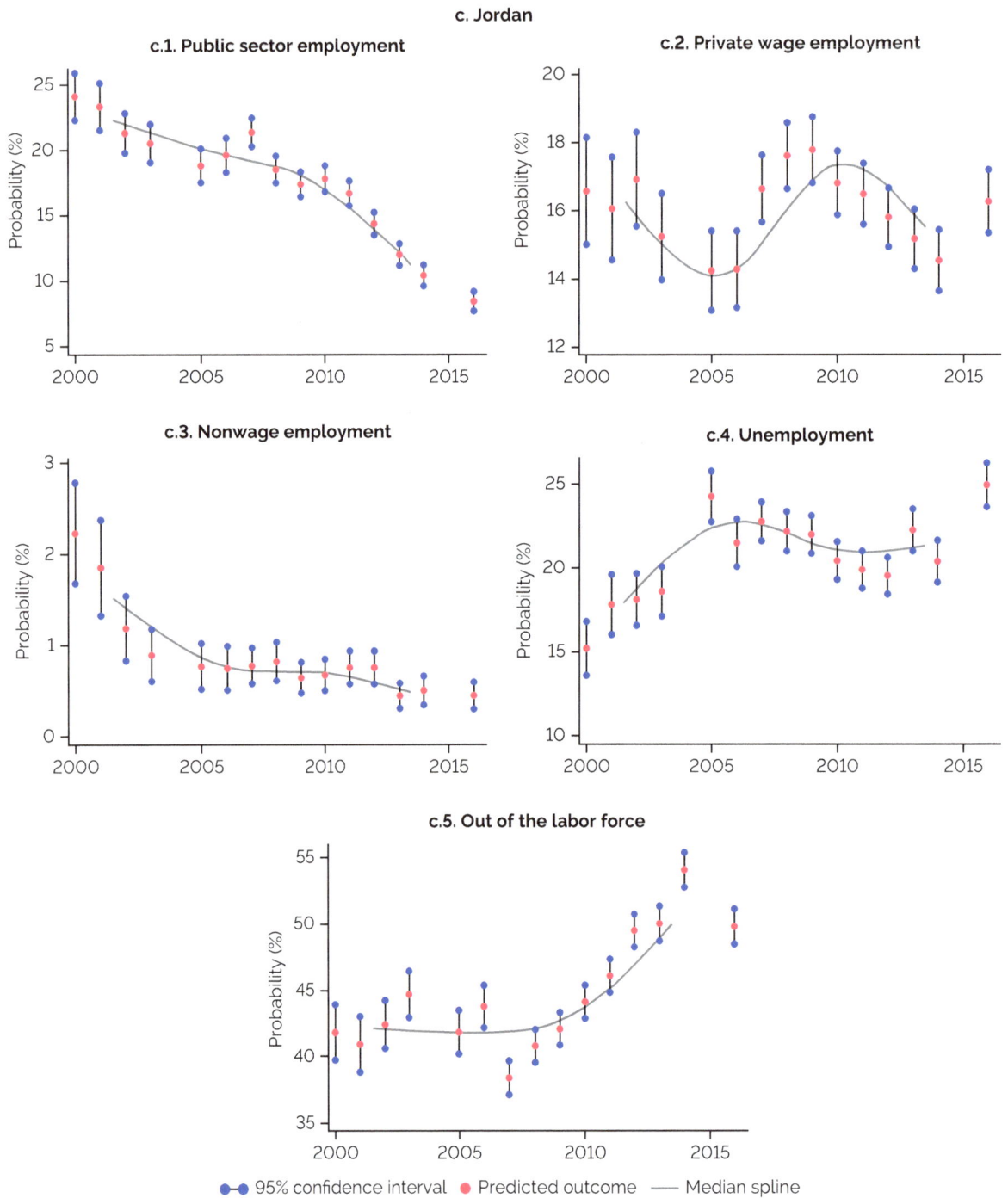

c. Jordan

c.1. Public sector employment

c.2. Private wage employment

c.3. Nonwage employment

c.4. Unemployment

c.5. Out of the labor force

● 95% confidence interval ● Predicted outcome — Median spline

(figure continues on next page)

Figure 2.7 The probability of a 25-year-old woman with a tertiary education working in the public sector has decreased in the Arab Republic of Egypt, Iraq, Jordan, and Tunisia in favor of unemployment and dropping out of the labor force *(continued)*

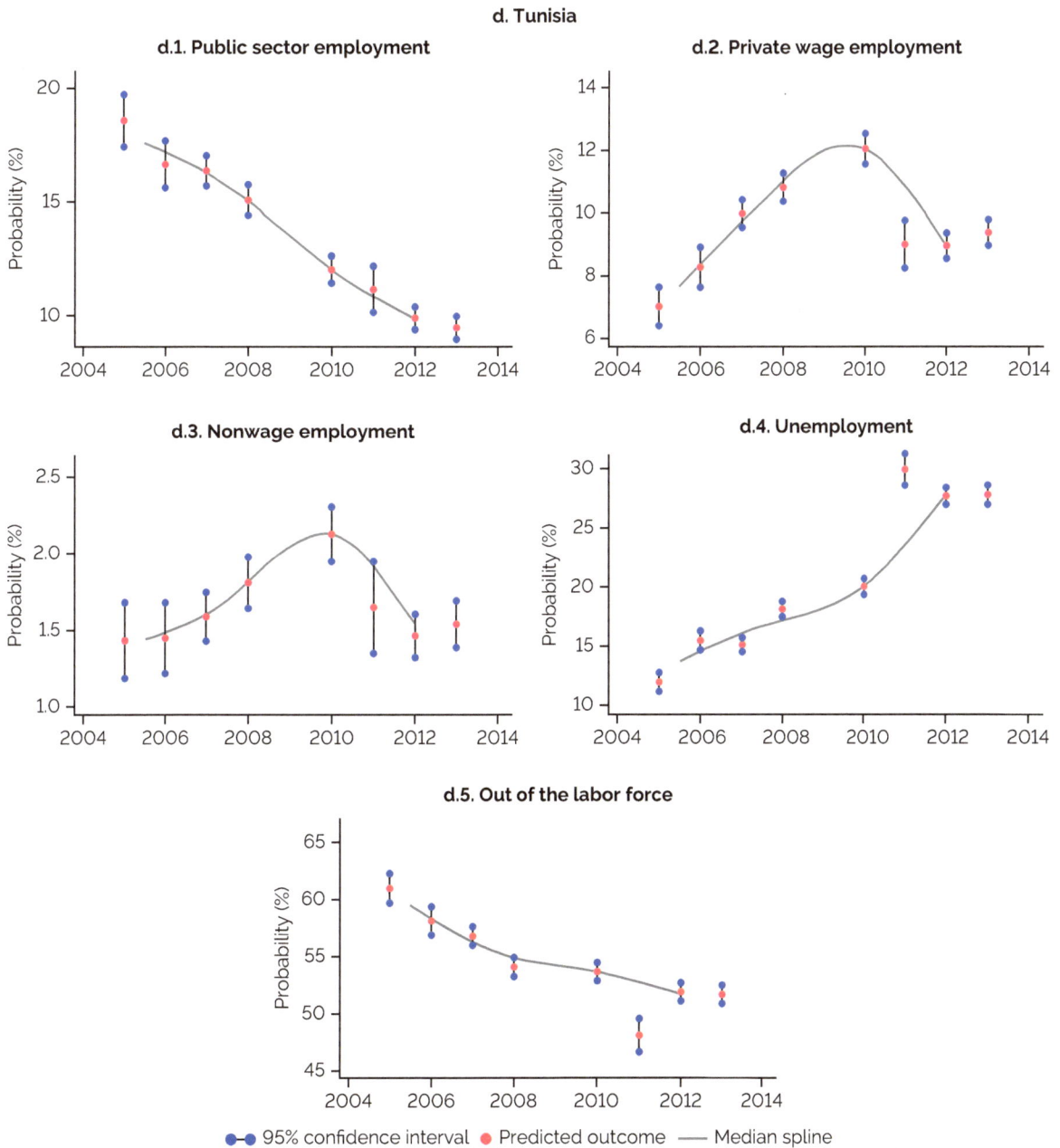

d. Tunisia

d.1. Public sector employment

d.2. Private wage employment

d.3. Nonwage employment

d.4. Unemployment

d.5. Out of the labor force

●—● 95% confidence interval   ● Predicted outcome   —— Median spline

Sources: Egypt Labor Force Surveys (2007–17); Iraq Household Socio-Economic Surveys (2007/08, 2012/13); Jordan Employment and Unemployment Surveys (2000–16); Tunisia Labor Force Surveys (2005–13).

graduates, with no previous contributions accumulated, noncontributory unemployment assistance is even more limited. Some GCC countries, such as Bahrain and Saudi Arabia, provide an allowance for a limited period of time, while it is nonexistent among middle-income countries in the region. Combined with the fact that active labor market policies are also limited, this leaves women in a particularly vulnerable situation.

Lastly, when women become self-employed, some evidence from the region shows a notable disadvantage in terms of income compared to men. In general, labor force surveys and household surveys provide limited information on the incomes of the self-employed, and quantifying these earnings can be fraught with errors. However, some descriptive evidence for Jordan, for instance, using available surveys, shows that self-employed women earned less than their male counterparts in 2016. Household enterprise data from Iraq using the available household surveys show that female-headed households earned significantly less from their economic activities than men, regardless of whether they operated in agricultural or nonagricultural activities. Male-headed households operating in some industrial activities earned 12 times more than their female counterparts in 2013. The difference was less evident in agricultural production, however.

Moreover, in Egypt, evidence on the dynamics of nonfarm household enterprises over the course of 14 years shows that while there is significant creation of enterprises over time, there is also a high rate of dissolution and exit altogether. The majority of these enterprises remain the same size, and they are significantly affected by the economic situation in the country. And while these dynamics are not different between male- and female-headed enterprises, women are far less likely to start and persist in this activity (Krafft 2016). The evidence on self-employment in the region, however meager, does not appear to be vastly different from the experience and disadvantages that face self-employed women around the world (Carranza, Dakhal, and Love 2018).

NOT THE JOBS OF THE FUTURE

The limited public and formal private sector employment in the region, and the prevalence of informality, has had many repercussions on both the quantity and quality of the jobs created for the region's increasingly ambitious and competent population.

As of 2018, only 24 percent of the region's employed workers were in high-skill occupations, whereas nearly half (48 percent) were in medium-skill occupations, and 28 percent were in low-skill occupations.[8] While the region's share of high-skill occupations is second to Europe and Central Asia, what is notable is that over the past two decades as the region shed low-skill occupations, the compensation was mostly in medium-skill jobs (figure 2.8). The share of low-skill occupations dropped by 6.7 percentage points between 2000 and 2018, while the share of medium-skill occupations increased by 4.5 percentage points, and the share of high-skill occupations climbed by 2.2 percentage points.

Medium-skill occupations, while important, are highly susceptible to automation and digitization, as they tend to be intensive in routine cognitive and manual tasks. They are among the jobs whose transformation could induce more productivity growth. The fact that the share of these occupations is still significant points to the type of lower-productivity jobs, and economic activity, that the region continues to rely on.

When comparing countries in the region to their income peers around the world, both lower-middle-income countries and high-income countries within the region have not added as many high-skill occupations to their mix as peers around the world (figure 2.9). While Djibouti, Egypt, Morocco, and Tunisia generally have higher shares of high-skill occupations in their economies, their income peers around the world appear to be catching up to them, growing their high-skill occupations much faster. This relative stagnation is also apparent among high-income countries in the region, the majority of

Figure 2.8 While MENA has shed low-skill jobs in the past two decades, the loss has mostly been offset by an increase in medium-skill jobs, not high-skill ones, unlike some other regional peers

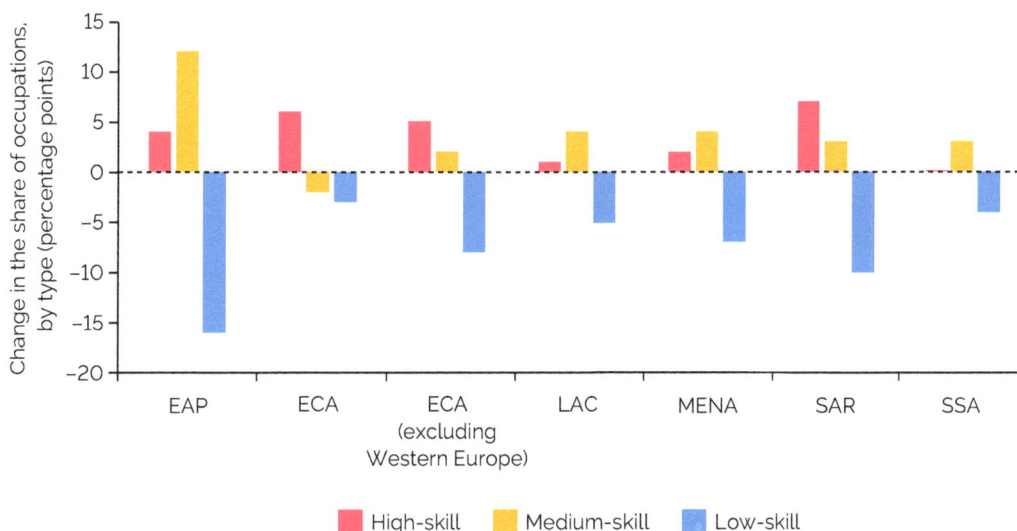

Source: International Labour Organization (ILO) ILOSTAT database.
Note: The figure covers the period from 2000 to 2018. High-skill occupations include managers, professionals, associate professionals, and technicians. Medium-skill occupations include clerical support workers, service and sales workers, craft and related trades workers, plant and machine operators and assemblers, as well as skilled agricultural, forestry, and fishery workers. Low-skill occupations include elementary occupations. EAP = East Asia and Pacific; ECA = Europe and Central Asia; LAC = Latin America and the Caribbean; MENA = Middle East and North Africa; SAR = South Asia; SSA = Sub-Saharan Africa.

Figure 2.9 MENA is growing its high-skill occupations much less than its income peers, while relying on medium-skill occupations

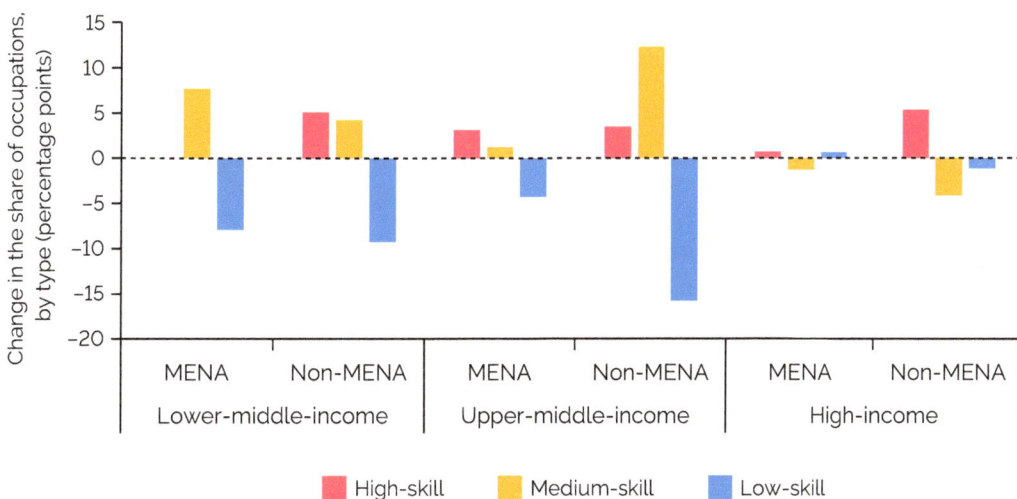

Source: International Labour Organization (ILO) ILOSTAT database.
Note: The figure covers the period from 2000 to 2018. High-skill occupations include managers, professionals, associate professionals, and technicians. Medium-skill occupations include clerical support workers, service and sales workers, craft and related trades workers, plant and machine operators and assemblers, as well as skilled agricultural, forestry, and fishery workers. Low-skill workers include elementary occupations.

which are the oil-reliant countries of the GCC. While their high-income peers around the world have continued to increase the share of their high-skill jobs, the share has changed little over the past two decades for the MENA countries, which still rely on middle-skill occupations, arguably driven by an outsize public sector. Upper-middle-income countries in the region, on the other hand, appear to have compensated their low-skill occupations with more high-skill and medium-skill ones, although the change in the composition is small.

Evidence from labor market data for several countries in the region shows that when looking at the private sector alone, the share of high-skill occupations is even lower than the entire economy. In a country like Egypt, where the share of high-skill occupations in the overall economy was 55 percent in 2018, it was only 30 percent among formal private jobs, and a meager 10 percent among informal ones. The case is similar for Jordan and Tunisia. Moreover, the continued existence and prevalence of the informal sector, and in the case of GCC countries the prevalence of low-skill and medium-skill expatriate labor, undoubtedly contribute to the stagnation that has been occurring.

Going deeper into the task content of jobs shows that workers in countries where the data are available, including Egypt, Jordan, and Tunisia, perform significantly fewer tasks that require nonroutine interpersonal and analytical skills—the jobs of the future. Compared to countries like Chile or Turkey (benchmarked against Germany), both the public and private sectors in these MENA countries use notably fewer nonroutine analytical and interpersonal tasks (figure 2.10), with the private sector performing even less. Even among higher-skill occupations such as managers, professionals, and technicians, the tasks that utilize nonroutine analytical and nonroutine interpersonal skills are still limited compared to other countries.

With the spread of COVID-19, working from home has become important. The feasibility of such work depends on the type of job and the tasks performed. Using data for Egypt, Jordan, and Tunisia, along with 50 other countries around the world, the results show that while Jordan performs better than Egypt or Tunisia in terms of working from home, the three still do not perform well compared to many other countries, including some of their own income peers. Moreover, less educated, older, and informal workers are much less likely to have jobs amenable to working from home (figure 2.11). This pattern can be traced to the fact that less educated and informal workers have jobs that are more intensive in physical tasks that cannot be done at home, while older workers are less likely to use information

Figure 2.10 **Jobs in MENA tend not to use nonroutine analytical and interpersonal tasks— the jobs of the future**

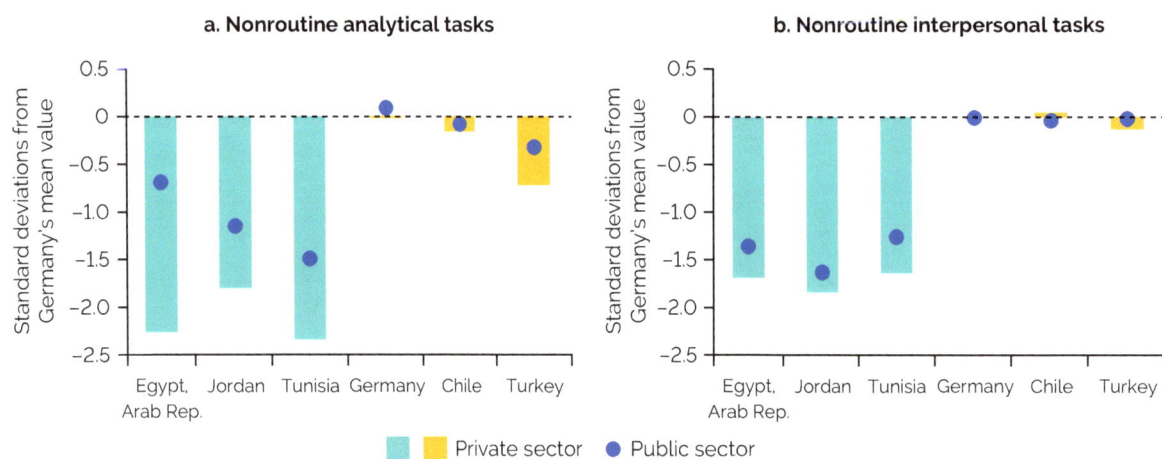

a. Nonroutine analytical tasks

b. Nonroutine interpersonal tasks

Private sector ● Public sector

Source: Viollaz and Winkler 2020.

Figure 2.11 Relatively few jobs in the Arab Republic of Egypt, Jordan, and Tunisia are amenable to working from home, especially among less educated, older, and informal workers

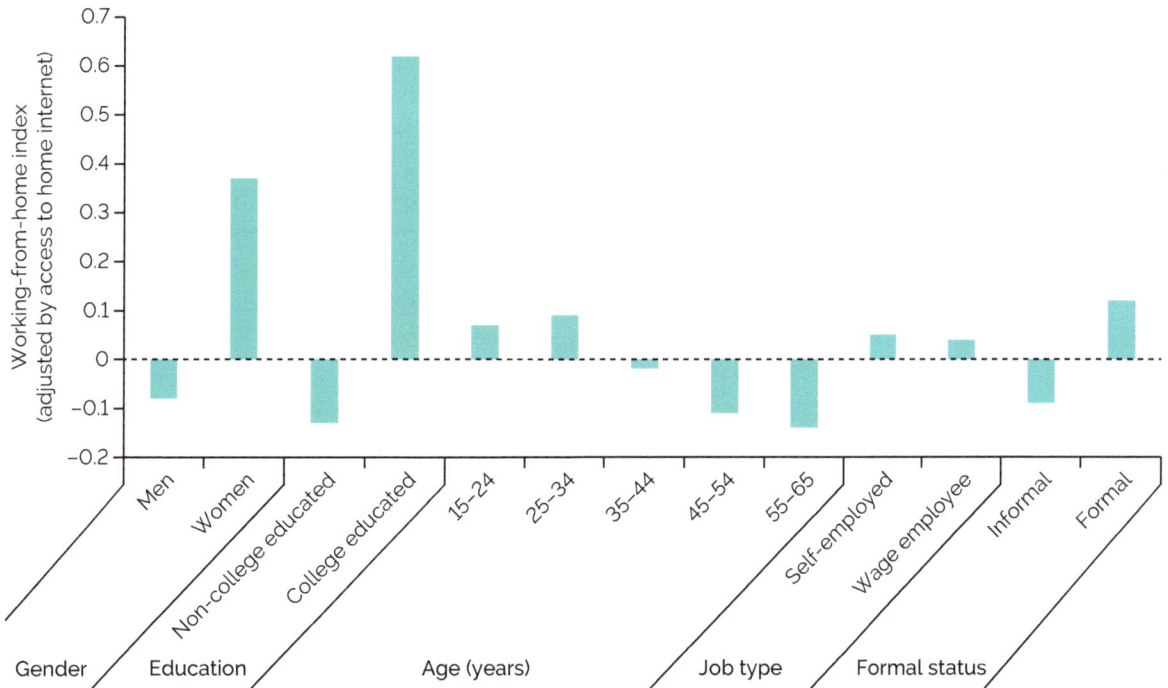

Source: Hatayama, Viollaz, and Winkler 2020.
Note: The figure presents data from the working-from-home (WFH) index adjusted by internet access at home, in standard deviations from the mean of the samples. A higher value indicates that jobs are more amenable to working from home.

and communication technologies. Women in MENA have jobs more amenable to working from home because they have jobs that are less intensive in physical tasks and less likely to be tied to a specific location and thereby can be done at home, especially with public employment.

THE IMPACT OF COVID-19

The COVID-19 pandemic has had a tremendous impact on the labor market and on workers and their households. As the virus began to spread, countries in the MENA region introduced measures to limit its spread, including curfews, lockdowns, and mobility restrictions, as well as various social distancing measures. In Iraq, for instance, this included nightly and weekend curfews that lasted for months during 2020 and continued intermittently into 2021 (Moosa and Moreira da Silva 2021). In Morocco, movements between major cities were banned for several weeks in 2020 as well as in 2021. In Saudi Arabia, citizens could not leave the country for months at a time, while internationals were forbidden from entering, including for religious pilgrimage.

Initial evidence from various phone surveys conducted during 2020 shows that shortly after the outbreak, many workers were unable to work altogether. About 41 percent of workers in Egypt and Tunisia, 19 percent of workers in Djibouti, and 16 percent in West Bank and Gaza had to stop working (Gansey 2020). The loss of work was even higher among private sector workers as governments deferred laying off their staff. In Iraq, 29 percent of private sector wage workers and 30 percent of the self-employed who responded to the surveys reported dropping into unemployment six months into the pandemic, while many other workers, especially women, dropped out of the labor force altogether (Krah, Phadera, and Wai-Poi 2021). In Morocco, only three months into the pandemic, 34 percent of responding households mentioned that they did not have any sources of income whatsoever, and this share was even higher among the poor (44 percent) and among some professions such as traders and manual laborers (Morocco High Commission for Planning 2020). For the GCC economies, little is known about the impact on jobs, but evidence from Bahrain shows that while nationals did not suffer a large negative impact, the nonnationals interviewed in the survey were significantly affected, with the share of respondents having a primary job dropping from 81 percent before the pandemic to 59 percent a few months into it (Abdulla et al. 2020). This is largely attributed to the fact that many nationals work in the public sector and that the Bahraini government has injected considerable enterprise and wage support into the private sector since the beginning of the pandemic—including deferring loan installments.

By February 2021, some signs of recovery emerged in the surveys conducted in Egypt, Morocco, Jordan, and Tunisia, including increases in labor force participation compared to November 2020. Employment rates also began to increase in Morocco (from 61 percent to 68 percent) and Tunisia (from 64 percent to 68 percent). Unemployment slightly decreased. However, the recovery a year into the pandemic appears to have been limited. This is especially the case for workers who were already vulnerable before the pandemic, namely informal workers and women, who have borne the brunt of the impact of the pandemic (Krafft, Assaad, and Marouani 2021).

These results demonstrate what many economies around the world already know: the recovery from the pandemic in terms of jobs and unemployment for the majority of the population will be slow. Despite the fact that some types of jobs have not come out as losers from the pandemic—namely, those that are based on digital skills—for the great majority of workers in the region, the jobs challenge remains a serious and difficult one. As variants of the coronavirus emerge throughout the world, the road to a full recovery remains a bumpy one.

NOTES

1. Regional estimates by the flagship team using International Labour Organization (ILO) data, calculated as a weighted average, where the weight is the ratio between the estimated number of youth in the country and the overall estimated number of youth in the region.

2. Country estimates are from the ILO. Note that the ILO definition of "employment" is all those who are engaged in any activity to produce goods or provide services for pay or profit during a short reference period. They comprise employed persons "at work": that is, who worked in a job for at least one hour; and employed persons "not at work" due to temporary absence from a job, or to working-time arrangements (such as shift work, flextime, and compensatory leave for overtime).

3. Flagship team calculations based on Open Access Micro Data Initiative (OAMDI) 2019. Labor Market Panel Surveys (LMPS), http://erf.org.eg/data-portal/. Version 2.0 of Licensed Data Files; ELMPS 1998–2018. Egypt: Economic Research Forum (ERF).

4. These are estimates by the International Labour Organization (ILO).

5. General Authority for Statistics, Kingdom of Saudi Arabia, https://www.stats.gov.sa/en/820 (accessed May 2021).

6. Simulated probabilities are analyzed for this section. Probabilities were derived with a series of multinomial logit models estimated on a polychotomous outcome variable including various employment alternatives using Labor Force Surveys in Egypt over the period 2000–18; Jordan (2003–16); Iraq (2006–07 and 2012); Tunisia (2004–13); and West Bank and Gaza (2013–18). The employment status used depends on the specifics of the survey questionnaire and includes public employment, private formal wage employment, private informal wage employment, nonwage employment, unemployment, and out of labor force as the base/reference outcome.

In cases in which a distinction could not be drawn between formal and informal wage employment due to lack of information about social security or health benefits, the separation of the two categories was dropped. The model accounts for individual characteristics such as age; age squared; gender (dummy variable); educational attainment (three dummies, with being illiterate as the reference group); marital status (equal to 1 if married and 0 otherwise); and geography (a dummy variable to account for urban/rural residency, that equals 1 if urban). The analysis also calculated 95 percent confidence intervals surrounding these probability simulations.

7. Multinomial logit regressions were performed on several harmonized surveys across the region, as mentioned in note 6.

8. According to the International Labour Organization (ILO), high-skill occupations include managers, professionals, associate professionals, and technicians. Medium-skill occupations include clerical support workers; service and sales workers; skilled agricultural, forestry, and fishery workers; craft and related trades workers; and plant and machine operators and assemblers. Low-skill workers are those in elementary occupations such as selling goods in streets and public places, or from door to door; providing various street services; cleaning, washing, pressing; taking care of apartment houses, hotels, offices, and other buildings; and washing windows.

REFERENCES

Abdulla, Ghada, Deema Almoayyed, Fatima Al-Sabaie, and Omar Al-Ubaydli. 2020. "Assessment of the Socioeconomic Impact of Covid-19 in Bahrain: Analysis of Survey Data from Bahrain and Comparative Surveys from the UK and the US." Bahrain Center for Strategic, International and Energy Studies, Awali, Bahrain.

Alfani, Federica, Fabio Clementi, Michele Fabiani, Vasco Molini, and Enzo Valentini. 2020. "Once NEET, Always NEET? A Synthetic Panel Approach to Analyze the Moroccan Labor Market." Policy Research Working Paper 9238, World Bank, Washington, DC.

Amer, Mona, and Marian Atallah. 2019. "The School to Work Transition and Youth Economic Vulnerability in Egypt." Working Paper 1359, Economic Research Forum, Cairo.

Angel-Urdinola, Diego F., and Kimie Tanabe. 2012. "Micro-Determinants of Informal Employment in the Middle East and North Africa Region." Social Protection Discussion Paper 1201, World Bank, Washington, DC.

Arezki, Rabah, Daniel Lederman, Amani Abou Harb, Nelly El-Mallakh, Rachel Yuting Fan, Asif Islam, Ha Nguyen, and Marwane Zouaidi. 2020. *How Transparency Can Help the Middle East and North Africa.* MENA Economic Update April 2020. Washington, DC: World Bank.

Assaad, Ragui, and Ghada Barsoum. 2019. "Public Employment in the Middle East and North Africa." *IZA World of Labor* 463, Institute of Labor Economics (IZA), Bonn. http://dx.doi.org/10.15185/izawol.463.

Assaad, Ragui, and Caroline Krafft. 2016. "Labor Market Dynamics and Youth Unemployment in the Middle East and North Africa: Evidence from Egypt, Jordan and Tunisia." Working Paper 993, Economic Research Forum, Dokki, Giza, Egypt.

Carranza, Eliana, Chandra Dakhal, and Inessa Love. 2018. "Female Entrepreneurs: How and Why Are They Different?" Jobs Working Paper 20, World Bank, Washington, DC.

Gansey, Romeo. 2020. "Socioeconomic Impact of COVID-19 in MENA Countries." World Bank, Washington, DC. Unpublished.

Gatti, Roberta, Diego F. Angel-Urdinola, Joana Silva, and András Bodor. 2014. *Striving for Better Jobs: The Challenge of Informality in the Middle East and North Africa.* Directions in Development—Human Development. Washington, DC: World Bank.

Gatti, Roberta, Matte Morgandi, Rebekka Grun, Stefanie Brodmann, Diego Angel-Urdinola, Juan Manuel Moreno, Daniela Marotta, Marc Schiffbauer, and Elizabeth Mata Lorenzo. 2013. *Jobs for Shared Prosperity: Time for Action in the Middle East and North Africa.* Washington, DC: World Bank.

Hatayama, Maho, Mariana Viollaz, and Hernan Winkler. 2020. "Jobs' Amenability to Working from Home: Evidence from Skills Surveys for 53 Countries." Policy Research Working Paper 9241, World Bank, Washington, DC.

Krafft, Caroline. 2016. "Understanding the Dynamics of Household Enterprises in Egypt: Birth, Death, Growth and Transformation." Working Paper 983, Economic Research Forum, Dokki, Giza, Egypt.

Krafft, Caroline, Ragui Assaad, and Mohamed Ali Marouani. 2021. "The Impact of COVID-19 on Middle Eastern and North African Labor Markets: Glimmers of Progress but Persistent Problems for Vulnerable Workers a Year into the Pandemic." ERF Policy Brief 57, Economic Research Forum, Dokki, Giza, Egypt.

Krah, Kwabena, Lokendra Phadera, and Matthew Grant Wai-Poi. 2021. "Iraq—High-Frequency Phone Survey (IHFPS) to Monitor Impacts of COVID-19: Results from August, September, and October 2020 Rounds (English)." World Bank Group, Washington, DC.

Lopez-Acevedo, Gladys, Gordon Betcherman, Ayache Khellaf, and Vasco Molini. 2021. *Morocco's Jobs Landscape: Identifying Constraints to an Inclusive Labor Market*. International Development in Focus. Washington, DC: World Bank. https://doi.org/10.1596/978-1-4648-1678-9.

Moosa, Dalal, and Vanessa Moreira da Silva. 2021. "Iraq—High-Frequency Phone Survey to Assess the Impact of COVID-19 on Firms." World Bank Group, Washington, DC.

Morocco, High Commission for Planning. 2020. *Survey of the Impact of the Coronavirus on the Economic, Social and Psychological Situation of Households in Morocco* [French]. Rabat: High Commission for Planning.

Narayan, Ambar, Roy Van der Weide, Alexandru Cojocaru, Christoph Lakner, Silvia Redaelli, Daniel Gerszon Mahler, Rakesh Gupta N. Ramasubbaiah, and Stefan Thewissen. 2018. *Fair Progress? Economic Mobility across Generations around the World*. Equity and Development Series. Washington, DC: World Bank. https://openknowledge.worldbank.org/handle/10986/28428.

Rother, Friederike, Carole Chartouni, Javier Sanchez-Reaza, Gustavo Paez Salamanca, and Belal Fallah. Forthcoming. *Enhancing Workers' Protection in Jordan*. Washington, DC: World Bank.

Saudi Arabia, Government of, General Authority for Statistics of the Kingdom of Saudi Arabia. 2019. "Labour Market 2019 Fourth Quarter: Main Data and Indicators of the Labour Market."

Tansel, Aysit, Halil Ibrahim Keskin, and Zeynel Abidin Ozdemir. 2020. "Is There an Informal Employment Wage Penalty in Egypt? Evidence from Quantile Regression on Panel Data." *Empirical Economics* 58: 2949–79. https://doi.org/10.1007/s00181-019-01651-2.

Tansel, Aysit, and Zeynel Abidin Ozdemir. 2014. "Determinants of Transitions across Formal/Informal Sectors in Egypt." IZA Discussion Paper 8773, Institute of Labor Economics (IZA), Bonn. http://ftp.iza.org/dp8773.pdf.

Wahba, Jackie. 2009. "Informality in Egypt: A Stepping Stone or a Dead End?" Working Paper 456, Economic Research Forum, Dokki, Giza, Egypt.

Viollaz, Marlana, and Hernan Winkler. 2020. "The Task Content of Jobs in MENA." World Bank, Washington, DC. Unpublished.

JORDAN: An Online Learning Platform to Deliver Accessible, Quality Education

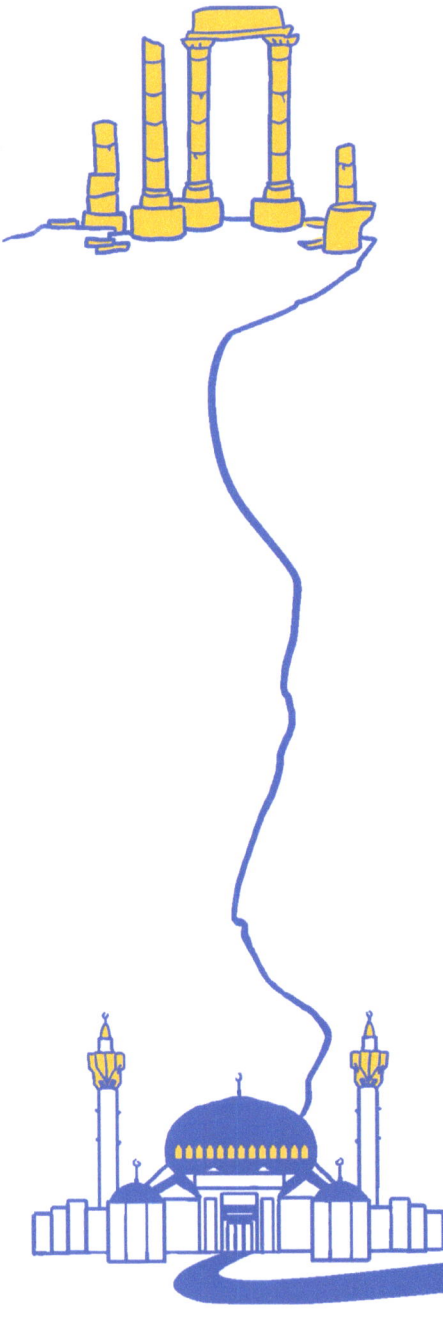

Hamdi is a 34-year-old entrepreneur in Amman who is the cofounder and chief executive officer (CEO) of a smart learning platform. Hamdi has been educated in some of the top education institutions in London, where he received his master's degree.

The key motivation behind this endeavor came from the simple question that Hamdi wished to answer: "Why am I among so few in the MENA region who can get exposed to such high-quality education?" Hamdi knew from experience that quality education systems move students away from rote memory as the sole tool of learning and encourage them to become self-reliant, independent thinkers. With several limitations in the existing education system in Jordan, including high fees and inaccessibility, especially for refugees, there was a market for a learning platform. Hamdi spent two years interviewing students, teachers, government officials, and parents regarding their needs and desires in relation to learning and after-school tutoring. He incorporated their input into his model and launched the first version of the platform in February 2020, when COVID-19 started picking up speed in the MENA region.

About 100,000 students are now registered on Hamdi's platform. More than 1 million students have learned from the platform since the onset of the COVID-19 pandemic, as the company opened it up for free during this crisis. The smart learning platform provides a seamless product and engaging content and uses the power of artificial intelligence to curate learning experiences for every student at a pace that works best for them. Today, the company employs more than 100 local staff and has offices in Amman and Cairo. In the next three years, Hamdi hopes to expand to the rest of the Arab world. He plans to establish offices across the MENA region with the goal of serving 10 million students in the coming five years.

Hamdi's entrepreneurship journey leveraged his education and experience in the tech sector. He built the platform after years of attempting to start various businesses, some of which succeeded and some of which failed. Hamdi's first-hand experience working with other established platforms in the transportation sector, seeing how technology positively disrupted the sector,

led him to consider how technology could have similar effects on education. Hamdi has identified several challenges that entrepreneurs such as him face, including access to finance, lack of a data infrastructure, and limited start-up services.

Hamdi has a few words of wisdom for his fellow entrepreneurs in the region. He believes that all entrepreneurs need to take risks to succeed. "Keep on iterating to find a product or a service that the customer needs and is willing to pay for. Surround yourself with solid team members who share your vision, and execute as hard as you can until you crack it. Also, remember that starting a new business in the MENA region has never been an easy journey; it is a marathon, not a sprint."

CHAPTER 3

What Prevents the Creation of More and Better Jobs in MENA?

INTRODUCTION

A dynamic private sector is the cornerstone of good jobs. The spirit of entrepreneurship and innovation can propel economies down serendipitous paths of prosperity. Youth are energized as they participate in the private sector, learn valuable skills, and gain a sense of purpose as they become stewards of their own destiny. But for far too long this has not been the case for the Middle East and North Africa (MENA) region, where the private sector has been sclerotic, not gender inclusive, and generally not in the business of creating jobs.

The lack of private sector dynamism in the region can be attributed to several factors. One of the most important ones is the barriers to firms entering or leaving markets—the lack of contestability—that characterizes most of the region's economies. The economies of MENA have favored incumbent firms, whether private-led or state-owned, resulting in job creation in the private sector that is too slow to absorb the rapidly growing population (Baduel, Geginat, and Pierre 2019).

PATHWAYS THAT LINK MARKET CONTESTABILITY WITH JOBS

Contestable markets are those in which there is costless entry and exit of firms, and where the pressure of potential competition always exists. Contestable markets encourage higher productivity among firms and workers and the efficient allocation of resources. This can consequently improve the state and speed of structural change; the rise in wages; and the creation of more, better, and inclusive jobs (Amable and Gatti 2001; Blanchard and Giavazzi 2003; Nicoletti and Scarpetta 2003; Spector 2004).

The theoretical and empirical literature identifies three channels through which reforms and policies that boost product market contestability can create more and better jobs (figure 3.1). First, competition encourages firms to upgrade their capabilities and innovate to become more efficient, contributing to *productive efficiency*. Second, it shifts the market toward more efficient producers, contributing to *allocative efficiency*. Third, it forces less efficient firms to exit the market and more efficient ones to enter and grow (encouraging *market selection*). There has been ample theoretical and empirical work on these mechanisms across various countries around the world (see, for example, Aghion et al. 2005; Cusolito and Maloney 2018; Eslava et al. 2013; Geroski 1990; Jovanovic 1982; Kitzmuller and Licetti 2012; Nickell 1996; Sekkat 2009; Vives 2008).

As firms get more productive, the jobs they create also become more productive. This induces the reallocation of labor toward more productive jobs, within firms, across firms, and eventually across sectors (*structural change*). Low-productivity firms are pushed out of the market, while high-productivity firms and their jobs remain, inducing productivity growth and structural transformation at the macro level (Amable and Gatti 2001; Blanchard and Giavazzi 2003; Boeri, Nicoletti, and Scarpetta 2000; Ebell and Haefke 2003; Krueger and Pischke 1997; Nickell and Layard 1999; Nicoletti et al. 2001; Nicoletti and Scarpetta 2005; Pissarides 2001). More productive jobs generally command better wages and are a better source of stable income and decent working conditions, especially as producers transmit some of their productivity gains to their workers.

Competition can also indirectly create more and better jobs in two additional ways. The first is when the cost savings from productivity gains are passed on to consumers in the form of lower prices (Dauda et al., forthcoming). In more competitive markets, firms are forced to align prices with marginal costs, and so prices tend to be lower than would have otherwise occurred in less competitive markets. Lower prices allow consumers (that is, workers and their families) to spend less of their disposable income on the same products[1] and spend more on other goods and services elsewhere in the economy. This consequent rise in demand can indirectly induce more job creation. Second, when firms invest their cost savings to expand their businesses, they increase the supply of goods and services, which ultimately also increases their demand for labor. Consequently, competitive pressure can create new pockets of demand. These new pockets could come from an expansion of the market, both domestically and abroad. In fact, the degree of competition in the domestic market is also a key determinant of international competitiveness (Goodwin and Pierola 2015).

Dynamic and fair competition can also ensure that income-earning opportunities are available to all people, including the poor, youth, women, and other disadvantaged groups. Research suggests that competition reduces the gender wage gap and reduces the level of informality in an economy, which tends to be associated with lower wages (Anand and Khera 2016; Ashenfelter and Hannan 1986; Belfield and Heywood 2006; Charlot, Malherbet, and Terra 2015).

However, it is worth noting that while dynamic markets are necessary for the creation of more and better jobs, it is quite likely that in the short term (the transition phase), competition may entail initial job losses when it weeds out low-productivity firms (Bouis et al. 2012; Bouis, Duval, and Eugster 2016). Hence, it becomes critical that labor market and social protection systems support workers and their families during these transitions to ensure welfare and inclusiveness. In the longer term, however, new innovative firms, induced by greater competition, may lead to net positive job creation.

Figure 3.1 The number and quality of jobs depend on the type and degree of competition and market contestability

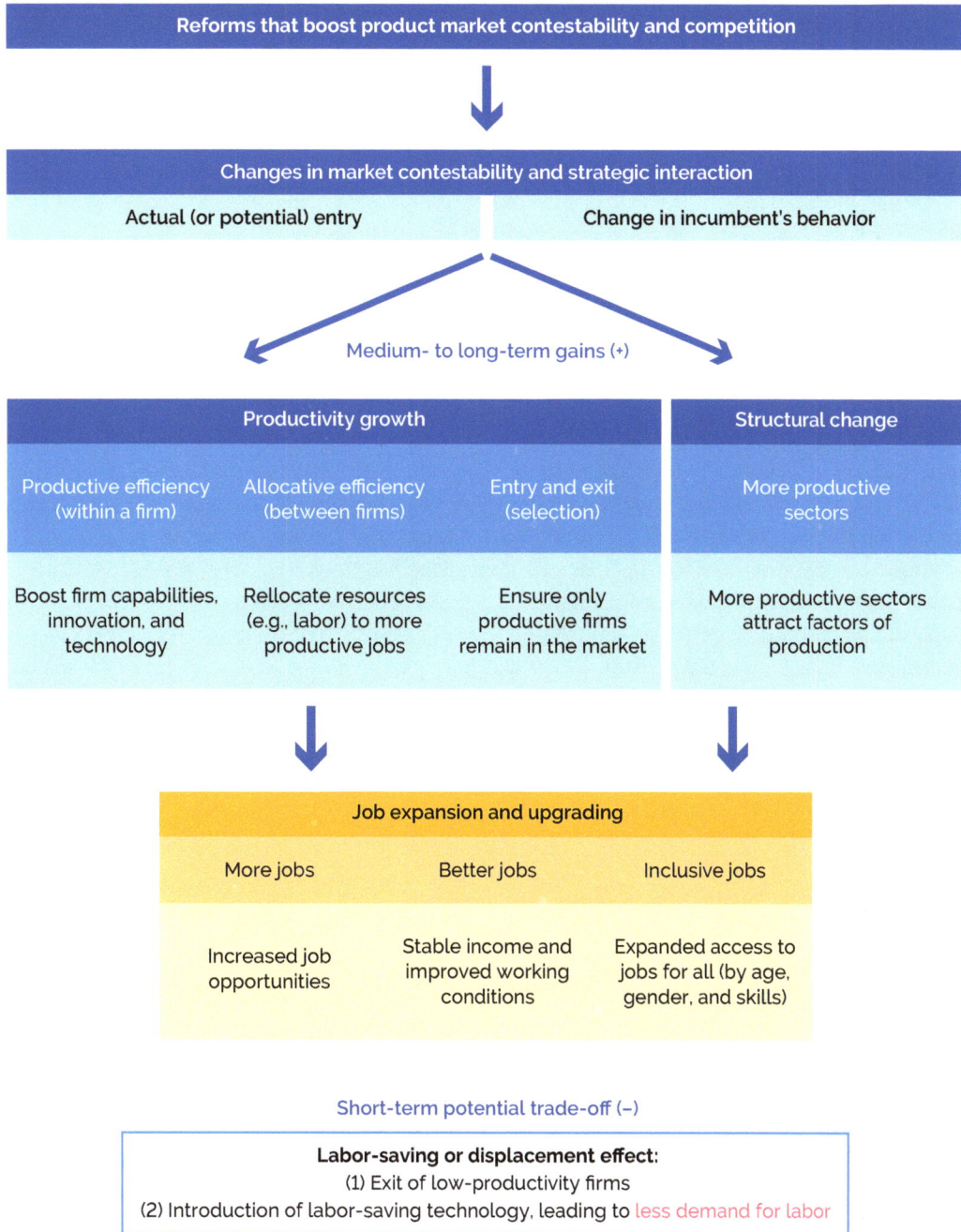

Reforms that boost product market contestability and competition

↓

Changes in market contestability and strategic interaction	
Actual (or potential) entry	Change in incumbent's behavior

Medium- to long-term gains (+)

Productivity growth			Structural change
Productive efficiency (within a firm)	Allocative efficiency (between firms)	Entry and exit (selection)	More productive sectors
Boost firm capabilities, innovation, and technology	Rellocate resources (e.g., labor) to more productive jobs	Ensure only productive firms remain in the market	More productive sectors attract factors of production

↓   ↓

Job expansion and upgrading		
More jobs	Better jobs	Inclusive jobs
Increased job opportunities	Stable income and improved working conditions	Expanded access to jobs for all (by age, gender, and skills)

Short-term potential trade-off (−)

Labor-saving or displacement effect: (1) Exit of low-productivity firms   (2) Introduction of labor-saving technology, leading to less demand for labor

Source: Flagship team elaboration, based on Dauda (2020).

THE REGION'S "SCLEROTIC" PRIVATE SECTOR

To better understand how these pathways manifest at the firm level in the MENA region, this section uses data from the World Bank Enterprise Surveys (WBES) that, for the first time, offered two rounds of surveys for several economies in the region, consequently allowing for a new glimpse into the evolution of the private sector over the years. The first round of the surveys was conducted in 2013–14, while the latest were in 2019–20 for the following six MENA economies: the Arab Republic of Egypt, Jordan, Lebanon, Morocco, Tunisia, and West Bank and Gaza. In addition, Malta was surveyed only for the 2019–20 wave. Income group comparisons include 88 countries surveyed in 2014 onward around the world.

Overall, the private sector in MENA is characterized by an evident and prevalent lack of dynamism, which manifests in mediocre job creation and labor productivity growth; and limited firm entry, growth, and exit; as well as low investments in physical capital, innovation, and worker training. Furthermore, the degree of political connections in the private sector is high.

The coronavirus (COVID-19) crisis is adding to this already suboptimal status quo, with important implications for the persistently unsatisfactory labor outcomes in the region (Apedo-Amah et al. 2020).

Job Creation and Labor Productivity

Overall, the private sector in the region has not seen much dynamism or productivity growth over the past few decades and has been a poor job creator. The growth rate of employment within firms for the latest round of the WBES was only 1 percent per year on average for MENA economies, which is markedly lower than the 5 percent average among middle-income peers (figure 3.2, panel a). The pattern of mediocre job creation and poor firm performance has been a mainstay for the MENA region (EBRD, EIB, and World Bank Group 2016; World Bank 2013, 2015), highlighting the fact that the (formal) private sector is unable to absorb the bulging workforce, leaving workers with few options but to seek opportunities in the informal sector. Moreover, firms in MENA economies to a large extent either contracted or remained the same in terms of employment between 2016 and 2019. The few expansions observed, on average, have been mainly among large firms (figure 3.2, panel b).

The limited role of small and medium enterprises in job creation is also evident when looking at labor force surveys, which show a bimodal distribution of formal employment across firm size in some countries (figure 3.3). In Egypt and Tunisia, for example, the majority of formal workers (those that have social security contributions) work in either microenterprises (1–4 workers) or relatively large public and private enterprises (100 or more workers). More precisely, about 57 percent of formal private sector workers in Egypt worked in large public or private sector enterprises and about 20 percent in microenterprises. In Tunisia in 2014, this bimodal distribution was also evident, with 34 percent of formal workers working in microenterprises, and 43 percent in large firms. When informal employment is added to the picture (panel b), the distribution tilts considerably more to the left, highlighting the fact that the majority of informal workers are in smaller firms (or self-employed). This pattern emphasizes the limited role of formal private sector firms in job creation.

Labor productivity growth has also been mediocre. Firms in five MENA economies (Egypt, Jordan, Lebanon, Tunisia, and Malta) registered negative labor productivity growth, while firms in two (Morocco and West Bank and Gaza) reported positive growth. On average the MENA region exhibited negative labor productivity growth, but this is on par with middle-income economies worldwide.

Figure 3.2 Job creation is mediocre in the MENA private sector

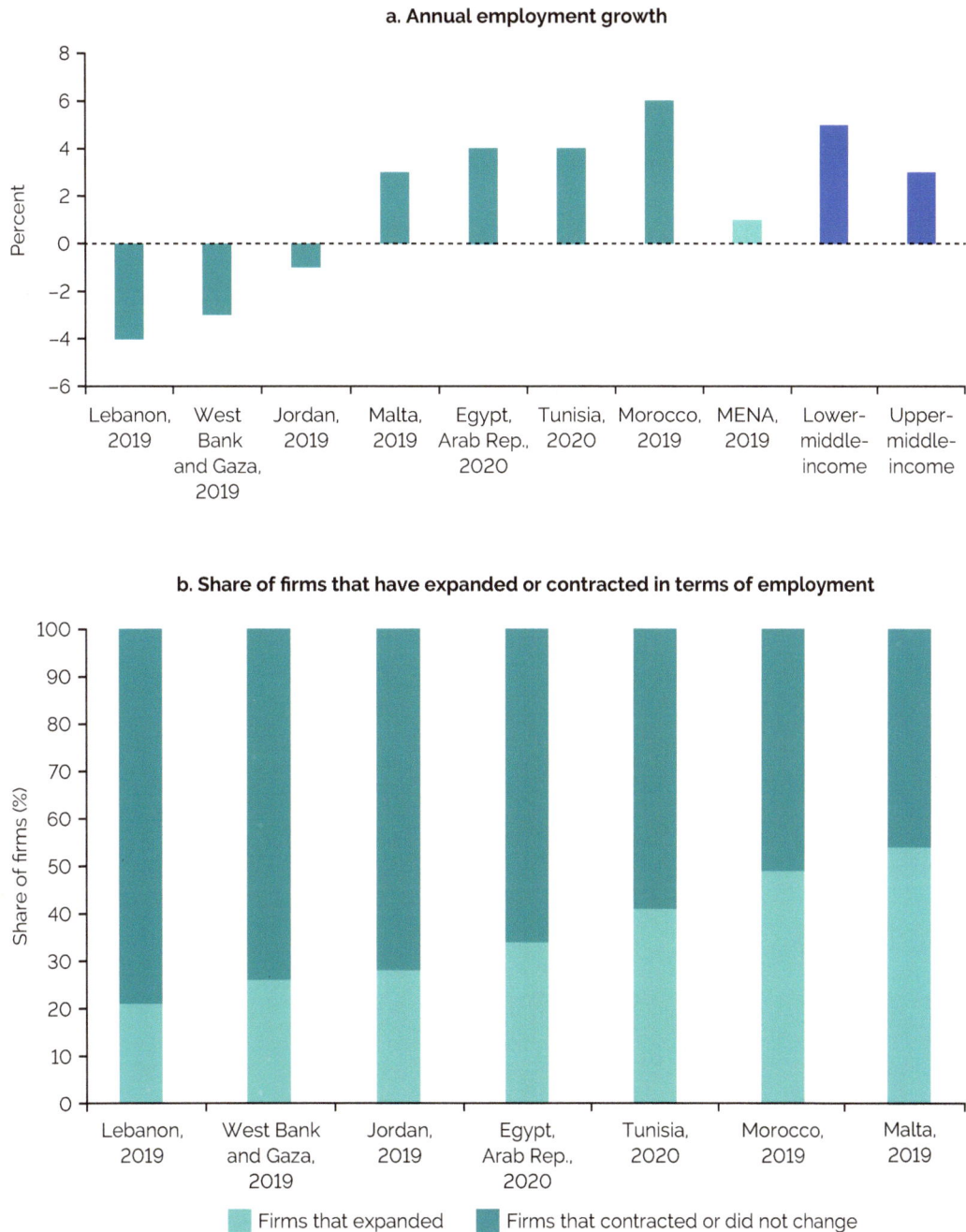

a. Annual employment growth

b. Share of firms that have expanded or contracted in terms of employment

☐ Firms that expanded   ☐ Firms that contracted or did not change

Source: World Bank Enterprise Surveys.
Note: Annual employment growth is calculated using employment from the last fiscal year, and employment recalled two fiscal years ago.
There are several limitations to this measure. First, firm entry and exit are not considered. Second, this employment growth is narrowly
defined for formal firms with five or more employees that are not fully government owned.

Figure 3.3 Formal employment is concentrated in the largest and smallest firms in some MENA countries

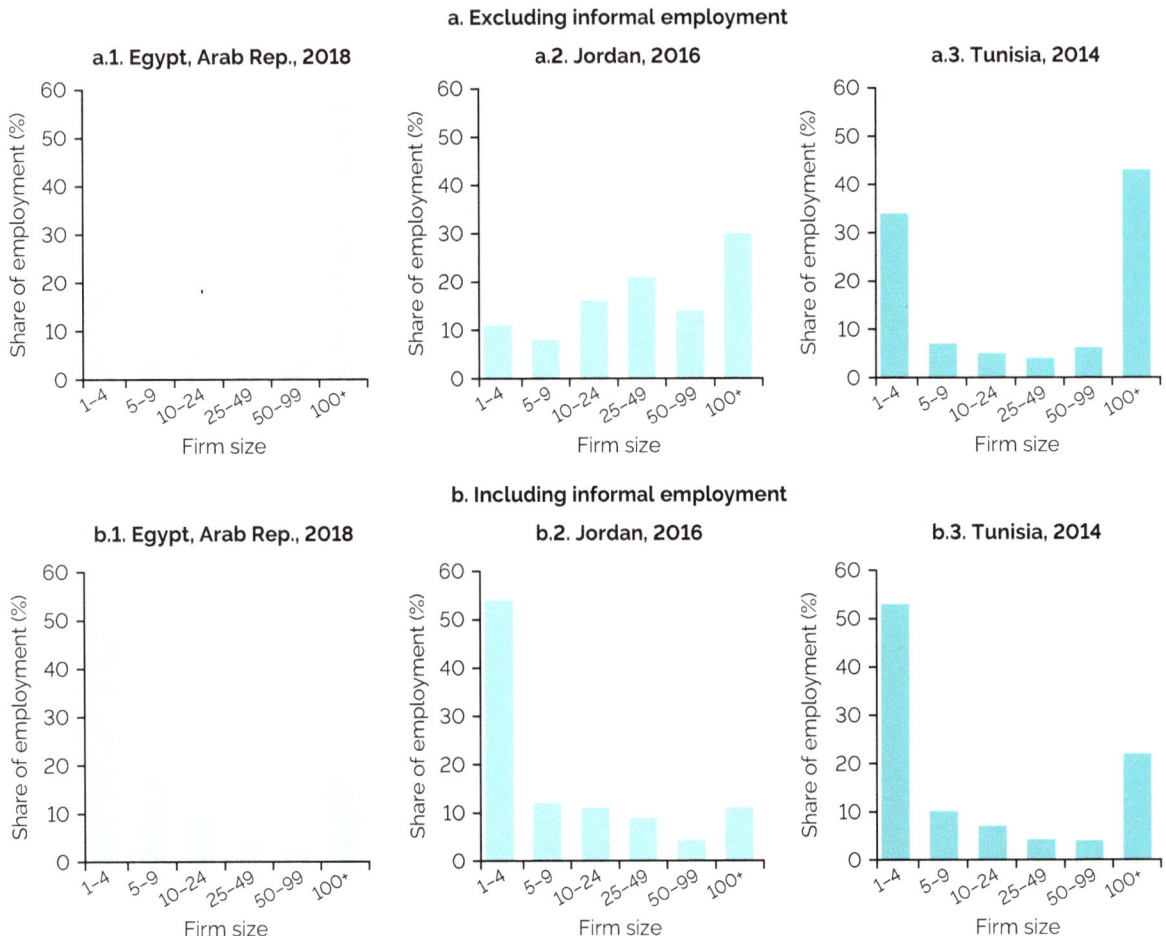

a. Excluding informal employment

a.1. Egypt, Arab Rep., 2018

Share of employment (%) — y-axis (0–60)
Firm size — x-axis (1–4, 5–9, 10–24, 25–49, 50–99, 100+)

a.2. Jordan, 2016

Share of employment (%) — y-axis (0–60)
Firm size — x-axis (1–4, 5–9, 10–24, 25–49, 50–99, 100+)

a.3. Tunisia, 2014

Share of employment (%) — y-axis (0–60)
Firm size — x-axis (1–4, 5–9, 10–24, 25–49, 50–99, 100+)

b. Including informal employment

b.1. Egypt, Arab Rep., 2018

Share of employment (%) — y-axis (0–60)
Firm size — x-axis (1–4, 5–9, 10–24, 25–49, 50–99, 100+)

b.2. Jordan, 2016

Share of employment (%) — y-axis (0–60)
Firm size — x-axis (1–4, 5–9, 10–24, 25–49, 50–99, 100+)

b.3. Tunisia, 2014

Share of employment (%) — y-axis (0–60)
Firm size — x-axis (1–4, 5–9, 10–24, 25–49, 50–99, 100+)

Sources: Economic Research Forum (ERF) Labor Market Panel Surveys for Egypt (2018), Jordan (2016), and Tunisia (2014).
Note: Firm size is based on number of employees. Informal employment is defined as those without social security contributions. The universe (for Egypt, Jordan, and Tunisia) is all those employed, between 15 and 64 years old, in both the public and private sectors, including both wage and nonwage employees.

Firm Entry, Growth, and Exit

The lack of dynamism can be seen in limited entry and growth of firms in the region (*market selection*).

In 2019, only 6 percent of firms surveyed across the MENA economies were young firms (at most five years old) (figure 3.4). This is only half the share of young firms seen in middle-income countries and indicates a relatively limited firm entry. What is even more startling is that the share of young firms on average fell for these MENA economies between 2012 and 2019, meaning that fewer firms seem to enter the market.

The role of young firms as important job creators has been well documented in advanced economies as well as in MENA (Adelino, Ma, and Robinson 2017; Heyman, Norback, and Persson 2018; Huber, Oberhofer, and Pfaffermayr 2017; Rijkers et al. 2014). The decline of young firms in the region is indicative of the weakening role of the formal private sector and potentially considerable barriers to firm entry.

Figure 3.4 The share of young firms is low and declining in MENA

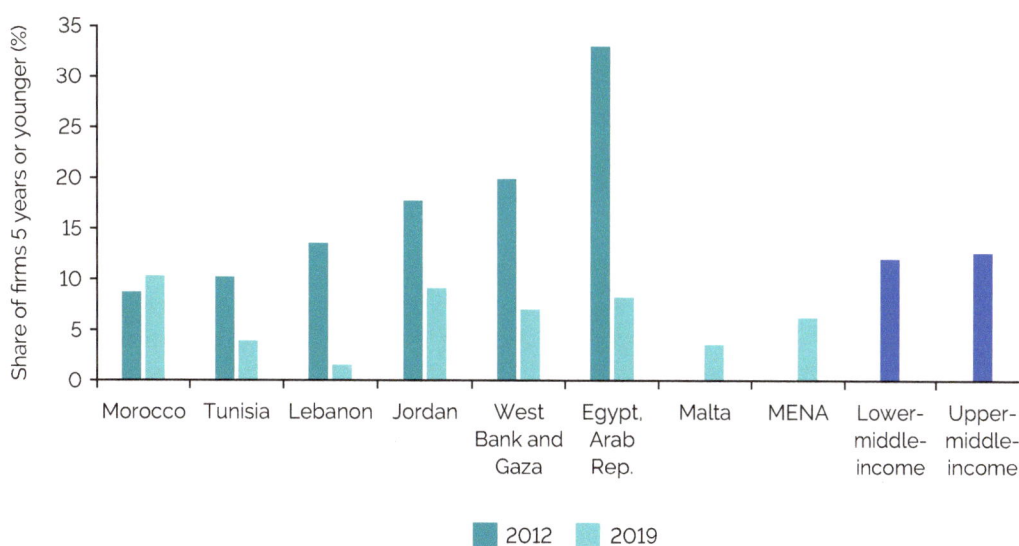

Source: World Bank Enterprise Surveys.
Note: Young firms are defined as those five years old or younger. Income group averages consist of economies surveyed between 2014 and 2019.

Table 3.1 Employment transition matrixes for MENA

Share of firms (%)

Size category in 2016	Size category in 2019			Size category at start of operations	Size category in 2019		
	Small (5–19)	Medium (20–99)	Large (100+)		Small (5–19)	Medium (20–99)	Large (100+)
Small (5–19)	95.42	4.41	0.17	Small (5–19)	78.30	20.29	1.41
Medium (20–99)	6.32	90.81	2.87	Medium (20–99)	26.06	59.63	14.31
Large (100+)	0.08	3.67	96.25	Large (100+)	7.67	20.35	71.98

Source: World Bank Enterprise Surveys.
Note: Firm size is based on number of employees. MENA economies include the Arab Republic of Egypt, Jordan, Lebanon, Malta, Morocco, Tunisia, and West Bank and Gaza. Firm exit and entry are not accounted for. The information is based on firms surveyed circa 2019, their size circa 2016, and their size when they started operations.

At the same time, when firms enter and operate in the private sector, very few of them seem to be able to grow in size, defined as number of workers (table 3.1).[2] Between 2016 and 2019, it was quite unlikely that a firm grew from small to large (0.17 percent of firms only). In fact, in this time period no small firm in Egypt, Jordan, Lebanon, Malta, Morocco, or West Bank and Gaza grew in size to a large firm, with the only exception being Tunisia (1.3 percent of firms). If this analysis is extended to the size of firms at birth, the probability that a firm that started small and became large by 2019 is still limited—a mere 1.4 percent. Excluding Malta from the sample drops this figure to less than 1 percent. For firms managed by women, the figure is far lower, at 0.11 percent. This is consistent with earlier reports based on census data, indicating not much has changed for at least a decade (World Bank 2015). Box 3.1 presents firm dynamics and job creation numbers for Egypt based on census data over a longer time horizon.

Box 3.1 Firm dynamics and job creation in the Arab Republic of Egypt

Egyptian firm-level data provide a longer time frame to observe transitions by firms across size categories. These are presented in table B3.1.1 and show that over two periods (1996–2006 and 2006–17) a very small proportion of firms outgrew their initial size category. These estimates do not account for entry and exit of firms because they are not based on panel data sets. Employment shares are based on average firm size within a cell of industry and geographical location (governorate). Also, these figures include only private sector nonagricultural firms.

Firm-level data from establishment censuses for 1996 (10 percent random sample), 2006, and 2017 indicate that Egypt experienced a 3.8 percent annual job growth rate over 1996–2006 and a 4.9 percent annual growth rate over 2006–17 (Assaad, Krafft, and Yassin 2020). The lack of dynamism and growth in the Egyptian formal private sector translates into poor job creation, especially by young firms (Krafft 2016). This is in contrast to other countries in the MENA region. Micro young firms achieved around 92 percent of the net job creation in Tunisia from 1996 to 2010 and 177 percent in Lebanon from 2005 to 2013 (World Bank 2015). However, there are signs that the role of small and medium enterprises in increasing employment may be rising in Egypt. Assaad et al. (2019) show that annual job creation in Egypt was only 1 percent in large firms over 2006–17 (from 9 percent over 1996–2006). On the other hand, small and medium private sector enterprises have witnessed increased shares of employment, decreasing the employment shares of micro and large establishments. Employment increased over 2006–17 by 50 percent and 60 percent faster in small and medium enterprises, respectively, compared to the overall employment in the private sector (Assaad, Krafft, and Yassin 2020).

Table B3.1.1 Employment transition matrixes for the Arab Republic of Egypt

Share of firms (%)

Size category in 1996	Size category in 2006				
	1–3	4–7	8–10	11–99	100+
1–3	**76**	20	3	0	0
4–7	26	**58**	14	2	0
8–10	14	44	**37**	5	0
11–99	20	32	37	**10**	1
100+	6	28	44	22	**0**

Size category in 2006	Size category in 2017				
	1–3	4–7	8–10	11–99	100+
1–3	**75**	20	4	1	0
4–7	20	**59**	18	3	0
8–10	7	23	**49**	21	1
11–99	9	17	28	**43**	3
100+	14	0	43	43	**0**

Source: Egypt Establishment Surveys. For more details, see Assaad, Krafft, and Yassin (2020).
Note: Firm size is based on number of employees.

(box continues on next page)

Box 3.1 Firm dynamics and job creation in the Arab Republic of Egypt *(continued)*

Weak overall formal private sector growth in Egypt implies that the informal sector may be taking up the slack. Household enterprises have a large role in providing employment opportunities in Egypt, comprising 56 percent of the employment share in 2017. Jobs created by household enterprises are very vulnerable and are substantially influenced by the macroeconomic environment.

In terms of exit, the results show that for the six MENA economies analyzed there is little correlation between various proxies for firm performance and whether or not a firm exited. In a few cases, there is some indication that productive firms may have exited—a positive correlation between labor productivity and firm exit. Exit rates are defined in two ways: if the discontinuation of the firm was confirmed (conservative definition) or if it was unreachable for the second round of the survey (extended definition). Thus, the evidence at best suggests that when firms exit, it is not the less productive firms that are exiting, indicating that competitive pressures may be absent.

Firm Investments

Few private sector firms in the MENA region invest in the physical capital (fixed assets) and in their workforce that could promote their *productive efficiency*. WBES data show that only 1 in 4 firms on average invested in physical capital over the previous fiscal year of the 2019/2020 survey (figure 3.5). The percentage of firms that invested in fixed assets also declined between 2012 and 2019. Similarly, the share of firms that offer formal training in MENA is lower than income peers. Formal training is mainly provided by large firms in the region. These insufficient investments make firms less dynamic and less able to expand and create the jobs to which the region's populations aspire. They are also symptomatic of a lack of competitive pressure that would otherwise drive firms to innovate and expand.

While the lack of investment by firms is one aspect, the type of investment matters too. Firms that operate in economies with the right structure and incentives are more likely to experiment with new ideas and then implement them. Research and development (R&D) spending is low in the region (figure 3.6), and it is lower than R&D spending by income peers. Furthermore, the share of firms that spent on R&D declined between 2012 and 2019. Women-led businesses are, however, more likely to spend on R&D (11.2 percent) than those led by men (6.8 percent).

Transforming MENA's economies entails creating the right incentives and institutional settings to transition from lower- to higher-productivity sectors and jobs. Entrepreneurship that pursues innovative ideas can exert new pressure on incumbents. This competitive pressure can improve productivity, especially if the threat from new firms induces innovation in existing firms.

To harness new opportunities, businesses—especially young ones—need to expand and invest, which necessitates access to finance. However, the financial sector in the region is dominated by a large banking sector that often lends to governments rather than to the private sector. The result of concentrated banking sectors in the MENA region may be low levels of engagement by the private sector with the financial sector. In fact, the share of firms having a bank loan or a line of credit is low: 26 percent of firms on average in the MENA region. The share of credit-constrained firms has also risen for most of the economies.

Figure 3.5 **The share of firms investing in physical capital is low and declining in MENA**

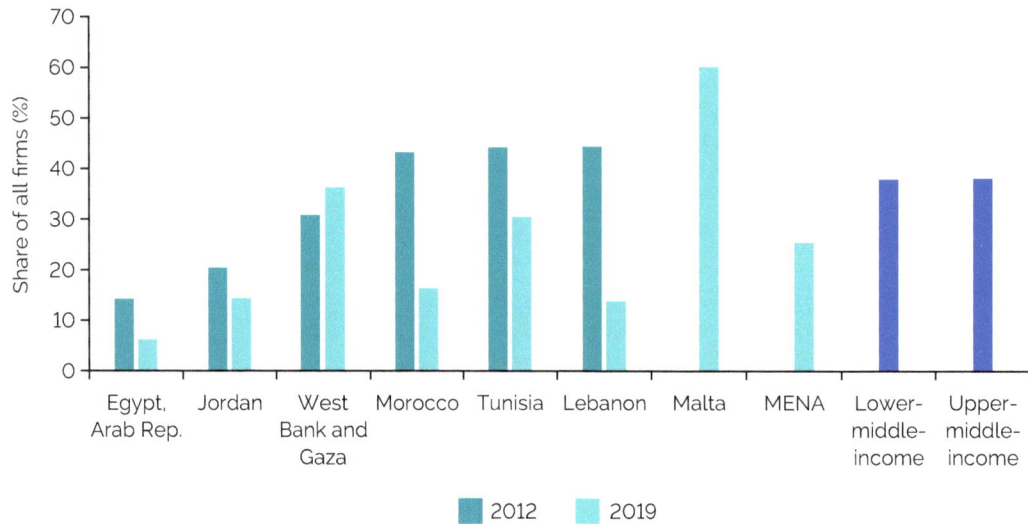

Source: World Bank Enterprise Surveys.
Note: Income group averages consist of economies surveyed between 2014 and 2019.

Figure 3.6 **The share of firms spending on R&D is low and declining in MENA**

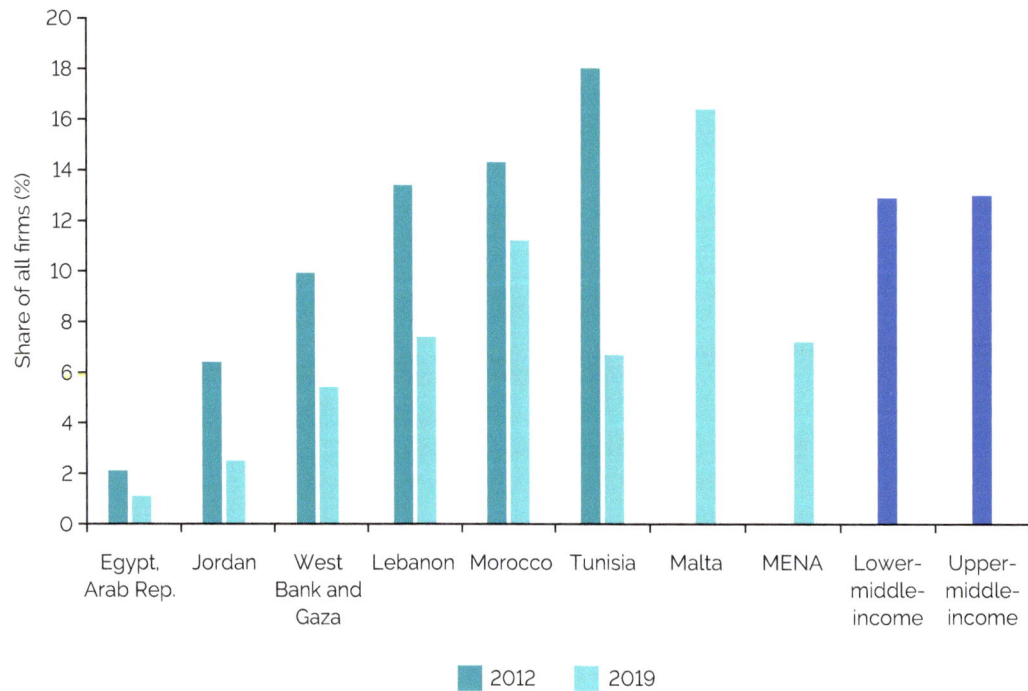

Source: World Bank Enterprise Surveys.
Note: Income group averages consist of economies surveyed between 2014 and 2019. R&D = research and development.

Still, despite access to finance being the second-biggest obstacle to operations cited by firms (next to political instability), a low share of firms in MENA in 2019 applied for loans at all, and this share declined between 2012 and 2019. This pattern further highlights a disconnect between the financial sector and the private sector, which has been well documented (EBRD, EIB, and World Bank Group 2016). The lack of competition in the banking sector may partly explain the disconnect between the financial and private sectors. The COVID-19 pandemic may accelerate digital financial services in the region that could fill the gap in financing needs. In fact, a survey of fintech firms has shown strong growth in the sector during the pandemic. The MENA region has witnessed the highest growth (up 40 percent) in fintech firms, consistent with a general pattern of emerging markets and developing countries experiencing faster growth than developed markets (World Bank 2020).

Political Connections

Political connections are one way by which market contestability can be debilitated. Politically connected firms can have access to privileges that deter the entry of new firms and inhibit unconnected firms from growing. The number of jobs created by politically connected firms as favors for economic privileges to politicians is unlikely to compensate for the larger loss in jobs due to enervated competitive forces. Moreover, the presence of politically connected firms in certain sectors may be indicative that such sectors face barriers to entry given that such firms may self-select into sectors where they can exercise their influence. Furthermore, politically connected firms may be capital intensive given privileged access to credit. Thus, when they grow, they may create fewer jobs as they substitute labor with physical capital.

The degree of political connections in the private sector is high in the MENA region. A sample of about 23,000 firms across Europe, Central Asia, Mongolia, and the MENA region were asked in the Enterprise Surveys, "Has the owner, CEO, top manager, or any of the board members of this firm ever been elected or appointed to a political position in this country?" This is the first time such a measure of political connection has existed for a broad range of countries, allowing for cross-country comparisons.

About 8 percent of firms in the MENA region responded Yes to this question, compared to much lower percentages among middle-income countries. The highest share was in Tunisia, with about 28 percent of firms responding Yes, while the lowest was in Lebanon, with only 1 percent responding Yes (figure 3.7, panel a). Larger firms in the region are more likely to be politically connected (figure 3.7, panel b).

At the same time, surveyed firms in Europe and Central Asia, Mongolia, and MENA that are politically connected are less likely to claim to have too many competitors, more likely to be part of a business organization, and more likely to use external sources of finance. Politically connected firms in the MENA region are also more likely to be part of a business organization and have access to external finance than the rest of the sample.

Studies about the region have documented that the presence of politically connected firms can hurt job creation. In Egypt, sectors that experienced entry of politically connected firms between 1996 and 2006 had lower aggregate employment growth than sectors that did not. Such politically connected firms enjoyed fiscal and regulatory privileges including trade protection and energy subsidies. They reduced competition and investment by unconnected firms (Diwan, Keefer, and Schiffbauer 2020). In Lebanon, while data from 2005 to 2010 show that politically connected firms create more jobs than politically unconnected firms, the presence of politically connected firms is correlated with lower aggregate job creation overall. This implies that the lack of contestability brought by politically connected firms hurts unconnected firms substantially such that overall employment growth falls. For every additional politically connected firm in a sector, 9.4 percent fewer net jobs were created (Diwan and Haidar 2020). In Tunisia, using data between 2000 and 2010, politically connected firms are found to have abused entry regulation for private gain, thereby reducing competition (Rijkers, Freund, and Nucifora 2017).

Figure 3.7 Politically connected firms are larger and more prevalent in MENA than in middle-income countries in general

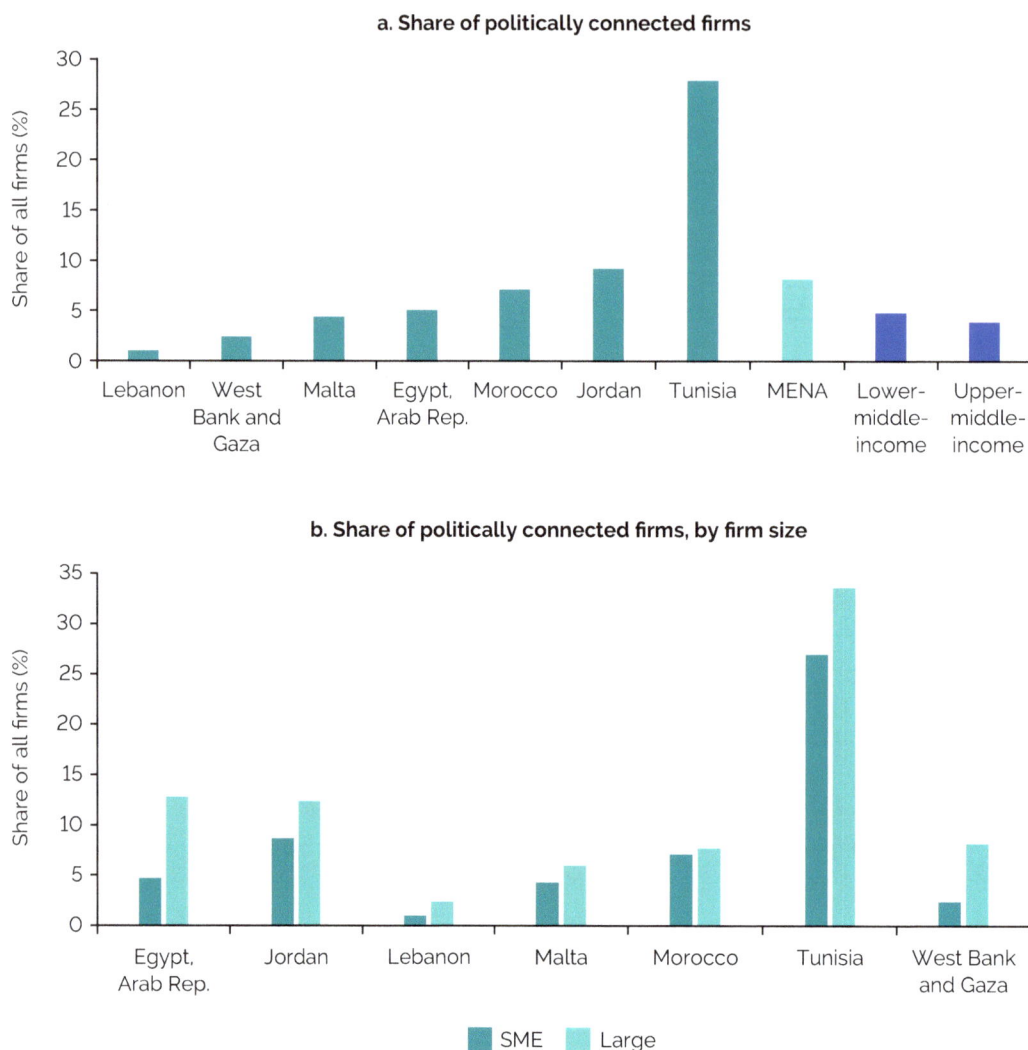

a. Share of politically connected firms

b. Share of politically connected firms, by firm size

Source: World Bank Enterprise Surveys.
Note: The sample includes firms in Europe and Central Asia, Mongolia, and the Middle East and North Africa surveyed in 2019. The question of political connectivity asks, "Has the owner, CEO, top manager, or any of the board members of this firm ever been elected or appointed to a political position in this country? SME = small and medium enterprise.

Politically connected firms were also more likely to avoid taxes in the form of import tariffs (Rijkers, Baghdadi, and Raballand 2017). In Morocco, sectors with politically connected firms received higher levels of nontariff protection than unconnected sectors (Ruckteschler, Malik, and Eib 2019).

The Impact of the COVID-19 Pandemic on Firms

The COVID-19 pandemic has brought about an existential threat to many private sector firms in the region. Phone surveys conducted in Algeria, Jordan, Morocco, Tunisia, and West Bank and Gaza right after the onset of the pandemic show that the MENA private sector is under duress. Firms in the MENA region experienced a larger drop in revenues than other regions despite on average being more likely to be open. The greatest declines in revenues occurred among micro and small firms, tourism-related activities, and women-owned businesses (Apedo-Amah et al. 2020).

The response by businesses in MENA to the fall in revenues has differed from firms surveyed in other regions. MENA businesses had the lowest likelihood of laying off workers (12 percent of firms laid off workers) compared to other developing economies (19 percent). They also had a higher likelihood of reducing hours/wages/granting leave (63 percent of firms) than other developing countries (48 percent). This pattern is mainly observed among large firms in MENA in comparison to other regions. Moreover, long-term adaptability to the pandemic has varied considerably by firm size. Compared to other developing countries, small firms in MENA have been disproportionately less likely to adopt digital technologies, less likely to receive public support, and more likely to fall into arrears than medium or large firms. The dominant reason behind small firms not accessing support is lack of information (40 percent).

The early findings from phone surveys indicate a growing disparity of small versus large firms in absorbing the effects of the pandemic. Programs that tend to help businesses are insufficiently targeted and may not be reaching the most vulnerable sections of the private sector. Finally, the digital divide between small and large firms implies that many smaller firms may have limited scope to adapt to stricter lockdown measures. If the pandemic increases the likelihood of large politically connected incumbent firms thriving while smaller unconnected firms falter, market contestability will deteriorate further. Governments should consider improving the targeting of their programs while enabling more firms to operate online. The full impact of the effects of the COVID-19 pandemic on the private sector may not have been realized. More recent rounds of phone surveys in Tunisia conducted in November–December 2021 found that 10.4 percent of businesses were permanently closed (IFC 2021). This is almost double the figure of 5.4 percent from the third quarter of 2020.

THE PLIGHT OF FEMALE ENTREPRENEURS

Like the region's labor market, MENA's private sector is not gender inclusive. Recent data on top managerial positions show that on average only 6 percent of firms in the MENA economies surveyed in the World Bank Enterprise Survey have a top woman manager (figure 3.8). This is less than half the average of low-income economies and less than one-third the high-income average. However, for most of the surveyed MENA economies, the percent of women top managers has risen between 2012 and 2019, albeit at a slow place.

Figure 3.8 **Few firms in MENA have a woman top manager**

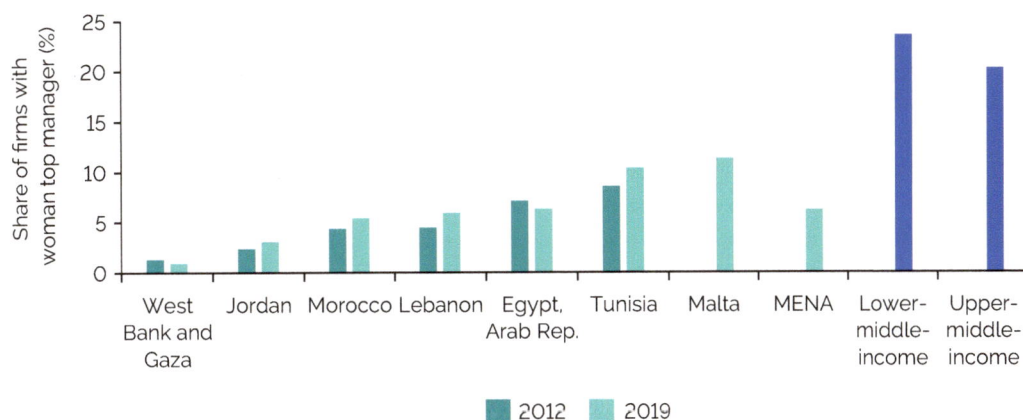

Source: World Bank Enterprise Surveys.
Note: Income group averages consist of economies surveyed between 2014 and 2019.

Women-managed firms in the region tend to be young firms engaged in activities in the retail sector. About 9.5 percent of businesses managed by women are young (five years or younger), in contrast to 5.8 percent of businesses led by men. Moreover, about 21 percent operate in the retail sector compared to 17 percent of firms managed by men.

There are certain similarities and differences between the operating environment of firms led by men and women in the region. While both cite political instability as the top obstacle to operating their businesses, a larger share of the women-led firms cite corruption as a major or severe constraint to running the business. Moreover, women-led firms are more likely to employ women workers than firms managed by men. On average 36.9 percent of permanent workers are women in firms led by women in contrast to 24.4 percent in firms managed by men.

In general, women-led businesses are doing the right things. They are more likely to invest in physical capital, train their workers, and invest in R&D. However, they are also facing challenges to productivity. A key insight of previous research based on 2012 data is that while fewer firms in the MENA region have a woman top manager, such firms tend to be as productive as those managed by male counterparts (EBRD, EIB, and World Bank Group 2016). This sets the region apart from other studies that have globally found that women-managed firms are less productive than male-managed firms (Islam et al. 2020). However, the 2019 wave of Enterprise Surveys show a gender labor productivity gap that did not exist in 2012. Firms managed by women are about 23 percent less productive than those managed by men. This figure is almost double that found by Islam et al. (2020) for a global sample. The absence of a labor productivity gap in 2012 was partly attributed to the fact that there was a high degree of selection of women into managerial positions. In other words, only few women attained higher-level positions in firms, but those that did ran businesses that were just as productive as businesses led by their male counterparts. However, the emerging productivity gap in 2019 is suggestive of the uneven playing field that women face in the private sector. The productivity gap is largely explained by country-level factors such as challenges of legal restrictions, childcare provisions, and social norms and factors unexplained by the data.

LIMITED OVERALL ECONOMIC GROWTH

Between 2000 and 2019, MENA's real GDP per capita grew by 37 percent, equivalent to an average annual compounded rate of about 1.7 percent (and a simple average of 1.9 percent per year). This growth exceeds only Latin America and the Caribbean and lags all other developing regions.

As growth is often dependent on the state of economic development, it is also evident that regardless of the income level of the countries in the region, they notably lag behind their income peers around the world (figure 3.9). For lower-middle-income economies in the region, which include Algeria, Egypt, Morocco, Tunisia, and West Bank and Gaza (data are limited for Djibouti), the annual growth rate of real GDP per capita was 2.6 percent over the two-decade period of 2000 to 2019, compared to a much higher rate of 6.8 percent among non-MENA countries. For upper-middle-income countries in the region, which include the Islamic Republic of Iran, Iraq, Jordan, Lebanon, and Libya, the growth rate was smaller, at 1.8 percent, compared to 12.2 percent for non-MENA countries (albeit driven by China). Finally, high-income countries in the region saw the least growth, of only 0.2 percent, and a contraction for Gulf Cooperation Council (GCC) economies of −0.1 percent, compared to a much higher rate of 1.6 percent among other high-income peers around the world.[3] These suboptimal macroeconomic outcomes reflect the labor and private sector realities in the region.

The growth of labor productivity, measured through real value added per worker, has also been generally limited, and particularly so among high-income countries. Growth prospects for developing countries often rely on the ability to increase the productivity of the economy. More productive economies are able to produce more with the resources they have, consequently generating higher income for their populations and more growth and prosperity.

Figure 3.9 The annual growth rate of GDP per capita in MENA economies lagged behind the rate among income peers worldwide between 2000 and 2019

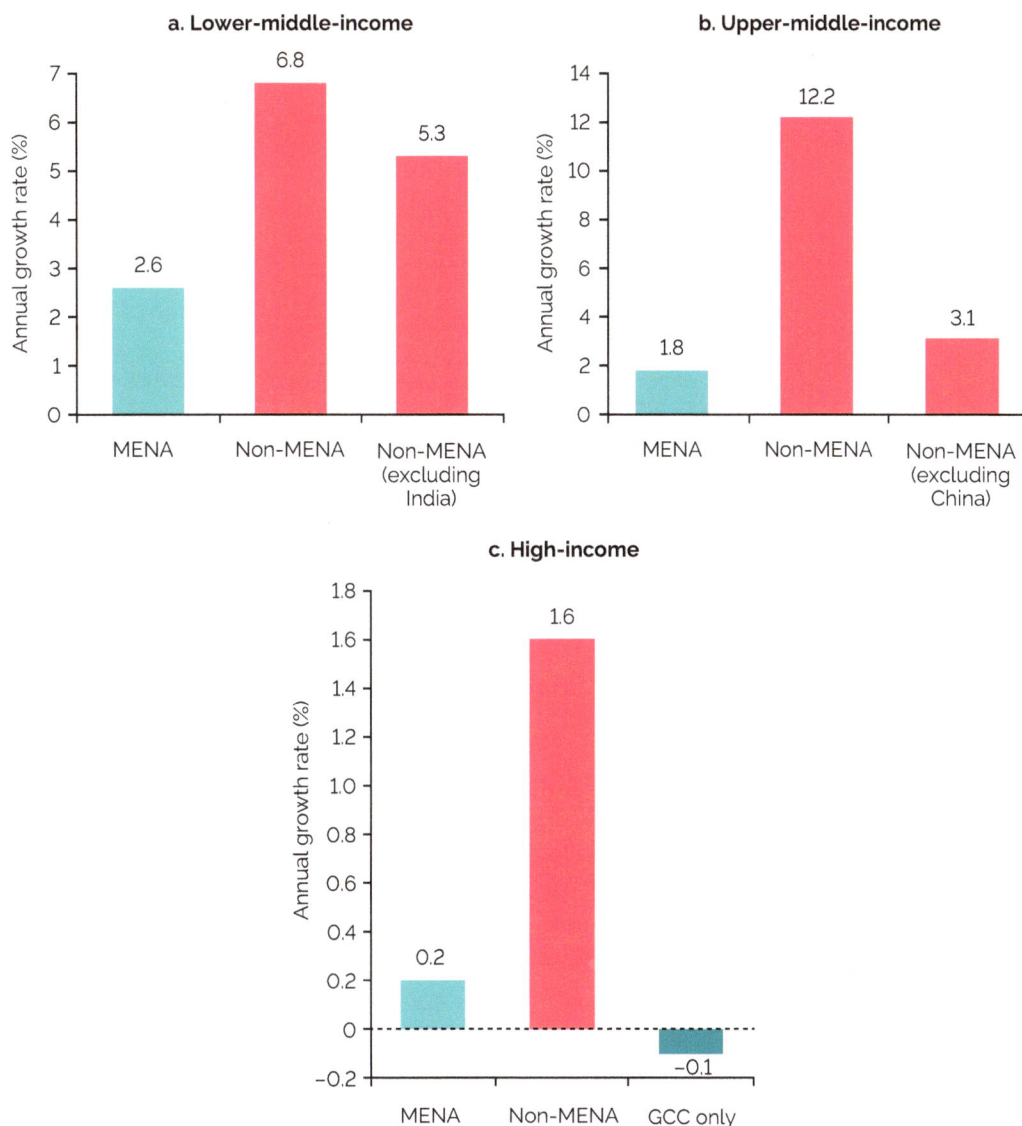

a. Lower-middle-income

b. Upper-middle-income

c. High-income

Source: World Bank World Development Indicators.
Note: Regional averages are weighted averages, where the weight is the share of the population size in the group. GCC = Gulf Cooperation Council; GDP = gross domestic product.

Between 2007 and 2018, the average annual labor productivity growth for lower-middle-income MENA economies was around 3 percent, significantly lower than 5.3 percent experienced by non-MENA peers. For upper-middle-income MENA countries, the growth rate was 2.4 percent per year, compared to 10.2 percent among non-MENA countries (driven significantly by the growth in China). Among high-income countries in the region, on the other hand, labor productivity contracted by an average of 1.1 percent per year, in contrast to non-MENA peers, whose productivity growth remained positive and grew by 1 percent.

Much of this labor productivity growth comes from growth within sectors, as opposed to growth between sectors (structural change). For lower-middle-income economies in the MENA region, 80 percent of labor productivity growth came from the fact that sectors became more productive during this period, while the remaining 20 percent came from the reallocation of workers from lower- to higher-productivity sectors.[4] This is comparable to other non-MENA peers.

However, for upper-middle-income countries in the region, there was negative structural change—meaning that workers reallocated to lower-productivity sectors. This is not the direction of labor mobility that supports further development, and it is the opposite of the experience of income peers around the world, who still saw both within-sector productivity growth (contributing 81 percent to overall growth) and structural change contributing 19 percent. The emphasis on structural change comes from the recognition that the composition of economic output and where workers are employed matter. Economies that are able to reallocate workers to higher-productivity sectors can grow faster than those where most workers are still employed in lower-productivity sectors.

Lastly, for the high-income countries in the region that saw negative labor productivity growth as mentioned above, much of this was driven by decreasing within-sector productivity—yet another concerning trend. Agriculture and industry saw decreasing value-added per worker during the period. This is also contrary to the experience of their income peers around the world, who still saw within-sector labor productivity growth.

Even when looking at the level of value-added per worker in 2018 for the three broad sectors of Agriculture, Industry and Services by each income group, upper-middle-income countries and high-income countries in the region especially do not perform well, and particularly so in Services. Only Lebanon, for instance, appeared to do relatively well compared to its peers in the value-added per worker in Services (while notably lagging in Industry)—which is likely now to be negatively affected as the country suffers from an ongoing economic and political crisis. All of the high-income countries trail their peers, and markedly so. When accounting for the fact that high-income countries and some middle-income countries, such as Algeria and Iraq, are heavy oil producers, which can pull up the value-added per worker in their Industry sector, their performance is notably below expectations.

These findings highlight the fact that it is not only a matter of growth where MENA faces challenges over time, but also the very level of productivity itself.

Contrary to economic growth and labor productivity, countries in the region have been able to attract flows of capital over the past couple of decades. The flows of gross fixed capital formation in the region have hovered around 20 percent to 25 percent of GDP. In 2018, these flows were higher than those of Europe and Central Asia, Sub-Saharan Africa, and Latin America and the Caribbean, although notably lower than those in East Asia and Pacific and South Asia (figure 3.10). Even when looking at these flows by the income level of the countries, MENA's shares have been comparable to those of their income peers around the world.

While the stock of capital per capita in MENA economies is also generally comparable to their income peers, the growth rate of this capital per capita has been notably lower over the past two decades, highlighting the fact that other countries around the world are catching up. In 2017, the average value of capital in lower-middle-income economies in the region was estimated at US$19,601 per person, compared to a slightly lower US$17,329 per person among non-MENA peers (figure 3.11). However, the growth rate of capital per capita was actually negative for the region, shrinking by 35 percent between 2000 and 2017, while growth has been more notable for other income peers. For upper-middle-income countries in the region, on the other hand, the estimated stock of capital per capita was US$35,485 in 2017 and considerably lower than non-MENA peers' US$46,076. As with lower-middle-income economies, income peers have been catching up rapidly in terms of growth. Finally, for the high-income countries in the region, the average estimated capital of US$125,793 per person is slightly higher

Figure 3.10 MENA's gross fixed capital formation as a share of GDP is in the middle compared to other regions and has been declining

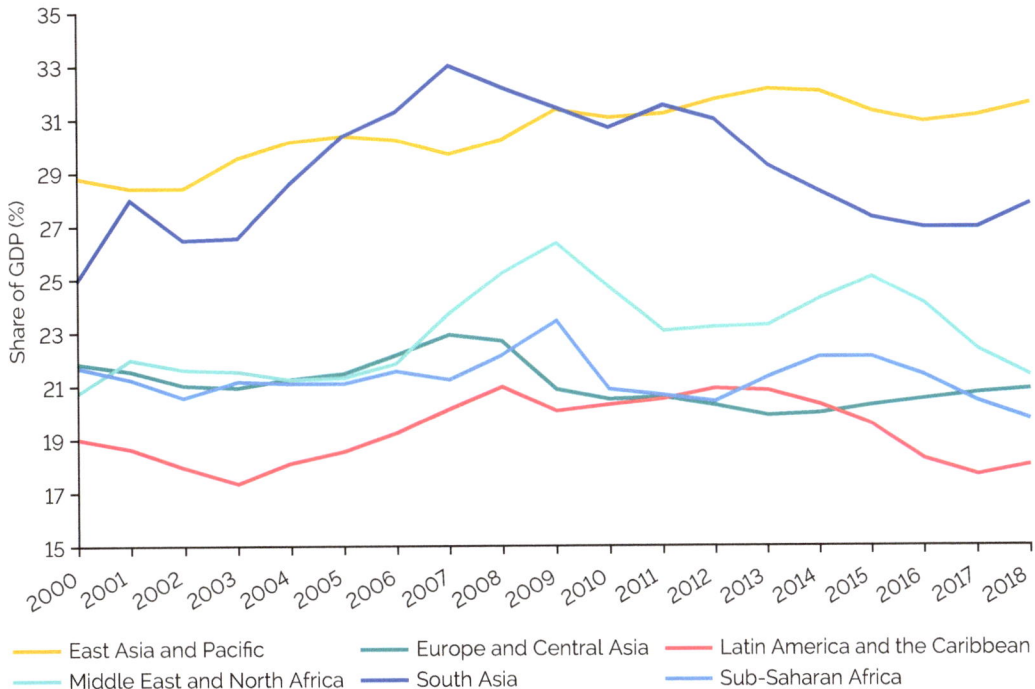

Source: World Bank World Development Indicators.

than non-MENA peers' estimate of US$123,494. However, like the other income groups in the region, the growth rate of capital per capita has also trailed behind income peers, contracting among MENA countries by 6 percent, while expanding by 21 percent among income peers, despite the high levels of capital they have already achieved.

These trends are generally similar when looking at capital per endowment of labor (that is, capital per person in the working-age population, 15–64 years old). However, it is worth noting than when looking at capital per worker (meaning the employed only), MENA countries generally exceed their peers. This is largely because much of the population is either too young or excluded from the workforce altogether through unemployment, underemployment, and female labor force participation. Capital is important for the entire economy, however, including its service as a public good for those who are not in the workforce.

The role of the state is evident in this capital accumulation. On average, the share of the stock of public capital in the total estimated stock of capital in MENA economies tends to be higher than income peers—regardless of income level (figure 3.12). The difference is not large for lower-middle-income economies and upper-middle-income countries. Lower-middle-income economies of the region have especially experienced a reduction in the share of public capital, considering the public sector legacy of the twentieth century. However, for high-income countries in the region, the share of public capital has increased over time (both in terms of flows and in terms of stock). This is particularly the case for Saudi Arabia and the United Arab Emirates.

The persistently significant share of public capital in MENA's overall capital accumulation may negatively affect the efficiency of the use of this capital and overall development. Some research

Figure 3.11 MENA's stock of capital per capita is comparable to that of its income peers worldwide, but income peers have been catching up

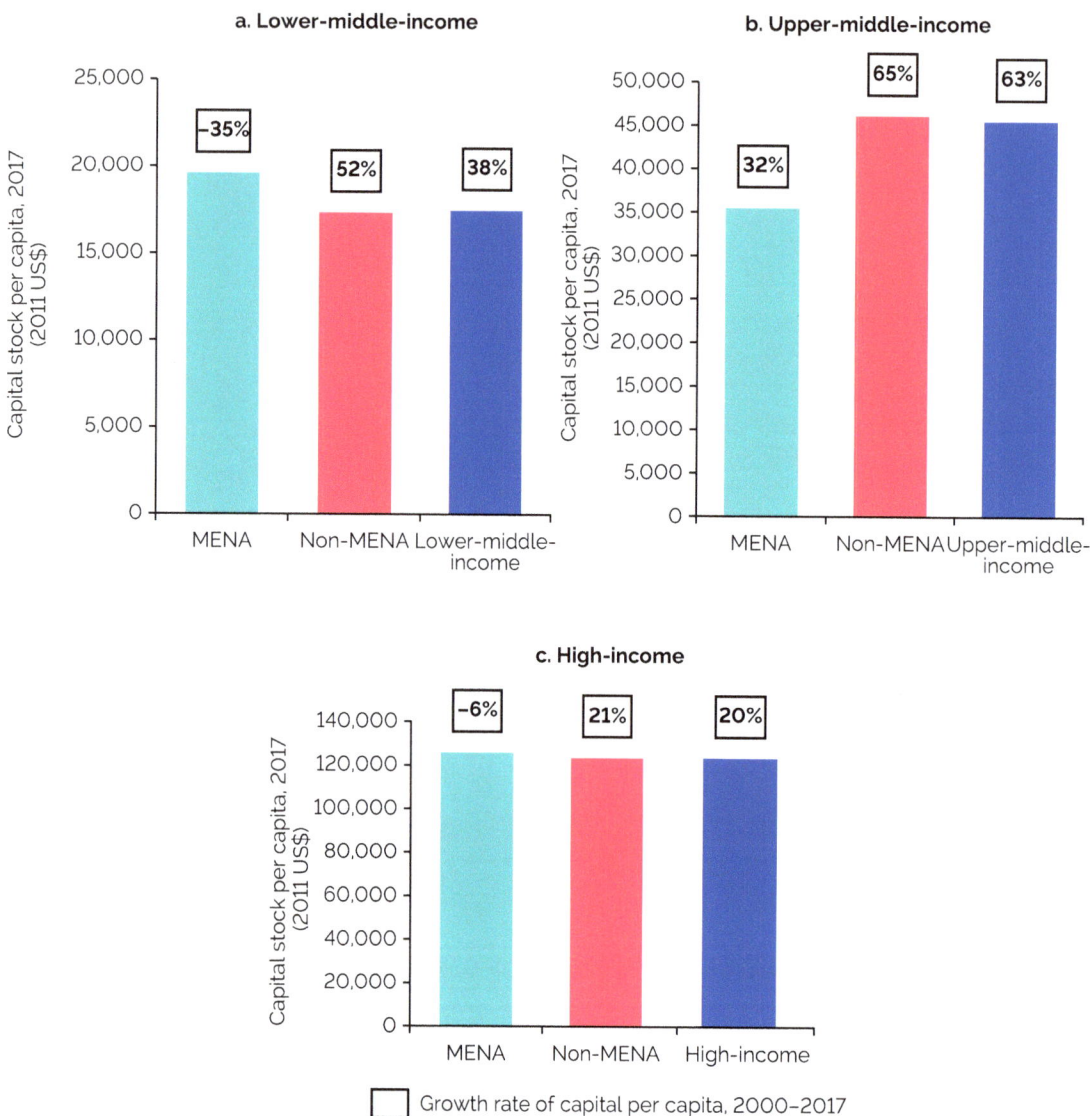

a. Lower-middle-income

Capital stock per capita, 2017 (2011 US$)

- MENA: ~19,500 [−35%]
- Non-MENA: ~17,200 [52%]
- Lower-middle-income: ~17,300 [38%]

(y-axis: 0 to 25,000)

b. Upper-middle-income

Capital stock per capita, 2017 (2011 US$)

- MENA: ~35,500 [32%]
- Non-MENA: ~46,000 [65%]
- Upper-middle-income: ~45,000 [63%]

(y-axis: 0 to 50,000)

c. High-income

Capital stock per capita, 2017 (2011 US$)

- MENA: ~125,000 [−6%]
- Non-MENA: ~122,500 [21%]
- High-income: ~122,000 [20%]

(y-axis: 0 to 140,000)

☐ Growth rate of capital per capita, 2000–2017

Source: Flagship team elaboration, based on IMF Investment and Capital Stock data set.
Note: The figures are calculated as weighted averages of the stock of capital per capita for the countries, such that the weight is the country's share of capital in its respective group. Higher levels of capital tend to have lower growth rates. IMF = International Monetary Fund.

suggests that public investment in developing countries especially may be used for unproductive projects that do not necessarily improve economic output (Pritchett 1996). The impact of public capital on productivity and growth also depends on the type of physical capital being supplied by the public sector. Some evidence has shown, for instance, that the impact of electricity and roads on growth is higher than other types of public investment (Canning and Bennathan 2000).

Moreover, while the impact of public capital on economic growth can be positive (Romp and de Haan 2005), there is always a risk that it can crowd out private investment, especially if it competes in profit-making sectors and if it is funded through domestic markets that are then constrained from lending to private stakeholders. A study on Egypt in the 1990s has shown that public investments crowded out private

Figure 3.12 Public capital continues to play an important role in the overall stock of capital in MENA

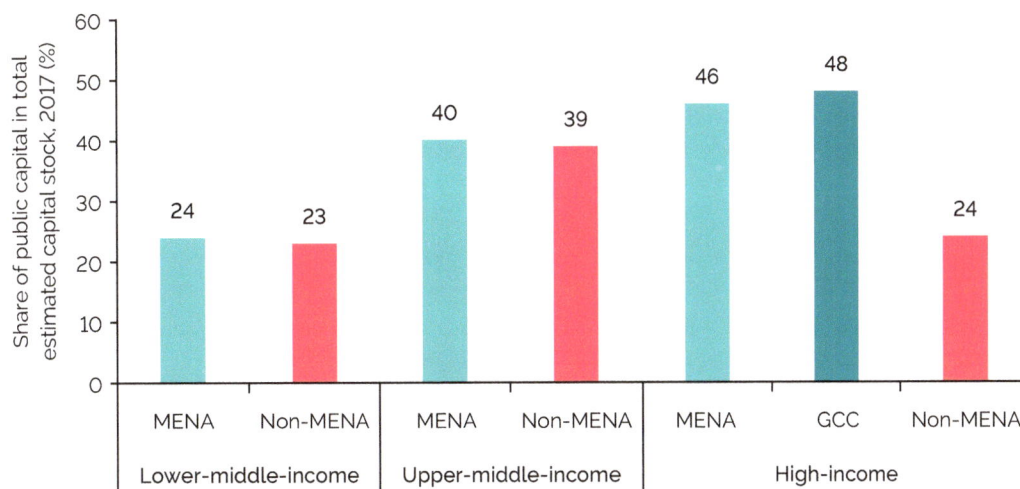

Source: IMF Investment and Capital Stock data set.
Note: Public capital here includes the estimates of both government capital as well as public-private partnerships. However, the share of these partnerships around the world is small for almost all countries. GCC = Gulf Cooperation Council; IMF = International Monetary Fund.

investment when accounting for the impact on credit markets, but it crowded in infrastructure investments (Shafik 1992). A later study found some crowding-out effect in oil-exporting countries of the region, but possible crowding-in for oil-importing countries (Dhumale 2000). A study on the impact of public infrastructure investments on private investments in Egypt, Jordan, and Tunisia shows that although public infrastructure investments have some positive impacts on the flows and stocks of private investment, they appear to be small and short-lived, highlighting issues related to unfavorable business environment as a major bottleneck for more and long-term capital investment growth (Agénor, Nabli, and Yousef 2005). However, much more research is needed in this area given the outdated and limited nature of existing analysis.

The macroeconomic repercussions of the COVID-19 pandemic have hit the MENA region in two primary ways. The first is the slowdown of business activity due to lockdowns, curtailments to mobility, and other restrictions that have had immediate impacts on domestic output, imports, and exports. This business slowdown has directly reduced jobs, and consequently household income and consumption. The second is the drop in oil prices that has directly squeezed oil-exporting countries in the region, which include the high-income countries of the GCC, as well as middle-income countries like Algeria, the Islamic Republic of Iran, Iraq, and Libya. GDP is estimated to have contracted by 5 percent in 2020, with a higher rate of 5.7 percent among oil exporters, while oil importers' GDP is estimated to have contracted by 2.2 percent (World Bank 2021). This economic downturn has negative ramifications on the fiscal space of MENA's economies. In 2020, the region was estimated to have experienced fiscal deficits equivalent to about 10 percent of GDP, with government debt climbing more than 7 percentage points, from 49 percent in 2019 to 56 percent in 2020 (IMF 2021).

Some signs of recovery were already apparent in 2021, including a rise in oil prices and a slow return of economic activity to some extent, with output expected to grow by 2.4 percent in 2021 (World Bank 2021). However, political fragility continues in a number of countries, including Lebanon, Libya, and Tunisia, while war and conflict persist in the Syrian Arab Republic, West Bank and Gaza, and the Republic of Yemen. The spread of different variants of the coronavirus further threatens to dampen expectations of recovery, especially as vaccination rates continue to be moderate in many countries.

NOTES

1. This depends on the products' price elasticity of demand.

2. The use of Enterprise Surveys to document size transitions is far from ideal and speaks to the inaccessibility or unavailability of census data. The information is based on recall data, and thus data on size are available at the time of the Enterprise Survey (2019), two fiscal years previous (2016), and when the business was founded (varies by firm). Given this is purely based on recall information, new firms that entered or exited within this time period are not accounted for. Furthermore, micro firms (fewer than five employees) as well as sectors not covered by the Enterprise Surveys are excluded. However, the results largely confirm earlier studies that have utilized census data where available.

3. High-income economies in the region include the six countries of the Gulf Cooperation Council (Bahrain, Kuwait, Oman, Qatar, Saudi Arabia, and the United Arab Emirates) as well as Israel and Malta.

4. To decompose labor productivity into structural change and within-sector productivity, this report utilized the following equation from McMillan, Rodrik, and Sepúlveda (2017)

$$\Delta P_t = \sum_{i=1}^{n} \theta_{i,t-k} \Delta p_{i,t} + \sum_{i=1}^{n} p_{i,t} \Delta \theta_{i,t}$$

where P refers to overall labor productivity in the economy and p refers to sectoral labor productivity levels, and where θ is the share of employment in sector i at time t. The Δ operator denotes the change in productivity or employment shares between time $(t - k)$ and (t), where k is the duration of the period of the analysis. What this equation implies is that the economywide labor productivity growth can be dissected into two sources: (1) "within-sector" productivity growth, captured through the first term on the right-hand side of the equation, which is expressed as the change in productivity within the sector multiplied by the share of the sector in employment at the beginning of the period under question; and (2) structural change that affects labor productivity, captured through the second term, which is expressed as the change in the sectors' employment shares, multiplied by the productivity at the beginning of the period under question.

REFERENCES

Adelino, Manuel, Song Ma, and David Robinson. 2017. "Firm Age, Investment Opportunities, and Job Creation." *Journal of Finance* 72: 999–1038.

Agénor, Pierre-Richard, Mustapha K. Nabli, and Tarik M. Yousef. 2005. "Public Infrastructure and Private Investment in the Middle East and North Africa." Policy Research Working Paper 3661, World Bank, Washington, DC.

Aghion, Philippe, Nick Bloom, Richard Blundell, Rachel Griffith, and Peter Howitt. 2005. "Competition and Innovation: An Inverted-U Relationship." *Quarterly Journal of Economics* 120 (2): 701–28.

Amable, B., and D. Gatti. 2001. "The Impact of Product Market Competition on Employment and Wages." IZA Discussion Paper 276, Institute of Labor Economics (IZA), Bonn.

Anand, Rahul, and Purva Khera. 2016. "Macroeconomic Impact of Product and Labor Market Reforms on Informality and Unemployment in India." IMF Working Paper 16/47, International Monetary Fund, Washington, DC.

Apedo-Amah, Marie Christine, Besart Avdiu, Xavier Cirera, Marcio Cruz, Elwyn Davies, Arti Grover, Leonardo Iacovone, Umut Kilinc, Denis Medvedev, Franklin Okechukwu Maduko, Stavros Poupakis, Jesica Torres, and Trang Thu Tran. 2020. "Unmasking the Impact of COVID-19 on Businesses: Firm Level Evidence from across the World." Policy Research Working Paper 9434, World Bank, Washington, DC.

Ashenfelter, Orley, and Timothy Hannan. 1986. "Sex Discrimination and Product Market Competition: The Case of the Banking Industry." *Quarterly Journal of Economics* 101 (1): 149–74.

Assaad, Ragui, Caroline Krafft, Khandkher Wahedur Rahman, and Irene Selwaness. 2019. "Job Creation in Egypt: A Sectoral and Geographical Analysis Focusing on Private Establishments, 1996–2017." Economic Research Forum Policy Paper, Economic Research Forum, Dokki, Giza, Egypt.

Assaad, Ragui, Caroline Krafft, and Shaimaa Yassin. 2020. "Job Creation or Labor Absorption? An Analysis of Private Sector Job Growth in Egypt." *Middle East Development Journal* 12 (2): 177–207.

Baduel, Bénédicte, Carolin Geginat, and Gaëlle Pierre. 2019. "Private Sector Job Creation in MENA: Prioritizing the Reform Agenda." IMF Working Paper WP/19/206, International Monetary Fund, Washington, DC.

Belfield, Clive, and John S. Heywood. 2006. "Product Market Structure and Gender Discrimination in the United Kingdom." In *Product Market Structure and Labor Market Discrimination*, edited by John S. Heywood and James H. Peoples. Albany, NY: State University of New York Press.

Blanchard, Olivier, and Francesco Giavazzi. 2003. "Macroeconomic Effects of Regulation and Deregulation in Goods and Labor Markets." *Quarterly Journal of Economics* 118 (3): 879–907.

Boeri, Tito, Giuseppe Nicoletti, and Stefano Scarpetta. 2000. "Regulation and Labour Market Performance." CEPR Discussion Papers 2420, Center for Economic and Policy Research, Washington, DC.

Bouis, Romain, Orsetta Causa, Lilas Demmou, Romain Duval, and Aleksandra Zdzienicka. 2012. "The Short-Term Effects of Structural Reforms: An Empirical Analysis." OECD Economics Department Working Paper 949, Organisation for Economic Co-operation and Development, Paris.

Bouis, Romain, Romain A. Duval, and Johannes Eugster. 2016. "Product Market Deregulation and Growth: New Country-Industry-Level Evidence." IMF Working Paper 16/114, International Monetary Fund, Washington, DC.

Canning, David, and Esra Bennathan. 2000. "The Social Rate of Return on Infrastructure Investments." Policy Research Working Paper 2390, World Bank, Washington, DC.

Charlot, Olivier, Franck Malherbet, and Cristina Terra. 2015. "Informality in Developing Economies: Regulation and Fiscal Policies." *Journal of Economic Dynamics and Control* 51 (February): 1–27.

Cusolito, Ana P., and William F. Maloney. 2018. *Productivity Revisited: Shifting Paradigms in Analysis and Policy*. Washington, DC: World Bank.

Dauda, Seidu. 2020. "The Effects of Competition on Jobs and Economic Transformation." Equitable Growth, Finance & Institutions Insight—Trade, Investment and Competitiveness. World Bank, Washington, DC.

Dauda, Seidu, Graciela Miralles Murciego, Georgiana Pop, and Azza Raslan. Forthcoming. "Restrictive Regulation as a Challenge for Competition, Productivity, and Jobs in the MENA Region: Closing the Gap." Background paper for *Jobs Undone: Reshaping the Role of Governments toward Markets and Workers in the Middle East and North Africa*. World Bank, Washington, DC.

Dhumale, Rahul. 2000. "Public Investment in the Middle East and North Africa: Towards Fiscal Efficiency." *Development Policy Review* 18 (3): 307–24.

Diwan, Ishac, and Jamal Ibrahim Haidar. 2020. "Political Connections Reduce Job Creation: Firm-Level Evidence from Lebanon." *Journal of Development Studies* 57 (8): 1373–96.

Diwan, Ishac, Philip Keefer, and Marc Schiffbauer. 2020. "Pyramid Capitalism: Political Connections, Regulation, and Firm Productivity in Egypt." *Review of International Organizations* 15 (1): 211–46.

Ebell, Monique, and Christian Haefke. 2003. "Product Market Deregulation and Labor Market Outcomes." Economics Working Paper, Department of Economics and Business, Universitat Pompeu Fabra, Barcelona.

EBRD (European Bank for Reconstruction and Development), EIB (European Investment Bank), and World Bank Group. 2016. "What's Holding Back the Private Sector in MENA? Lessons from the MENA Enterprise Survey." EBRD, London; EIB, Luxembourg; and World Bank, Washington, DC.

Eslava, Marcela, John C. Haltiwanger, Adriana D. Kugler, and Maurice Kugler. 2013. "Trade and Market Selection: Evidence from Manufacturing Plants in Colombia." *Review of Economic Dynamics* 16 (1): 135–58.

Geroski, Paul A. 1990. "Innovation, Technological Opportunity, and Market Structure." *Oxford Economic Papers* 42 (3): 586–602.

Goodwin, Tanja, and Martha Denisse Pierola. 2015. "Export Competitiveness: Why Domestic Market Competition Matters." Viewpoint No. 348, World Bank, Washington, DC.

Heyman, Fredrik, Pehr-Johan Norback, and Lars Persson. 2018. "Who Creates Jobs and Who Creates Productivity? Small versus Large versus Young versus Old." *Economics Letters* 164 (C): 50–57.

Huber, Peter, Harald Oberhofer, and Michael Pfaffermayr. 2017. "Who Creates Jobs? Econometric Modeling and Evidence for Austrian Firm Level Data." *European Economic Review* 91 (C): 57–71.

IFC (International Finance Corporation). 2021. "Impact of the COVID-19 Crisis on the Private Sector in Tunisia," Business Pulse Survey Tunisia. https://www.ifc.org/wps/wcm/connect/9d414d73-a5c9-4517-ac8d-5fd685e87ade /Tunisia+BPS_Third+wave_Executive+Summary.pdf?MOD=AJPERES&CVID=nuQ.iEG.

IMF (International Monetary Fund). 2021. *Fiscal Monitor April 2021: A Fair Shot*. Washington, DC: IMF.

Islam, Asif M., Isis Gaddis, Amparo Palacios Lopez, and Mohammad Amin. 2020. "The Labor Productivity Gap between Formal Businesses Run by Women and Men." *Feminist Economics* 26 (4): 228–58.

Jovanovic, Boyan. 1982. "Selection and the Evolution of Industry." *Econometrica* 50 (3): 649–70.

Kitzmuller, Markus, and Martha M. Licetti. 2012. "Competition Policy: Encouraging Thriving Markets for Development." Viewpoint Note 331, World Bank, Washington, DC.

Krafft, Caroline. 2016. "Understanding the Dynamics of Household Enterprises in Egypt: Birth, Death, Growth and Transformation." Economic Research Forum Working Paper 983, Economic Research Forum, Dokki, Giza, Egypt.

Krueger, Alan B., and Jorn-Steffen Pischke. 1997. "Observations and Conjectures on the U.S. Employment Miracle." NBER Working Paper 6146, National Bureau of Economic Research, Cambridge, MA.

McMillan, Margaret S., Dani Rodrik, and Claudia Sepúlveda, eds. 2017. *Structural Change, Fundamentals, and Growth: A Framework and Case Studies*. Washington, DC: International Food Policy Research Institute (IFPRI).

Nickell, Stephen J. 1996. "Competition and Corporate Performance." *Journal of Political Economy* 104 (4): 724–46.

Nickell, Stephen, and Richard Layard. 1999. "Labor Market Institutions and Economic Performance." Chapter 46 in *Handbook of Labor Economics*, edited by Orley C. Ashenfelter and David Card, Vol. 3, Part C, 3029–84. Elsevier.

Nicoletti, Giuseppe, Andrea Bassanini, Ekkehard Ernst, Sébastien Jean, Paulo Santiago, and Paul Swaim. 2001. "Product and Labour Market Interactions in OECD Countries." OECD Economics Department Working Paper No. 312, OECD Publishing, Paris.

Nicoletti, Giuseppe, and Stefano Scarpetta. 2003. "Regulation, Productivity and Growth: OECD Evidence." *Economic Policy* 18 (36): 9–72. https://doi.org/10.1111/1468-0327.00102.

Nicoletti, Giuseppe, and Stefano Scarpetta. 2005. "Product Market Reforms and Employment in OECD Countries." OECD Economics Department Working Paper No. 472, OECD Publishing, Paris. https://doi .org/10.1787/463767160680.

Pissarides, Christopher. 2001. "Employment Protection." *Labour Economics* 8 (2): 131–59.

Pritchett, Lant. 1996. "Mind Your P's and Q's: The Cost of Public Investment Is *Not* the Value of Public Capital." Policy Research Working Paper 1660, World Bank, Washington, DC.

Rijkers, Bob, Hassen Arouri, Caroline Freund, and Antonia Nucifora. 2014. "Which Firms Create the Most Jobs in Developing Countries? Evidence from Tunisia." *Labour Economics* 31 (C): 84–102.

Rijkers, Bob, Leila Baghdadi, and Gael Raballand. 2017. "Political Connections and Tariff Evasion: Evidence from Tunisia." *World Bank Economic Review* 31: 459–82.

Rijkers, Bob, Caroline Freund, and Antonnio Nucifora. 2017. "All in the Family: State Capture in Tunisia." *Journal of Development Economics* 124 (C): 41–59.

Romp, Ward E., and Jakob de Haan. 2005. "Public Capital and Economic Growth: A Critical Survey." *EIB Papers* 10 (1): 41–70.

Ruckteschler, Christian, Adeel Malik, and Ferdinand Eib. 2019. "The Politics of Trade Protection: Evidence from an EU-Mandated Tari Liberalization in Morocco." CSAE Working Paper 2019-12, Centre for the Study of African Economies, University of Oxford.

Sekkat, Khalid. 2009. "Does Competition Improve Productivity in Developing Countries?" *Journal of Economic Policy Reform* 12 (2): 145–62.

Shafik, Nemat. 1992. "Modeling Private Investment in Egypt." *Journal of Development Economics* 39 (2): 263–77.

Spector, David. 2004. "Competition and the Capital-Labor Conflict." *European Economic Review* 48 (1): 25–38.

Vives, Xavier. 2008. "Innovation and Competitive Pressure." *Journal of Industrial Economics* 56 (3): 419–69

World Bank. 2013. *Jobs for Shared Prosperity: Time for Action in the Middle East and North Africa.* Washington, DC: World Bank.

World Bank. 2015. *Jobs or Privileges: Unleashing the Employment Potential of the Middle East and North Africa.* Washington, DC: World Bank.

World Bank. 2020. "Fintech Market Reports Rapid Growth during COVID-19 Pandemic." Press release, December 3, 2020. https://www.worldbank.org/en/news/press-release/2020/12/03/fintech-market-reports-rapid-growth-during-covid-19-pandemic.

World Bank. 2021. *Global Economic Prospects, January 2021.* Washington, DC: World Bank.

WEST BANK: A Food Processing Factory That Empowers Women

Haneen is the founder and chief executive officer (CEO) of a food processing factory. Haneen graduated from Bethlehem University with an undergraduate degree in psychology but struggled to find the right job in her sector. She accepted a modest job at a local telecommunication firm, but she felt unproductive working in a sector in which her skills were going to waste. Haneen started to explore the idea of launching a factory to produce high-quality homemade organic products. Initially, Haneen sold her products to extended family, friends, and neighbors. Not long after, she expanded her sales to festivals, exhibitions, and a few local mini markets. Through these small steps, Haneen's business took off.

Each year, Haneen's factory produces about 1,500 different types of jarred makdos (stuffed eggplant); 1,500 jars of labneh (traditional processed yogurt with olive oil); 1,800 jars of shatta (traditional Mediterranean hot sauce); and 1,000 jars of stuffed olives. Haneen intentionally buys raw materials from female suppliers and farmers living in the rural West Bank. She works with a network of about 100 local female suppliers and small farmers operating in the informal sector. Through these relationships, Haneen provides her suppliers with financial security. She employs 15 people at the factory, a combination of part-time and full-time workers, mainly women between the ages of 18 and 45. Haneen sells her products through a network of retailers across the West Bank, and recently she started to export to Doha, Qatar, through local representatives.

Haneen points to several challenges through her entrepreneurial journey. Beyond the political situation, there are many costs related to registering a business and obtaining a health license for food processing machinery. Haneen says that the process of applying for and receiving proper business licensing is lengthy and complex, requiring interactions with several ministries such as health, economy, and agriculture. Haneen has identified a lack of funding with reasonable interest as a major limitation for small and medium-size enterprises' growth in West Bank. Haneen believes the Palestinian Authority can help by bringing experts from overseas to provide small businesses with quality assurance training and other knowledge, tools, and resources and also facilitate export capabilities to the Gulf (Kuwait, Qatar, Saudi Arabia, and the United Arab Emirates).

Over the years, many men have questioned Haneen's personal competency and skills as an entrepreneur simply because she is a woman. Her advice to other woman entrepreneurs in the region is clear: "There is no magical way to overcome challenges in Palestine. Women entrepreneurs need to innovate and persist. It's not easy to become an entrepreneur in Palestine, especially as a woman, but it is possible."

TUNISIA: A Beverage Manufacturer That Brings Instant Tea and New Flavors to New Markets

Tarek is the 36-year-old chief executive officer (CEO) and cofounder of a company that manufactures beverages. Born and raised in France by Tunisian parents, he attended business school in France, where he earned a master's degree in business management. After completing his education, he went to work for a business consulting firm in France as a strategy and organization consultant for three years and for three years as an assistant to the CEO of a French firm in Morocco. It was there that he gained his initial experience as a business professional. He then decided to move to Tunisia, where he felt he could be an asset to the Tunisian economy due to his French education and knowledge.

Initially Tarek convinced his business partner, the CEO of an agricultural and tree-treatment company in Tunisia, to raise funds with him for a factory to produce energy bars. However, further market research convinced them that instant tea had greater global potential.

Tarek's company manufactures hot beverages using local ingredients such as mint leaves processed with special machinery. The company officially launched in 2013 with the help of local investors and took off in 2017 after Tarek's arrival. Tarek and his partner (the Kyufi team) worked hard to design the factory's production line by contracting local engineers. The contracting, design, and construction process took almost two years to complete, and the cofounders now maintain all proprietary rights for their machinery. The company exports its products by contracting one to two carefully selected distributors per country in Tunisia, Morocco, France, and Canada. Tarek was able to infiltrate the North American market in 2019 after befriending and convincing a Canadian distributor to sell the products in Canada. Tarek now hopes to export his products and beverage flavors to the United States. The company's annual revenue grew by 300 percent per year for the past three years. Tarek notes that the revenues might have been even higher if the pandemic had not complicated his production process and reduced sales. Nonetheless, in 2019, Tarek sold 1 million sachets of tea, and in 2020, he sold another 3 million. The company in Tunis currently has 39 employees, all hired since early 2019.

Tarek acknowledges several challenges that entrepreneurs in the region face. Getting access to funds is difficult. Tarek credits his cofounder as being instrumental in obtaining financing and also having considerable experience in the entrepreneurial sphere. Tarek believes the entrepreneurs in Tunisia could benefit from progressive laws and regulations. Tarek spent two days filling out registration paperwork to register a business in France. The same registration process in Tunisia took Tarek one month to complete. Digital infrastructure and business training are ways Tarek believes the government could help. Tarek also notes that while it is easy to access talented engineers in Tunisia, it was the soft skills that he found missing in employees—skills that he had acquired through his experience in France.

CHAPTER 4

The Suspects That Limit Market Contestability and Job Creation

INTRODUCTION

Market contestability can transform economies in the Middle East and North Africa (MENA) region into modern states where innovative firms thrive and allocate resources to their best use. However, governments across the region, through their regulatory arm, have fostered an uneven playing field, hindering competition in multiple ways. This section scrutinizes the regulatory role of the state through three dimensions: (1) product market regulations (PMRs) and state-owned enterprises (SOEs); (2) labor market regulations and related taxes; and (3) gendered laws. How these three dimensions are addressed is highly influential in providing private businesses a fair chance to succeed and workers more and better jobs to live and prosper.

PRODUCT MARKET REGULATIONS AND SOEs

Understanding the policies and regulations that can hinder market contestability in the MENA region is key for reforms. PMRs are particularly relevant in this context because they affect the costs that firms face when they enter the market, and the degree of competition between the firms that already exist in this market (Ebell and Haefke 2003; Griffith and Harrison 2004; Nicoletti and Scarpetta 2005). The rigidity or flexibility of these regulations directly affect the number of firms that operate, their growth, and their ability to create jobs.

Between 2020 and 2021, this report supported an extensive data collection effort and associated analysis carried out by the World Bank of key features of PMRs for eight middle- and high-income economies in the MENA region: the Arab Republic of Egypt, Jordan, Kuwait, Morocco, Saudi Arabia,

Tunisia, the United Arab Emirates, and West Bank and Gaza. The analysis was built on the methodology of the Organisation for Economic Co-Operation and Development (OECD) Indicators of Product Market Regulation (see appendix A).[1]

The collected data allowed a comparison to be drawn for the first time of several indicators that capture economywide distortions induced by the presence of the state in product markets against two sets of comparators: 37 high-income countries and 14 upper-middle-income countries included in the 2018 PMR database.[2]

Among the areas measured are the scope of SOEs (namely, ownership and control and the governance of SOEs) (appendix tables A.1 through A.4); competitive neutrality (appendix table A.5); public procurement (appendix table A.6); government involvement in business operations through price controls (appendix tables A.7 and A.8); and simplification and evaluation of regulations that relate to contestability (namely, the assessment of the impact on competition and the complexity of regulatory procedures) (table A.9).[3] Appendix tables A.10 and A.11 explore barriers to trade and investment. Appendix tables A.12 and A.13 show the barriers in network industries and professional services.

Results from PMR analysis show three aspects that weaken the private sector and reduce market contestability for most countries in the MENA region. First, state presence through SOEs is still visible and significant, even in sectors where there is unclear economic rationale for it. Second, there is little competitive neutrality that would level the playing field between these SOEs and their private sector peers. Third, price controls are still prevalent, and often seen as a pillar of the welfare state, reducing incentives for more productivity and efficiency, while mechanisms to assess the negative impact of regulations are limited (Dauda et al., forthcoming). Detailed PMR data for each economy covered are presented in appendix A.

The Prevalence of State Presence in Product Markets

SOEs in MENA play a dominant role in many sectors, including those that are typically served by the private sector in other countries around the world. In Egypt, the government controls at least one SOE in all 29 sectors analyzed. The state has at least one SOE in 23 sectors in Saudi Arabia, 22 sectors in the United Arab Emirates, and 18 sectors in Morocco. This is much higher than the average for high-income countries (12 sectors) and upper-middle-income countries (15 sectors). What is more striking is that in the MENA economies examined, there is an unusual SOE presence in subsectors that can better benefit from private sector involvement, such as manufacturing, accommodation, trade, and even construction (figure 4.1).

Moreover, SOE decision-making remains heavily influenced by governmental bodies in most MENA economies analyzed. The exercise of ownership rights is typically carried out by specialized agencies that are not far from the government. Often, sector regulators and chief executive officers (CEOs) are appointed by public authorities in the region, as opposed to being appointed by the board of directors as in most high-income countries. This implies a larger control over firm decision-making and higher risks for potential conflict of interests. In Egypt, the National Telecommunications Regulatory Authority is under the authority of the Ministry of Communications and Information Technologies, which owns 80 percent of Telecom Egypt. These governance and ownership structures create incentives to favor SOEs over private competitors. In Egypt and Kuwait, the government controls the national air carriers, which benefit from preferential treatment, in terms of time slots in Egypt and fuel (kerosene) prices in Kuwait.[4] A key recommendation is for governments in the region to focus on improving the performance and the oversight of SOEs while adopting safeguards to ensure equal treatment with private sector firms where they are present.

Figure 4.1 **MENA has more SOEs operating in various sectors compared to income peers**

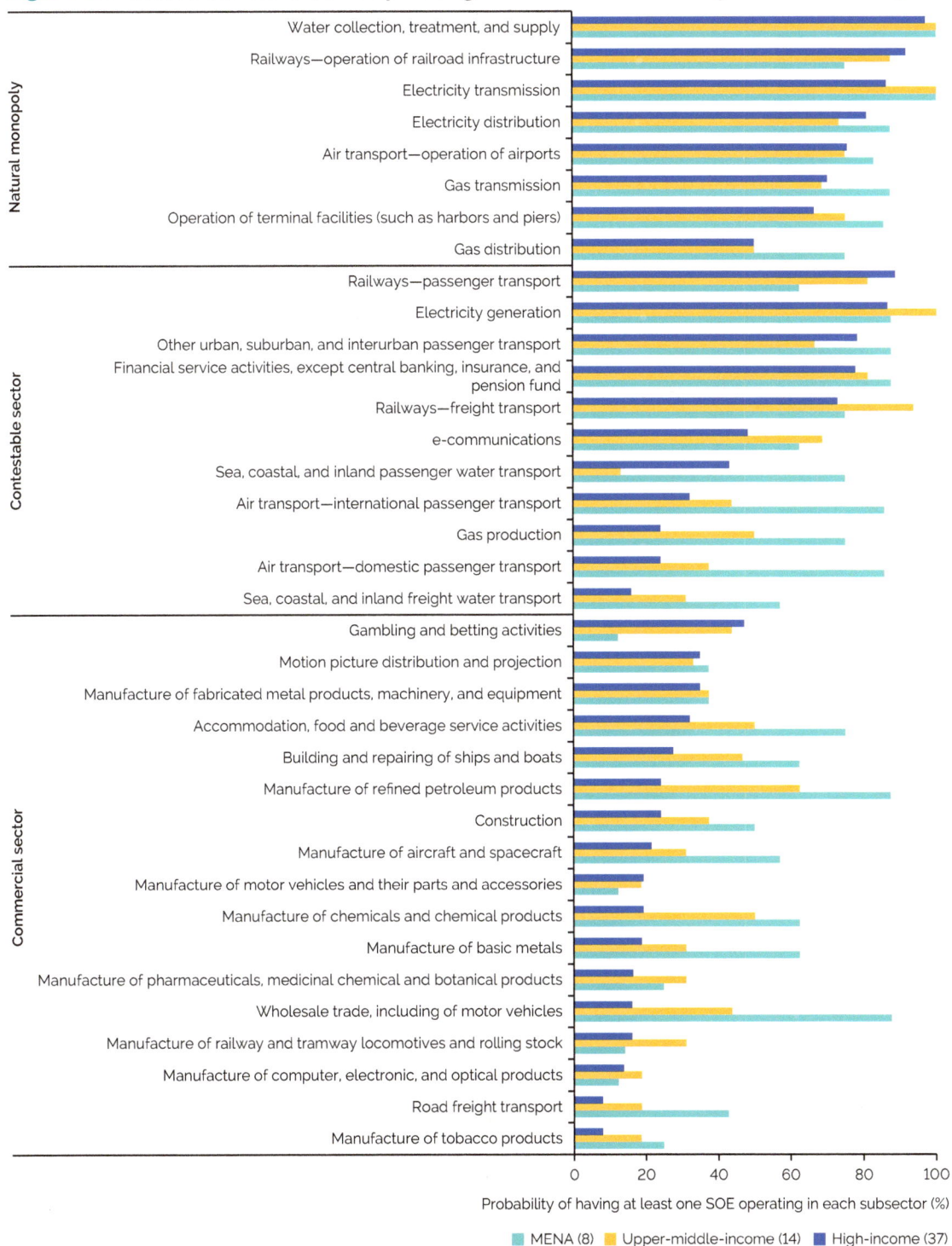

Natural monopoly
- Water collection, treatment, and supply
- Railways—operation of railroad infrastructure
- Electricity transmission
- Electricity distribution
- Air transport—operation of airports
- Gas transmission
- Operation of terminal facilities (such as harbors and piers)
- Gas distribution

Contestable sector
- Railways—passenger transport
- Electricity generation
- Other urban, suburban, and interurban passenger transport
- Financial service activities, except central banking, insurance, and pension fund
- Railways—freight transport
- e-communications
- Sea, coastal, and inland passenger water transport
- Air transport—international passenger transport
- Gas production
- Air transport—domestic passenger transport
- Sea, coastal, and inland freight water transport

Commercial sector
- Gambling and betting activities
- Motion picture distribution and projection
- Manufacture of fabricated metal products, machinery, and equipment
- Accommodation, food and beverage service activities
- Building and repairing of ships and boats
- Manufacture of refined petroleum products
- Construction
- Manufacture of aircraft and spacecraft
- Manufacture of motor vehicles and their parts and accessories
- Manufacture of chemicals and chemical products
- Manufacture of basic metals
- Manufacture of pharmaceuticals, medicinal chemical and botanical products
- Wholesale trade, including of motor vehicles
- Manufacture of railway and tramway locomotives and rolling stock
- Manufacture of computer, electronic, and optical products
- Road freight transport
- Manufacture of tobacco products

Probability of having at least one SOE operating in each subsector (%)

■ MENA (8)   ■ Upper-middle-income (14)   ■ High-income (37)

Sources: Flagship team elaboration, based on OECD and OECD-WBG Product Market Regulation (PMR) database 2018–2020 and PMR data for the Arab Republic of Egypt collected in 2017, for Kuwait in 2018, and for Tunisia in 2017.
Note: In the legend, the numbers in parentheses indicate the number of observations available per income or country group. Data for the MENA countries were collected by the flagship team using the 2018 OECD PMR methodology. OECD = Organisation for Economic Cooperation and Development; SOE = state-owned enterprise; WBG = World Bank Group.

Lack of Competitive Neutrality

The framework of competitive neutrality can help level the playing field between private enterprises and government-run businesses. Competitive neutrality is a principle according to which all enterprises—public or private, domestic or foreign—should face the same set of rules. The government's contact, ownership, or involvement in the marketplace, in practice or in law, should not confer an undue competitive advantage to any actual or potential market participant. The effective implementation of this principle is important to decrease the risk of anticompetitive behavior and economic distortions due to the participation of SOEs in markets.

Most MENA economies lag in key components that can help ensure competitive neutrality (figure 4.2 and table A.5). They lack the separation (and identification/allocation) of costs related to commercial and noncommercial activities of SOEs. Their SOEs have cumbersome structures. They provide subsidies (and loans) to support the provision of public services that result in advantages to SOE commercial activities and cause ripple effects on private participants in those markets. Moreover, they have regulations that facilitate the operation of SOEs such as statutory monopolies, exemptions from competition law, and preferences in public procurement—all of which distort the level playing field further and affect the ability of private firms to remain competitive and expand.

The closeness of these SOEs to governments results in favoritism and exemptions. In Saudi Arabia, SOEs do not fall within the scope of the application of competition law. Egypt, Kuwait, Tunisia, and the United Arab Emirates all have several exemptions in their competition regulatory frameworks that make life easier for SOEs: (1) targeted exemptions in Egypt and Tunisia based on case by case assessments related to market effects;[5] (2) exemptions granted to certain categories of SOEs, such as those providing utilities in Egypt, Kuwait, and Tunisia; and (3) exemptions for certain sectors altogether, such as telecommunications, financial services, and oil and gas among others in the United Arab Emirates (table 4.1).[6] Bankruptcy laws in Kuwait also exempt SOEs but apply to their peers. These exemptions greatly hinder competitive neutrality, resulting in an uneven playing field between SOEs and their peers in the same sectors and the same market.

The fact that many MENA countries also have agencies that act as both regulators and operators further weakens competitive neutrality. With the exception of West Bank and Gaza, SOEs in MENA operate in all transportation subsectors and they also sometimes hold regulatory powers at the same time. In some sectors, SOEs enjoy legal monopolies as in the case of port operations in Kuwait and air transport in Egypt. SOEs in Morocco manage infrastructure in ports, road transport, and airports (World Bank 2020). For example, the SOE in charge of developing and managing highways also has many roles and responsibilities as owner, administrator, manager, and supplier all at once. The United Arab Emirates has a publicly owned provider for generation, transmission, and distribution of electricity, which can also set prices and connection fees.

Moreover, procurement policies should be transparent and nondiscriminatory to allow for competitive pressure—both foreign and domestic—and not provide any preferences for SOEs. While public procurement laws in MENA economies are transparent and base the adjudication of tenders or bids on objective criteria, some exemptions or preferences still exist (appendix table A.6). In Egypt, for example, agency-to-agency contracts remain possible. Jordanian SOEs have specific tender rules. Moreover, procurement laws include a wide range of provisions to benefit domestic firms that may affect the competitive nature of tenders. For instance, Egypt, Kuwait, Tunisia, and West Bank and Gaza reserve a share of the contract for domestic firms, and most MENA economies analyzed require domestic content (personnel and/or goods). In addition, most MENA economies, except Kuwait and Morocco, explicitly permit access discrimination in favor of local firms.

Tax exemptions remain in place that favor SOEs. While SOEs are theoretically subject to the same tax system as private companies in Egypt, Jordan, Kuwait, Saudi Arabia, and Tunisia, some exemptions

Figure 4.2 **Most MENA economies lag in key components that can help ensure competitive neutrality**

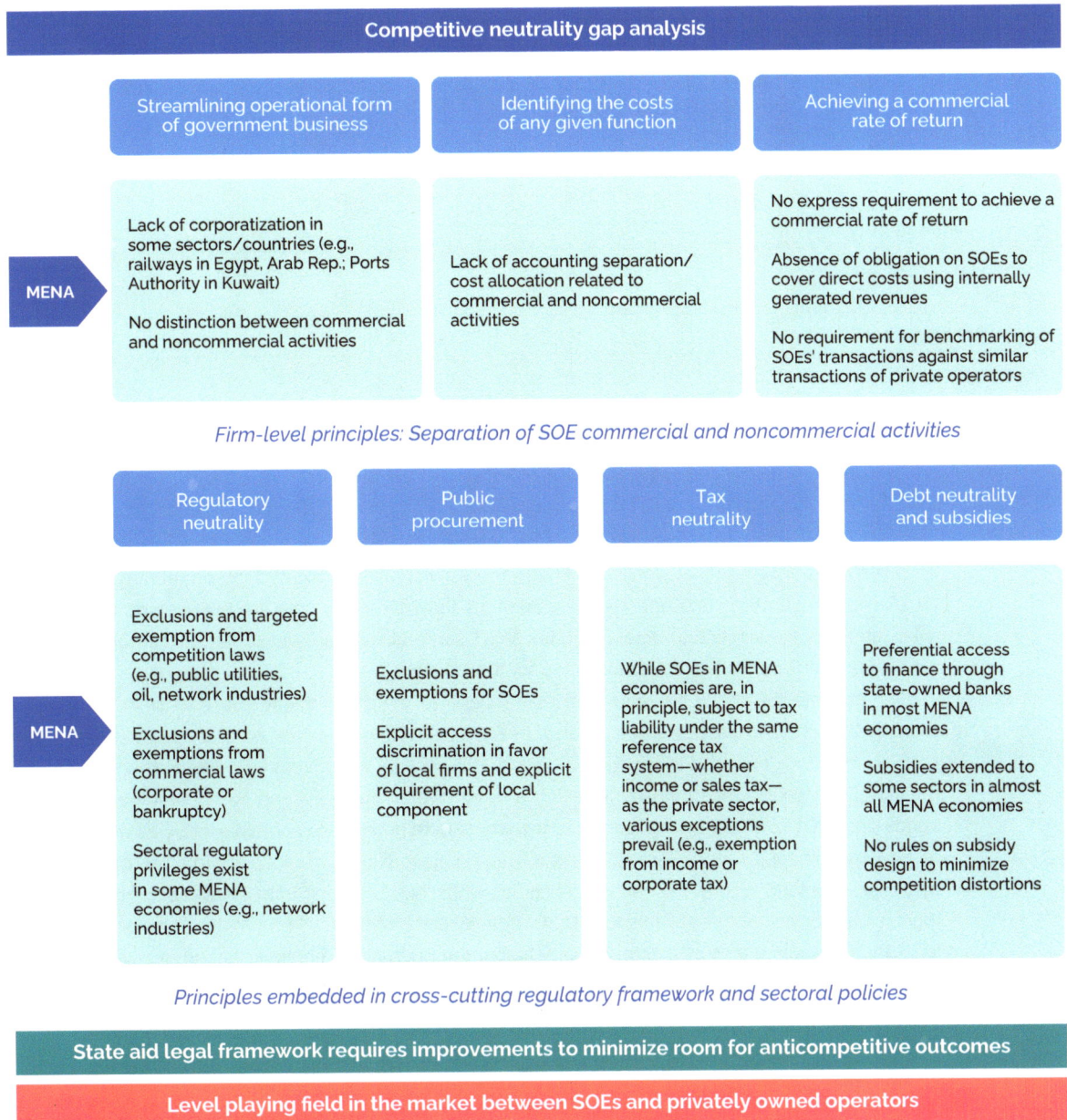

Competitive neutrality gap analysis		
Streamlining operational form of government business	Identifying the costs of any given function	Achieving a commercial rate of return

MENA → Lack of corporatization in some sectors/countries (e.g., railways in Egypt, Arab Rep.; Ports Authority in Kuwait) No distinction between commercial and noncommercial activities	Lack of accounting separation/ cost allocation related to commercial and noncommercial activities	No express requirement to achieve a commercial rate of return Absence of obligation on SOEs to cover direct costs using internally generated revenues No requirement for benchmarking of SOEs' transactions against similar transactions of private operators

Firm-level principles: Separation of SOE commercial and noncommercial activities

Regulatory neutrality	Public procurement	Tax neutrality	Debt neutrality and subsidies
MENA → Exclusions and targeted exemption from competition laws (e.g., public utilities, oil, network industries) Exclusions and exemptions from commercial laws (corporate or bankruptcy) Sectoral regulatory privileges exist in some MENA economies (e.g., network industries)	Exclusions and exemptions for SOEs Explicit access discrimination in favor of local firms and explicit requirement of local component	While SOEs in MENA economies are, in principle, subject to tax liability under the same reference tax system—whether income or sales tax— as the private sector, various exceptions prevail (e.g., exemption from income or corporate tax)	Preferential access to finance through state-owned banks in most MENA economies Subsidies extended to some sectors in almost all MENA economies No rules on subsidy design to minimize competition distortions

Principles embedded in cross-cutting regulatory framework and sectoral policies

State aid legal framework requires improvements to minimize room for anticompetitive outcomes

Level playing field in the market between SOEs and privately owned operators

Source: Flagship team elaboration.
Note: The figure applies the competitive neutrality framework to the MENA region and identifies key gaps. The eight MENA economies are the Arab Republic of Egypt, Jordan, Kuwait, Morocco, Saudi Arabia, Tunisia, United Arab Emirates, and West Bank and Gaza. SOEs = state-owned enterprises.

Table 4.1 Exemptions from competition law in eight MENA economies

Exemptions	Egypt, Arab Rep.	Jordan	Kuwait	Morocco	Saudi Arabia	Tunisia	United Arab Emirates	West Bank and Gaza
State-owned enterprises (SOEs)	X		X			X	X	NA
Conduct required or authorized by other government authority	X	X		X	X	X	X	
Certain sectors of economy			X	X		X	X	
Legal monopolies			X	X		X		
Certain goods or services	X	X	X	X		X		
Other state bodies	X		X					

Sources: Review by the flagship team of national competition laws; Mahmood and Slimane 2018, pp. 77–89.
Note: NA = not applicable.

from corporate income taxes persist. In Egypt and Kuwait, unincorporated government operations[7]—for example, when the state offers services directly through a ministry—are tax exempt. In Morocco, although SOEs are subject to value added tax (VAT), some of them are not subject to corporate tax and may enjoy parafiscal tax[8] revenues instituted for their benefit.[9]

The advantages that SOEs reap from being close to the government also appear in the form of preferential access to finance and subsidies. In Egypt, explicit guarantees are provided to some SOEs or the public body engaged in commercial activity.[10] In Jordan, the government provides support to the National Electrical Power Company (NEPCO) and the Water Authority, and has guaranteed corporate bonds since 2011.[11] In the United Arab Emirates, where debt guarantee is possible for SOEs wholly owned by the government,[12] reports show that some have received capital infusions and preferential treatment by the government, such as the national air carrier, which has benefited from initial capital injections and regular loans on concessional terms (OECD 2012). In Kuwait,[13] Morocco,[14] and Tunisia,[15] the state provides financing to or guarantees SOE debt. In Saudi Arabia, the budget law mentions that government agencies whose budgets are attached to the state's general budget can borrow or issue any type of debt instruments with the approval of the Minister of Finance.[16] Meanwhile none of the MENA economies in the study require SOEs to show a positive rate of return—whether calculated in terms of net present value or internal rate of return.[17] More on SOE presence and regulations in network sectors can be found in box 4.1.

Price Controls and Limited Mechanisms to Assess the Negative Impact of Regulations

Retail price controls also remain prevalent among many MENA economies. For instance, all the MENA economies analyzed control the price of staples (such as milk and bread) and liquefied petroleum gas (LPG). Almost all of them control prices for gasoline and medicine (figure 4.3 and appendix table A.7). This is far higher than the share of countries that do so among upper-middle-income countries and high-income countries. While these prices can help secure most needed foods for the poor and vulnerable, they are not targeted to them exclusively. MENA economies have long used these price controls and their subsidies as a pillar of the welfare state, especially in the absence of rigorous and targeted social

Figure 4.3 MENA has more retail price controls and regulations compared to income peers

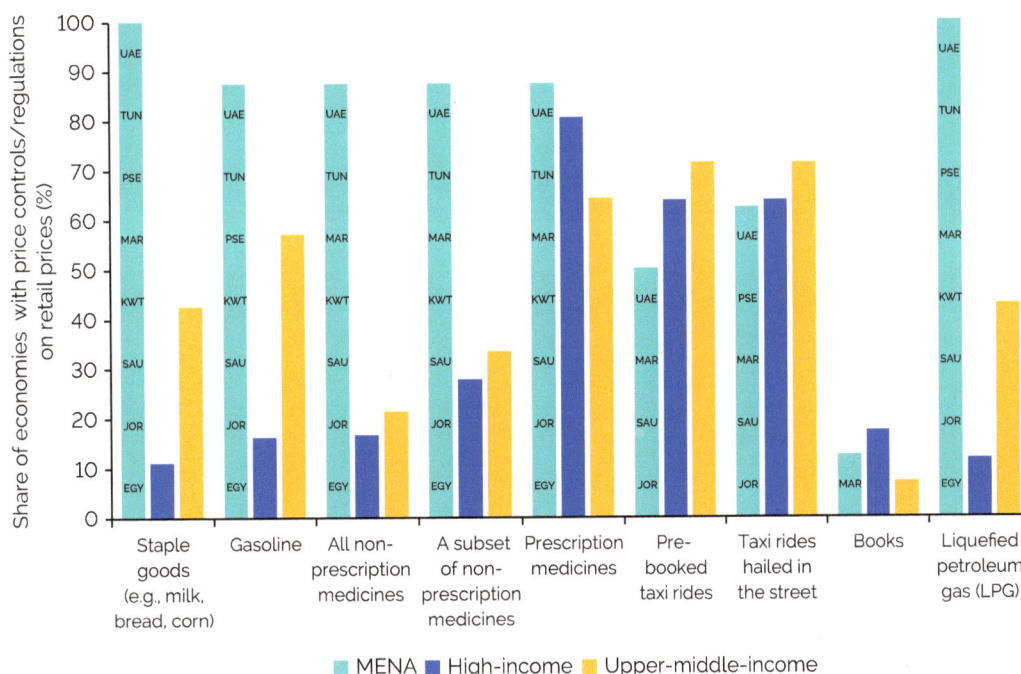

Sources: Flagship team elaboration, based on OECD and OECD-WBG Product Market Regulation (PMR) database 2018–2020, as well as data collected on selected aspects of the 2018–2020 PMR for eight Middle East and North Africa (MENA) economies. PMR data for Egypt were collected in 2017, for Kuwait in 2018, and for Tunisia in 2017.
Note: The eight MENA economies are Egypt (EGY), Jordan (JOR), Kuwait (KWT), Morocco (MAR), Saudi Arabia (SAU), Tunisia (TUN), United Arab Emirates (UAE), and West Bank and Gaza (PSE). The economies shown in the MENA group indicate economies with retail price controls. OECD = Organisation for Economic Co-operation and Development; WBG = World Bank Group.

Box 4.1 Sector-specific restrictive regulations in network industries and professional services in MENA economies

The eight MENA economies analyzed feature a number of sector-specific regulatory restrictions in network industries such as electricity and gas transmissions,[a] product market regulation (PMR) data reveal. These restrictions are associated with the significant presence of state-owned enterprises (SOEs) in segments of the market where competition is viable, as well as vertical integration with no separation of the competitive components of the market segments (figure B4.1.1), and weak access regulations to enable entry in those segments and price controls. This results in suboptimal market outcomes that possibly hamper the entire economy.

In regulated professional services, restrictions in countries analyzed remain moderate compared to their comparator country groups, especially regarding pricing policies. However, in all countries analyzed restrictions on the form of business, such as the purpose and shareholding in Morocco and Tunisia or on the basis of nationality in Gulf countries, exist for the four surveyed professions (accountants, lawyers, architects, and engineers), except in Saudi Arabia for accountants and lawyers; and Saudi Arabia and Jordan, for architects and engineers. Regulations pertaining to advertising of regulated professional services in countries analyzed remain more restrictive than the averages in high-income countries and upper-middle-income countries, with the legal profession facing the strongest restrictions, following the same trend as in high-income countries

(box continues on next page)

Box 4.1 Sector-specific restrictive regulations in network industries and professional services in MENA economies *(continued)*

and upper-middle-income countries. The ability of firms to advertise can improve the quality of services and overcome information asymmetries inherent in these industries, but advertising bans restrict the competitive options of new firms and make it more difficult for them to challenge incumbents.

Lack of structural separation and third-party access (TPA) may insulate public incumbents from competition (figure B4.1.2). In the energy sector, Kuwait, Morocco, Saudi Arabia, and Tunisia have vertically integrated SOEs with no separation among market segments. Egypt and the United Arab Emirates are aligned with the majority of high-income countries and upper-middle-income countries by having a legal separation between SOEs present in segments where competition is possible (generation and distribution), and the SOE in charge of transmission segments that constitute natural monopolies. Jordan has legal separation in the generation/production segment of energy and Kuwait in gas segments. Nevertheless, most countries analyzed do not establish adequate TPA as opposed to the prevalent regulations model in high-income countries and upper-middle-income countries. In telecom, mandated network access and infrastructure sharing paired with measures supporting client mobility are widely adopted; however, implementation remains challenging in some countries, such as Morocco.

Figure B4.1.1 Vertical integration with separation of the competitive components of market segments is limited in MENA

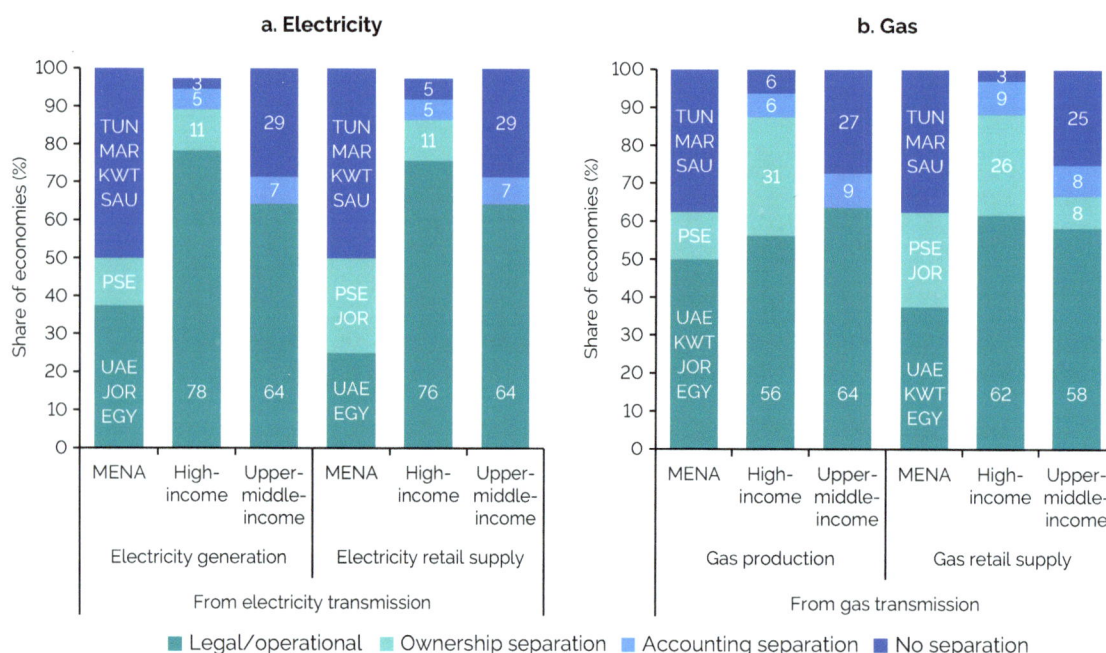

Source: Flagship team elaboration on product market regulation (PMR) data.
Note: The economies shown in the Middle East and North Africa (MENA) group indicate those with specific separation arrangements. The eight MENA economies are Egypt (EGY), Jordan (JOR), Kuwait (KWT), Morocco (MAR), Saudi Arabia (SAU), Tunisia (TUN), United Arab Emirates (UAE), and West Bank and Gaza (PSE).

(box continues on next page)

Figure B4.1.2 Third-party access to the energy transmission grid is rare in MENA

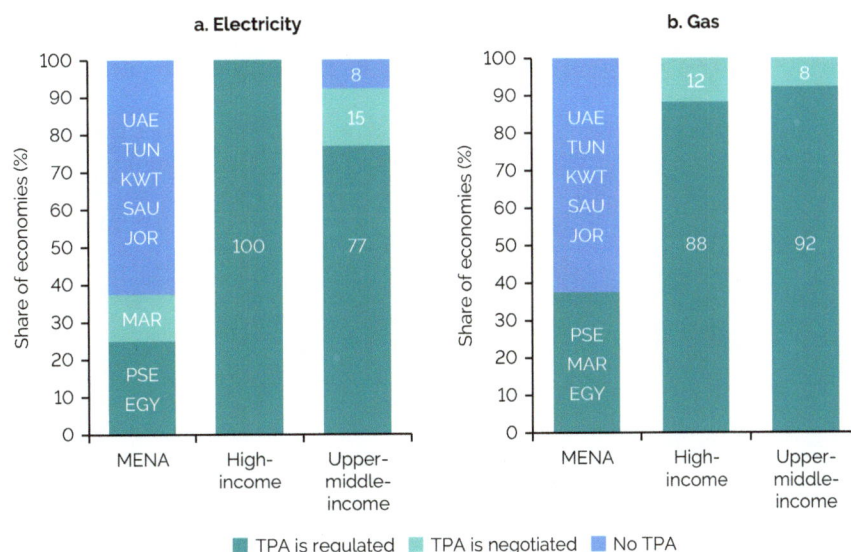

a. Electricity

b. Gas

Legend: ■ TPA is regulated   ■ TPA is negotiated   ■ No TPA

Source: Flagship team elaboration on product market regulation (PMR) data.
Note: The economies shown in the Middle East and North Africa (MENA) group indicate those with the various third-party access (TPA) arrangements. The eight MENA economies are Egypt (EGY), Jordan (JOR), Kuwait (KWT), Morocco (MAR), Saudi Arabia (SAU), Tunisia (TUN), United Arab Emirates (UAE), and West Bank and Gaza (PSE).

Sources: OECD and OECD-WBG Product Market Regulation (PMR) database 2018–2020, as well as data collected on selected aspects of the 2018–2020 PMR for eight Middle East and North Africa (MENA) economies and PMR data for Egypt collected in 2017, for Kuwait in 2018, and for Tunisia in 2017. See also Dauda et al., forthcoming.
Note: The eight MENA economies are Egypt, Jordan, Kuwait, Morocco, Saudi Arabia, Tunisia, United Arab Emirates, and West Bank and Gaza.
a. The network sectors are key upstream services sectors that are important for firms in downstream sectors, such as manufacturing. The network sectors (industries in parentheses) covered in the 2018 version of the PMR include energy (electricity and natural gas), transport (rail, air, road, and water), and communications (fixed and mobile telecommunications).

assistance programs for those who need it the most. An upcoming World Bank report on the future of social protection in the region emphasizes the importance of streamlining and targeting support for the poor and vulnerable. On the other hand, for digital operators in the taxi business, MENA economies do not have as much control as upper-middle-income and high-income peers. In Jordan for example, ride-sharing companies are obliged to set prices 15 percent higher than taxis.[18]

In addition, systematized Regulatory Impact Assessments (RIAs) have yet to be adopted, especially regarding competition effects of regulations and policies (appendix table A.9). RIA frameworks have been adopted by the majority of high-income countries (95 percent) and half of the upper-middle-income countries as they offer a critical filter to evaluate the costs and benefits of new regulations and policies (figure 4.4, panel a). The impact on competition constitutes a critical aspect to cover in the RIA. While Morocco and the United Arab Emirates have adopted general RIA frameworks,[19] no other MENA economy analyzed currently preforms an analysis of competition impact of regulations (figure 4.4, panel b). This omission presents higher risks for those economies with no independent agency entrusted to advocate for competition, including Jordan, the United Arab Emirates, and West Bank and Gaza.

Figure 4.4 **MENA economies do not systematically analyze the competitive impact of their regulations**

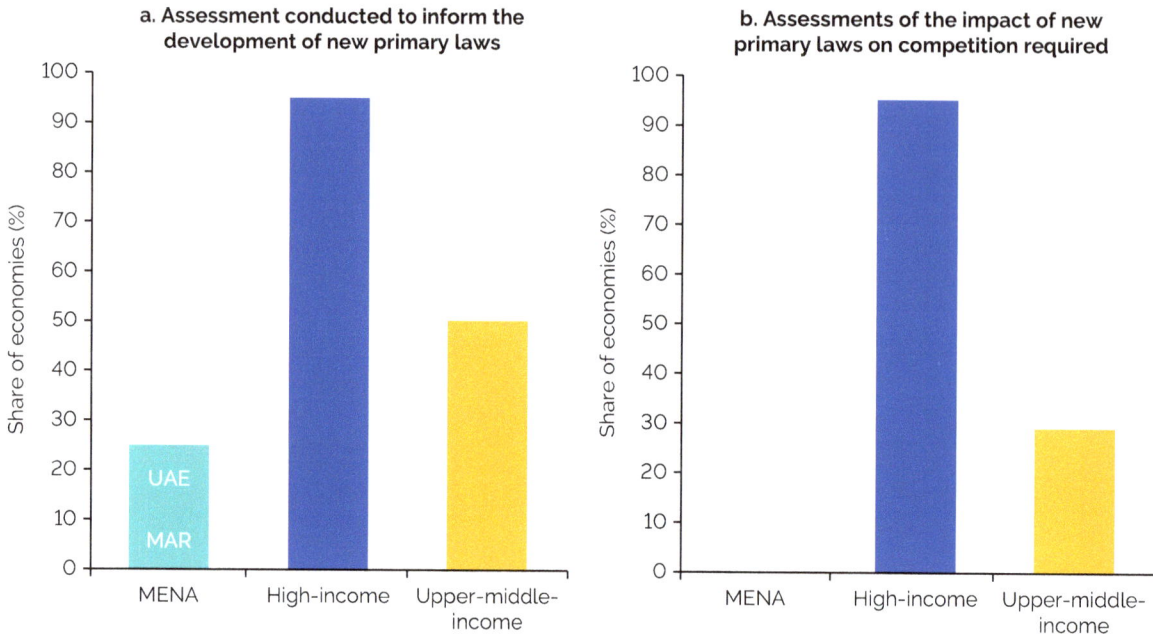

a. Assessment conducted to inform the development of new primary laws

b. Assessments of the impact of new primary laws on competition required

Sources: Flagship team elaboration, based on OECD and OECD-WBG Product Market Regulation (PMR) database 2018–2020, as well as data collected on selected aspects of the 2018–2020 PMR for eight Middle East and North Africa (MENA) economies. PMR data for Egypt were collected in 2017, for Kuwait in 2018, and for Tunisia in 2017.

Note: The eight MENA economies are Egypt, Jordan, Kuwait, Morocco, Saudi Arabia, Tunisia, United Arab Emirates, and West Bank and Gaza. The economies shown in the MENA group indicate those with the requirements. MAR = Morocco; OECD = Organisation for Economic Co-operation and Development; UAE = United Arab Emirates; WBG = World Bank Group.

LABOR MARKET REGULATIONS AND RELATED TAXES

Labor regulations are important determinants of resource allocation and productivity. They can protect workers' rights, enhance job security, and improve working conditions. At the same time, if they are too strict, they can also act as a barrier to formal work and hinder dynamism, imposing a high cost on firms and excluding some workers, especially youth and the low-skilled (Packard et al. 2019; World Bank 2013, 2019). For instance, while employment protection rules are important to reduce the negative impacts of income loss for workers, they can potentially limit the movement of workers from low- to high-productivity jobs, while resulting in longer unemployment spells (Betcherman 2014).

Furthermore, some evidence has shown that stricter labor regulations, specifically with burdensome dismissal procedures, are associated with lower technology adoption (Bartelsman, Gautier, and de Wind 2016; Packard and Montenegro 2017), as well as lower entry and exit of firms—especially small ones—in industries with higher worker reallocation (Bottasso, Conti, and Sulis 2017). This is an especially important issue today as countries slowly recover from the repercussions of the pandemic and worker movements become essential.

The vital principle for policy makers to follow when setting labor regulations is to avoid extremes. Being on a "plateau"—between the extremes of very strict and very loose labor regulations—is a compelling and powerful metaphor and one that should be used as a policy principle to guide the design of labor market regulation (World Bank 2013). However, it has not yet been sufficiently developed to be quantified for actionable policy guidance. It is also safe to assume that the features that can define the "plateau" may vary significantly according to countries' economic and institutional development (Packard et al. 2019).

With these reflections in mind, this section analyzes and compares labor regulations in 19 MENA economies in four areas that are important to facilitate the transitions of workers while ensuring businesses are not burdened: (1) firing rules and unemployment benefits; (2) labor taxes; (3) the flexibility of work arrangements; and (4) the minimum wage (Hatayama 2021).[20] The results show that some MENA economies have limiting labor regulations, including relatively high severance pay (end-of-service compensation) for certain classes of workers. However, general unemployment schemes that would cover more workers are scarce. Labor taxes constitute a significant share of the larger tax obligations of firms and worker earnings in some countries, while the use of fixed-term contracts—which could encourage employment, especially for young workers through flexible hiring—is sometime restricted. Coverage of a minimum wage is also limited in certain countries, while some countries do not have a minimum wage at all.

Firing Rules and Unemployment Benefits

Labor regulations can use different types of firing provisions to protect workers. In middle- and low-income countries, severance pay is the most common way to protect workers when they get laid off and fall into unemployment. However, while it provides some means of income protection for workers, it increases firing costs and pools risk at the firm level, potentially failing to protect workers when firms have liquidity constraints and cannot afford to pay or compliance is limited (Kuddo, Robalino, and Weber 2015). Moreover, high firing costs and strict job security regulations can reduce aggregate employment and productivity, and promote inequality across workers (Bassanini, Nunziata, and Venn 2009; Harasty 2004; Kugler and Saint-Paul 2004).

When faced with rigid employment protection laws, firms have incentives to hire workers informally. There is a negative relationship between firing costs and formal employment, measured by the share of active contributors to pension schemes out of the labor force (figure 4.5, panel a). Moreover, high firing costs are also associated with a large number of self-employed workers, who are nonwage workers and are overwhelmingly informal in most countries around the world (figure 4.5, panel b). Although these relationships are not causal, they corroborate past empirical literature showing that stringent labor regulations, including high redundancy costs, potentially reduce employment and worker flows (Botero et al. 2004; Kugler and Pica 2008; Kugler and Saint-Paul 2004).

Results from the MENA region show that firing costs are relatively high, and dismissal rules are rather complex in many countries. Fourteen MENA economies require employers to notify a third party and obtain approval from that third party before an employer can make a worker redundant or issue collective dismissals (making a group of nine or more workers redundant).[21] Half of the 14 economies also require approval from third parties.[22]

Moreover, the region mandates higher severance payments compared to international benchmarks. The average amount of severance payment in the MENA region stands at 17 weeks of salary, which is higher than the global average of severance payments of 14.7 weeks. The average of non-Gulf Cooperation Council (GCC) countries is 18.4 weeks, while the average for GCC countries is lower, at 13.9 weeks. All the income groups in the MENA region have more generous severance payments compared to comparator groups in the rest of the world (figure 4.6).

Figure 4.5 High firing costs are associated with a large number of informal workers and self-employed workers in MENA

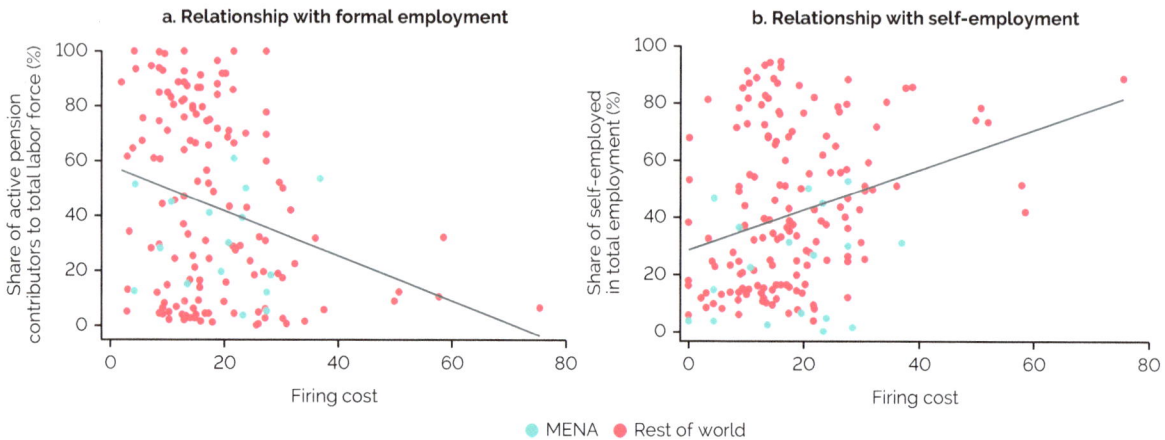

a. Relationship with formal employment

b. Relationship with self-employment

● MENA ● Rest of world

Sources: World Bank Employing Workers 2020 database. For panel a, ILO (International Labour Organization) World Social Protection Database, based on the Social Security Inquiry (SSI). For panel b, International Labour Organization, ILOSTAT database.
Note: Firing cost is the sum of severance cost and advance notice period as weeks of salary. The number of active contributors is those who contribute to national existing contributory pension schemes. This total number of active contributors is then set in relation to the size of the labor force population. In each country, data are from the latest available year (2003–15).

Figure 4.6 Severance pay in MENA is the most generous in the world

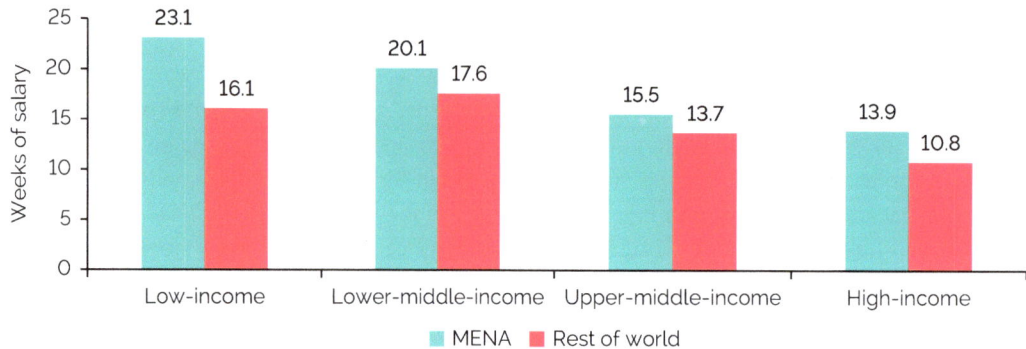

■ MENA ■ Rest of world

Source: World Bank Employing Workers 2020 database.
Note: Low-income countries include Syrian Arab Republic; Yemen, Rep. Lower-middle-income economies include Algeria; Djibouti; Egypt, Arab Rep.; Iran, Islamic Rep.; Morocco; Tunisia; West Bank and Gaza. Upper-middle-income countries include Iraq; Jordan; Lebanon; Libya. High-income countries include Bahrain; Kuwait; Oman; Qatar; Saudi Arabia; United Arab Emirates.

In economies with less rigid and less costly firing regulations, well-designed unemployment insurance schemes can provide adequate protection for workers' transitions. Unemployment protection schemes can be more reliable options to provide income support for workers because they can support workers in transition or long-term unemployed workers. In fact, reasonable levels of social protection, including well-designed unemployment benefits, have been found to reduce poverty and vulnerability (Renahy et al. 2018). In the MENA region, there is a dearth of unemployment insurance schemes; only nine MENA countries have such schemes.[23] This leads to income protection through mandated severance pay and dismissal rules.

Even when unemployment insurance systems exist (particularly contributory), the majority of the population is not entitled to related benefits. The share of unemployed individuals receiving unemployment insurance is less than 10 percent. The coverage rate is 8.8 percent in Algeria, 9.8 percent in Bahrain, and 0.1 percent in Egypt.[24] The underutilization of unemployment insurance could be due to strict eligibility conditions, the difficulty of documenting a firing decision, and low layoff risks of insured permanent employees, in addition to potentially less awareness by the public (Angel-Urdinola and Kuddo 2010). These limited unemployment benefits are particularly stark when looking at the level of unemployment, underemployment, and informality in the region.

Labor Taxes

Labor taxes refer to social security contributions incurred by employers and employees as well as personal income taxes levied on employees. Labor taxes create a tax wedge—a gap between the labor costs to the employer and the worker's gain. A higher tax wedge can increase labor costs for employers and reduce labor demand. It can also create an incentive for employers to hire workers informally, on a temporary basis, or reduce working time/hours. Moreover, the burden of taxes could induce some firms to underreport wages or avoid registration requirements or mandatory contributions, increasing the size of the informal sector. If contributions by employees exceed the benefits, this can also create incentives for workers to work informally to avoid paying contributions. A sizable body of empirical research has already confirmed that high labor taxes can reduce labor demand and increase unemployment rates and affect levels of employment and informality (Antón 2014; Kugler and Kugler 2009; Lehmann and Muravyev 2012; World Bank 2009).

Statutory social security contribution rates are relatively high in some MENA countries compared to international benchmarks. For example, the average rate of non-GCC countries stands at around 22 percent, with Egypt having the highest insured and employer contribution rates in the MENA region (40 percent), followed by Algeria (34 percent). This is significantly higher than the global average of around 20 percent (figure 4.7). Regarding taxes actually paid by the business, labor taxes in non-GCC countries are estimated at around 18.8 percent of the corporate profit compared to the global average of around 16 percent. The cost on labor is very high in Algeria, the Islamic Republic of Iran, Egypt, Tunisia, Lebanon, and Morocco; nearly one-fourth of corporate profits are spent on labor taxes and contributions. In contrast, GCC countries, whose public revenues predominantly rely on oil exports, have low tax rates. An average labor tax rate in GCC countries is around 13 percent of a firm's profit, which is relatively low compared to non-GCC countries. Moreover, GCC countries generally require little tax on corporate profit. This, in turn, means that the proportion of labor taxes to total tax is very high in these countries. The fact that some GCC countries have also begun to impose some other taxes, such as VAT in Bahrain and Saudi Arabia, could also mean future changes in the tax system on businesses and workers, especially with tightening fiscal space.

Flexibility of Work Arrangements

Flexible work arrangements, which include flexible working hours, part-time work, and fixed-term contracts and other arrangements, can have a number of advantages. They can provide opportunities for workers to join the formal sector and benefit from new forms of employment. They can also provide employers with the flexibility they may need to adjust employment levels in response to changes in market demand without excessive firing costs. Firms can use such contractual arrangements to conduct new or short-term projects and complement permanent staff on holiday or maternity leave (ILO 2016a).

Figure 4.7 Statutory social security contribution rates are relatively high in MENA

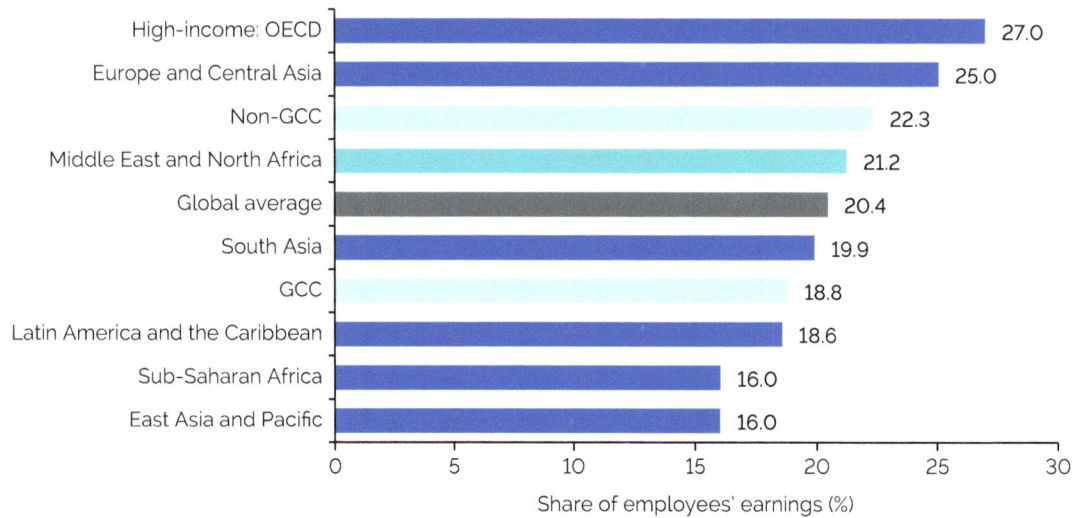

Share of employees' earnings (%)

High-income: OECD — 27.0
Europe and Central Asia — 25.0
Non-GCC — 22.3
Middle East and North Africa — 21.2
Global average — 20.4
South Asia — 19.9
GCC — 18.8
Latin America and the Caribbean — 18.6
Sub-Saharan Africa — 16.0
East Asia and Pacific — 16.0

Sources: International Social Security Association (ISSA) 2018, 2019a, 2019b, 2020.
Note: The figure excludes countries without statutory social security contribution rates by employers or/and employees. Data are for 2018–19. Social security contribution rates are the total for the insured person and the employer in a country and averaged over each region. Contribution rates are not directly comparable across programs and countries, and the definition of earnings used to calculate contributions can vary. Detailed sources, notes, and definitions by country are available at International Social Security Association (ISSA) 2018, 2019a, 2019b, 2020. GCC = Gulf Cooperation Council; OECD = Organisation for Economic Co-operation and Development.

The use of fixed-term contracts can potentially become a stepping-stone to permanent employment and can be beneficial for workers, especially new labor market entrants and young workers, to gain work experience and skills (ILO 2016a). For women, they can also provide an opportunity to tackle work and caregiving more flexibly, especially in societies where the predominant caregiver is the woman. Technological progress has also increased the importance of flexibility for firms in the management of human resources, and the digital economy has increased the role of freelance and fixed-term type of contracts.

While many MENA countries have flexible working arrangements, some countries do not. For countries like Algeria, Djibouti, Iraq, and Morocco, there are limitations on fixed-term contracts, including the prohibition of fixed-term contracts for permanent tasks. Moreover, the maximum cumulative duration of fixed-term contracts is short (less than 24 months) for some countries, and renewal is further restricted. For regulations affecting work hours, most MENA countries allow worker overtime arrangements. While the number of legal working hours follows international practices in most MENA countries, several countries have restrictive regulations on overtime such as notification to the competent authority or limitations on the number of working hours. Djibouti, Jordan, Kuwait, Lebanon, Oman, and Qatar have these restrictions.

It is important to note, however that while flexible work arrangements are important today, they can also represent a risk of insecurity for workers (ILO 2013a). Temporary workers, especially the young and less skilled, tend to have limited access to social security benefits such as pensions, health insurance, and unemployment insurance. They earn lower wages, receive less training, and have limited collective bargaining power (ILO 2016a). Therefore, the use of fixed-term contracts should be supported by appropriate enforcement and comprehensive social protection to avoid abuse. If economies have social protection measures for temporary jobs, more flexible employment contracts and work arrangements can provide flexibility while facilitating workers' transitions toward productive jobs and allowing workers that need flexibility to have it.

Statutory Minimum Wage

Governments set minimum wages with the aim of providing adequate income for workers, especially low-paid workers, as well as reducing wage inequality (ILO 1971; Kuddo, Robalino, and Weber 2015). Minimum wages can also be important when certain firms monopolize local markets, leaving little bargaining power to workers. Empirically, some of the literature shows that a minimum wage has positive effects on workers' productivity while reducing turnover (for example, Brochu and Green 2011). However, when the minimum wage is higher than the marginal product of labor, it becomes a constraint for firms by increasing the labor cost, particularly for less-skilled workers (Gatti et al. 2014), thereby potentially reducing demand for formal labor and increasing unemployment and informality, particularly for low-wage workers (Betcherman 2014; Maloney and Mendez 2004). The statutory minimum wage should protect all workers and be regularly revised to reflect changes in local economic conditions and changes in productivity (ILO 2016b).

Some MENA economies set a high level of the minimum wage compared to value added per worker. While the regional average of the ratio of the minimum wage to value added per worker is similar to the global average at 0.45, there are considerable variations among economies. West Bank and Gaza, Djibouti, and Morocco show high ratios at 0.75, 0.71, and 0.68, respectively.

More important, the minimum wage in MENA tends to be static and not adaptive to existing circumstances. Out of 14 economies where some minimum wage exists for private sector workers, 6 have not revised it since 2014 (table 4.2). Only the Islamic Republic of Iran has implemented an adjustment of the minimum wage every year. At the same time, some economies have just introduced a statutory minimum wage. In October 2012, for instance, West Bank and Gaza introduced a minimum wage of NIS 1,450 per month (ILO 2013b). More recently, Djibouti amended the Labor Code of 2006 in January 2018, which set a minimum wage for the private sector. Limited revisions of minimum wage levels mean that they fail to reflect changes in the cost of living and economic conditions, which may reduce workers' purchasing power and impede a fair wage structure (ILO 1971, 2016b). The International Labour Organization (ILO) recommends annual adjustments in periods of low or moderate inflation, which allow workers and employers for smooth adjustment and predictability.

While governments need to find an appropriate level of minimum wage, this minimum wage should protect all workers, regardless of their nationalities and types of employment. One-quarter of countries in the MENA region do not have a national minimum wage for workers in the private sector, and for those that have it, many workers are excluded, or the minimum wage is different between nationals and non-nationals (table 4.3). This is especially the case for domestic workers, who represent a significant share of the labor force in the region, especially in GCC countries.

Table 4.2 Minimum wage in selected MENA economies, 2014–19

Monthly amounts (local currency)

Economy	2014/15	2015/16	2016/17	2017/18	2018/19	Local currency
Algeria	DA 18,000	DA 18,000	DA 18,000	DA 18,000	DA 18,000	Algerian dinar
Djibouti	O	O	O	O	DF 35,000	Djibouti franc
Iran, Islamic Rep.	Rls 7,124,250	Rls 8,121,660	Rls 9,299,310	Rls 11,112,691	Rls 15,168,810	Iranian rial
Iraq	ID 120,000	ID 120,000	ID 120,000	ID 350,000	ID 350,000	Iraqi dinar
Jordan	JD 190	JD 190	JD 220	JD 220	JD 220	Jordanian dinar
Kuwait	KD 60	KD 60	KD 60	KD 75	KD 75	Kuwaiti dinar
Lebanon	LL 675,000	LL 675,000	LL 675,000	LL 675,000	LL 675,000	Lebanese pound
Libya	LD 450	LD 450	LD 450	LD 450	LD 450	Libyan dinar
Morocco	DH 2,450	DH 2,566	DH 2,566	DH 2,566	DH 2,566	Moroccan dirham
Oman	RO 325	RO 325	RO 325	RO 325	RO 325	Omani rial
Syrian Arab Republic	LS 13,670	LS 16,175	LS 16,175	LS 16,175	LS 16,175	Syrian pound
Tunisia	TD 476	TD 476	TD 502	TD 595	TD 634	Tunisian dinar
West Bank and Gaza	NIS 1,450	NIS 1,450	NIS 1,450	NIS 1,450	NIS 1,450	Israeli new shekel
Yemen, Rep.	YRl 20,000	YRl 20,000	YRl 20,000	YRl 20,000	YRl 20,000	Yemeni rial

Source: World Bank Employing Workers 2020 database.
Note: The information on minimum wages was collected from May in one year to May in the subsequent year.

Table 4.3 Applicability of minimum wage in selected MENA economies

Applicability of minimum wage	Economy/economies
National minimum wage applicable to domestic workers	Kuwait, Qatar
No minimum wage	Saudi Arabia, United Arab Emirates
Minimum wage only in the public sector	Bahrain; Egypt, Arab Rep.
A different minimum wage for migrant and national workers	Jordan

Sources: International Labour Organization; World Bank Employing Workers 2020 database.

GENDERED LAWS

Laws and regulations that discriminate on the basis of gender restrict women's participation in the labor market (Amin and Islam 2015; Hallward-Driemeier and Gajigo 2015; Islam, Muzi, and Amin 2019) and result in wage gaps between men and women (World Bank 2015). Moreover, more equal legal treatments are associated with a reduction in the wage gap, and less occupational segregation between men and women (Hyland, Djankov, and Goldberg 2020). Evidence shows that it is crucial to eliminate legal discriminations to enhance women's employment. The 2021 Women, Business and the Law (WBL) report highlights that the region on average ranks the lowest in the WBL index score of legal equality (figure 4.8).[25] While various MENA countries have undertaken some notable reforms recently, women in the MENA region face unfair laws that economically disempower them (see appendix C).

Women in the region face multiple layers of legal restrictions and inequality to enter and participate in the labor market. Ten economies (Bahrain, Djibouti, Egypt, Jordan, Kuwait, Lebanon, Morocco, the Syrian Arab Republic, Tunisia, and West Bank and Gaza) prohibit women from working in certain industries. For instance, in Lebanon, women are not allowed to drive machines with large engines. Moreover, nine countries in the region link women's work to their husband's or legal guardian's permission in some way or allow for legal ramifications when this permission is not granted. Globally, there are only 19 countries where women face these permission restrictions, of which 9 are in the MENA region and 10 are in the Sub-Saharan Africa region (table 4.4).

Once women enter labor markets, they face additional restrictions in the workplace. The MENA region has the highest share of countries with restrictions on women's work at night (figure 4.9). Restrictions on working hours at night for women who are not pregnant or nursing are most common in the MENA region compared to other countries. Globally, only 12 percent of economies have such conditions. Moreover, none of the GCC countries has a law establishing paid leave for mothers that

Figure 4.8 **MENA ranks lowest in the world on the Women, Business and the Law index**

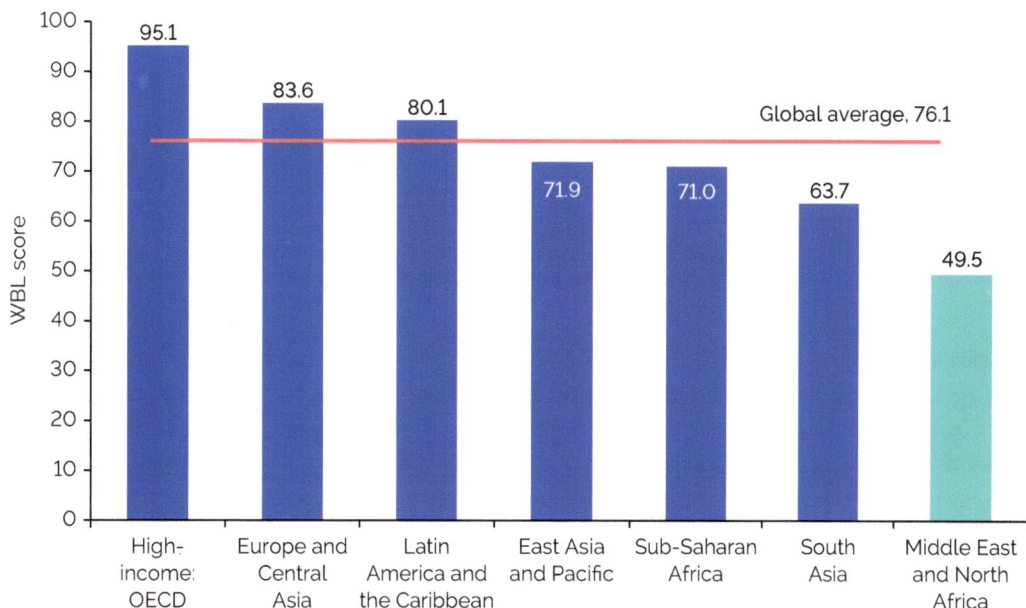

Source: World Bank, Women, Business and the Law 2021.
Note: OECD = Organisation for Economic Co-operation and Development; WBL = Women, Business and the Law.

Table 4.4 Economies where a woman needs her husband's permission to get a job

Middle East and North Africa	Sub-Saharan Africa
Bahrain	Cameroon
Egypt, Arab Rep.	Chad
Iran, Islamic Rep.	Comoros
Jordan	Gabon
Kuwait	Guinea-Bissau
Qatar	Equatorial Guinea
Syrian Arab Republic	Eswatini
West Bank and Gaza	Mauritania
Yemen, Rep.	Niger
	Sudan

Source: World Bank, Women Business and the Law 2021.

Figure 4.9 MENA has more restrictions on women working night shifts than nearly every other world region

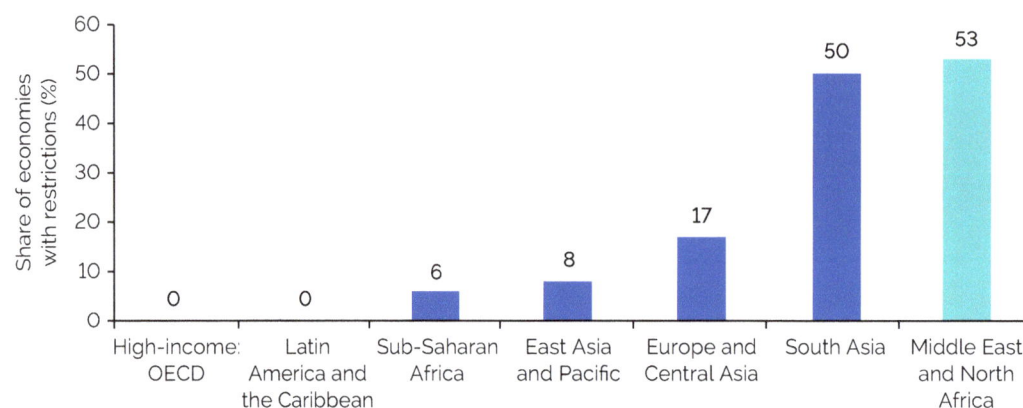

Source: World Bank, Women, Business and the Law 2021.
Note: OECD = Organisation for Economic Co-operation and Development.

meets international standards. The ILO Maternity Protection Convention (2000) recommends 14 weeks (98 days) as necessary paid maternity leave. Globally, 117 out of 190 economies legally allow mothers to have at least 14 weeks of paid leave (maternity leave, parental leave, or a combination of both) for childbirth. In the MENA region, only seven countries provide more than 14 weeks of paid leave. When paid maternity leave is available, employers often bear the costs, implying that they may be induced to discriminate against female employees, particularly women of childbearing age due to the associated direct and indirect costs of maternity leave. The government administers 100 percent of maternity leave benefits in only five countries (Algeria, the Islamic Republic of Iran, Jordan, Morocco, and Tunisia). By contrast, governments cover maternity leave benefits in nearly 90 percent of countries in the OECD and the Europe and Central Asia regions.

Laws that protect women from discrimination raise labor force participation (figure 4.10). Many governments have established laws enhancing gender equality in the workplace, such as laws that prohibit discrimination in employment based on gender, that mandate equal remuneration for work of equal value, and that prohibit the dismissal of pregnant workers. However, in the MENA region, Algeria, the Islamic Republic of Iran, Jordan, Kuwait, Oman, and Qatar still do not have laws prohibiting discrimination in employment based on gender. Moreover, less than half of the MENA economies have legislation mandating equal remuneration for work of equal value. The establishment of nondiscrimination laws can provide a legal framework for action on women's rights and is an essential step toward reducing gender inequality in the labor market.

In some countries in the region, progress has been made toward gender equality. For example, in 2020, Saudi Arabia eliminated all restrictions on women's employment in sectors considered unsafe, such as mining, setting men and women on equal terms in the choice of employment opportunities. In 2019, it also amended laws discriminating against women in employment, including job advertisements and hiring, and prohibited employers from dismissing a woman during her entire pregnancy and

Figure 4.10 **There is a positive relationship between women empowerment and their labor force participation**

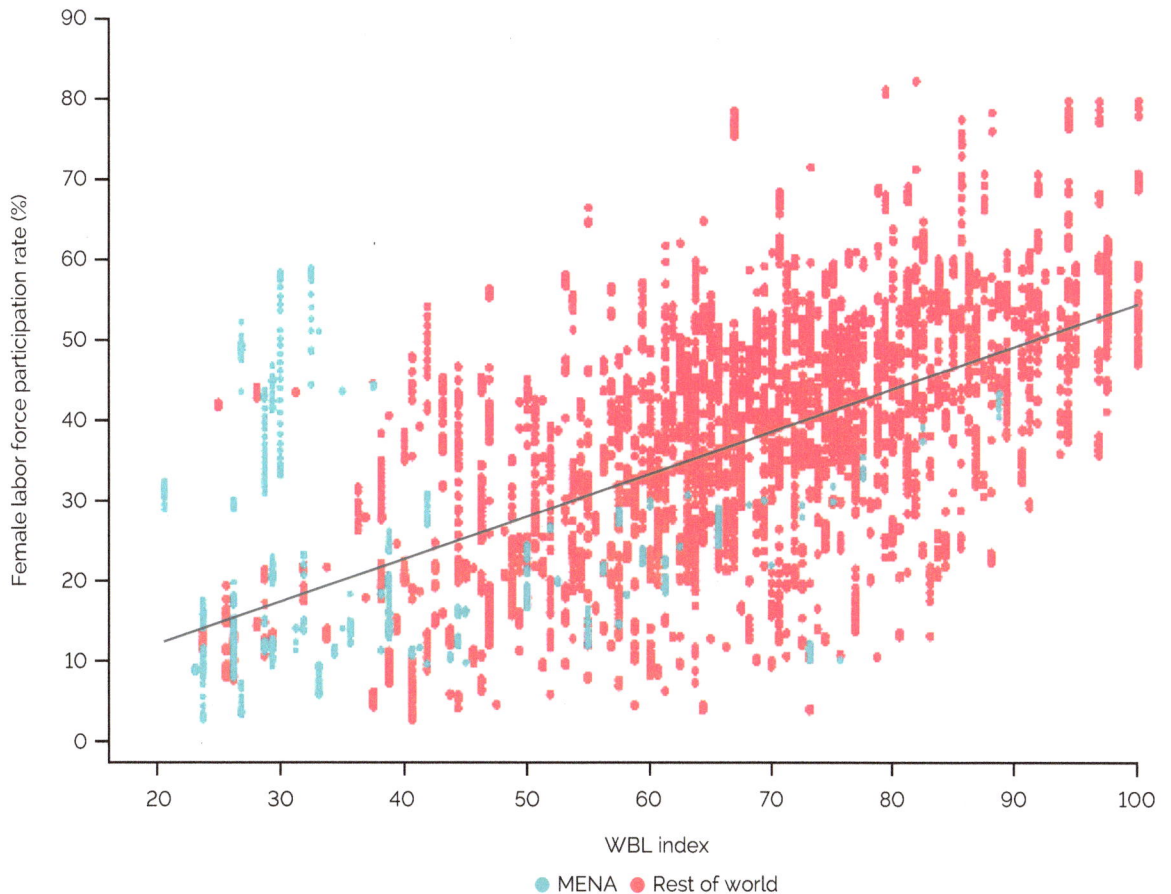

Sources: World Bank, Women, Business and the Law 1970–2019; International Labour Organization.
Note: The figure covers 190 economies for 50 years. WBL = Women, Business and the Law.

maternity leave. In 2005, the United Arab Emirates established a federal agency, the Gender Balance Council, to foster efforts to remove legal barriers to women's work. In 2019, the government removed all job restrictions on women, and women are allowed to work the same hours and in the same jobs and industries as men. In 2020, the United Arab Emirates introduced five days of parental leave, becoming the first and only country in the region to have paid parental leave.

Realizing the positive impact of these initiatives on women and the world of work may take more time. But the potential of women in the region is and will be large. This is evident not only in the general increase in women's educational achievement, as they surpass their male peers in international tests, but also in the way that they handle and operate their businesses. While few women lead firms in the region, the firms that they lead, as seen in chapter 3, tend to invest more in physical capital, in worker training, and in R&D. Moreover, the firms that are managed by women have had higher employment growth over the past few years than those managed by men, and they were more likely to employ female workers. Lastly, women-led firms are more likely to be digitally connected than firms led by men, as defined by the business having its own website, highlighting the potential and opportunity that the region can leverage for change.

NOTES

1. https://www.oecd.org/economy/reform/indicators-of-product-market-regulation/.

2. Data used and collected for these comparator countries are based on the 2018 PMR methodology. This section uses the following income categorizations: High-income countries consist of Australia, Austria, Belgium, Canada, Chile, Croatia, Cyprus, the Czech Republic, Denmark, Estonia, Finland, France, Germany, Greece, Hungary, Iceland, Ireland, Israel, Italy, Japan, the Republic of Korea, Latvia, Lithuania, Luxembourg, Malta, the Netherlands, New Zealand, Norway, Poland, Portugal, Romania, the Slovak Republic, Slovenia, Spain, Sweden, Switzerland, and the United Kingdom. Upper-middle-income countries consist of Albania, Argentina, Brazil, Bulgaria, Colombia, Costa Rica, Indonesia, Kazakhstan, Mexico, Peru, the Russian Federation, Serbia, South Africa, and Turkey. The classifications for MENA economies are high-income (Kuwait, Saudi Arabia, and the United Arab Emirates); upper-middle-income (Egypt, Jordan, Morocco, and Tunisia), and lower-middle-income (West Bank and Gaza).

3. More details on the PMR data collection methodology can be found in appendix A. Additional data were collected and analyzed, but were not presented in this report, including administrative burdens (licensing); barriers in service and network sectors; barriers to trade and investment (barriers to foreign direct investment, tariff barriers, deferential treatment of foreign suppliers, and barriers to trade facilitation); and sectoral analysis covering the energy sector, the telecommunications sector (focusing on government involvement in the sector, vertical integration, third-party access, and pricing policy), the service sectors of legal, accounting, engineering, and architecture (focusing on conduct regulations), and retail services (focusing on price regulations). The background paper "Restrictive Regulation as a Challenge for Competition, Productivity, and Jobs in the MENA Region: Closing the Gap" (Dauda et al., forthcoming) presents a full analysis of PMR data.

4. In Kuwait, Chapter 25 of the 2020–2021 budget stipulates subsidies for public corporations and nonfinancial public corporations, support to refined products and liquefied gas locally marketed, and a fuel subsidy for Kuwait Airways. Available at https://www.mof.gov.kw/MofBudget/PDF/Budget20-19eng.pdf (last accessed February 10, 2021). For Egypt, see Decree no. 934/2001, which stipulates that regular domestic or international flights shall not be operated in the same operating time of Egypt Air.

5. For Egypt this refers to hard-core cartels, where an exemption can be granted provided said agreement would achieve economic efficiencies that have a clear benefit to the consumer that exceed the effects of reducing competition (Article 6 of the Competition Law no. 3 of 2005); and Tunisia, where the relevant minister may set the prices for temporary measures not exceeding six months to deal with market irregularities such as sudden excessive increase or collapse in prices (Articles 2-4 of Law 36 of 2015).

6. Article 4 of Federal Law 4 of 2012.

7. Unincorporated operations refer to business undertakings rendered by entities that are not formed into a legal corporation and thus lack corporate status.

8. Parafiscal taxes are essentially the charges that the state levies without necessarily providing a service. They include some nontax fees.

9. Article 6 of the General Tax Code exempts certain SOEs from income tax.

10. As per a 2019 report by the Egyptian Ministry of Finance (MoF), subsidies extended to the public sector (including electricity subsidies) amounted to LE 32,178.9 million; loans amounted to LE 73.8 million; and participation in SOEs amounted to LE 2,633.9 million (total LE 34,886.5 million) for fiscal year 2017/2018. The report also disclosed the amounts of the guarantees of external loans granted by the MoF and the refinancing/restructuring extended through the MoF to SOEs. Ministry of Finance, Financial Relation between SOEs and the Government, available at http://www.mof.gov.eg/MOFGallerySource/Arabic/Financial-Egypt-report2018/Relationship_between_companies_treasury.pdf (last accessed September 2, 2019).

11. US Department of State, "2020 Investment Climate Statements: Jordan," available at https://www.state.gov/reports/2020-investment-climate-statements/jordan/ (last accessed December 5, 2021).

12. Article 77 of Law 26 of 2019 addresses requirements to issue government guarantees to federal entities, the definition of which does not seem to include the SOEs (Article 3). However, Article 11 of Law 9 of 2018 regarding public debt includes SOEs that are wholly owned by the government under the definition of government entities for which debt can be guaranteed.

13. See "Kuwait—Competition from State-Owned Enterprises," available at https://www.export.gov/article?id=Kuwait-Competition-from-State-Owned-Enterprises (last accessed February 18, 2021).

14. The total amount of subsidies paid to Moroccan public entities and enterprises (EEPs) amounted to DH 30.792 million by the end of 2018, of which 44 percent was for investment (capital and equipment) and 56 percent was for operating expenses. EEPs of a commercial nature benefited by DH 2.988 million. The transport and energy sector benefited by more than DH 900 million. See EEP Report of the MoF 2020, "Report on the Public Entities and Enterprises (EEP) Sector Accompanying the 2020 Draft Finance Law," available at https://www.finances.gov.ma/en/Pages/finance-act-2020.aspx (last accessed February 18, 2021).

15. Publicly controlled companies may receive financing guaranteed by the state. The amount of the state guarantee is decided each year in the Finance Law (as stipulated in Article 9 of 2013 Finance Law).

16. Article Four C, the State Budget 1441-1442 AH (2020), available at https://www.mof.gov.sa/financialreport/budget2020/Pages/default.aspx (last accessed February 18, 2021).

17. For a detailed explanation of both net present value and internal rate of return, see the EU Commission: "Guide to Cost-Benefit Analysis of Investment Projects: Structural Funds, Cohesion Fund and Instrument for Pre-Accession, 2008," https://ec.europa.eu/regional_policy/en/information/publications/evaluations-guidance-documents/2008/guide-to-cost-benefit-analysis-of-investment-projects.

18. Article 10 of the Regulations on Transportation Services through the Use of Smartphone Applications.

19. Article 19 of Law No. 13-065 relating to the organization and conduct of government affairs and the legal status of its members. "Twenty-five economies worldwide, including the European Union, the United Arab Emirates and Taiwan (China) measure all of these impacts [spectrum of the impacts covered by RIA]." World Bank Global Indicators of Regulatory Governance: Worldwide Practices of Regulatory Impact Assessments, available at https://documents.worldbank.org/en/publication/documents-reports/documentdetail/905611520284525814/global-indicators-of-regulato-ry-governance-worldwide-practices-of-regulatory-impact-assessments.pdf.

20. The MENA region in this analysis includes Algeria; Bahrain; Djibouti; Egypt, Arab Rep.; Iran, Islamic Rep.; Iraq; Jordan; Kuwait; Lebanon; Libya; Morocco; Oman; Qatar; Saudi Arabia; Syrian Arab Republic; Tunisia; United Arab Emirates; West Bank and Gaza; and Yemen, Rep.

21. The fourteen economies are Algeria; Bahrain; Djibouti; Egypt; Iran, Islamic Rep.; Iraq; Jordan; Lebanon; Libya; Morocco; Syria; Tunisia; West Bank and Gaza; and Yemen, Rep.

22. The seven countries are Egypt; Iran, Islamic Rep.; Iraq; Jordan; Morocco; Syria; and Tunisia.

23. The nine countries are Algeria; Bahrain; Egypt; Iran, Islamic Rep.; Jordan; Kuwait; Morocco; Saudi Arabia; and Tunisia.

24. Data for Algeria, Bahrain, and Egypt refer to 2003, 2010, and 2015, respectively. ILO Social Security database.

25. The MENA region for this analysis consists of 19 economies: Algeria; Bahrain; Djibouti; Egypt; Iran, Islamic Rep.; Iraq; Jordan; Kuwait; Lebanon; Libya; Morocco; Oman; Qatar; Saudi Arabia; Syria; Tunisia; United Arab Emirates; West Bank and Gaza; and Yemen, Rep.

REFERENCES

Amin, Mohammed, and Asif Islam. 2015. "Does Mandating Nondiscrimination in Hiring Practices Affect Female Employment? Evidence Using Firm-Level Data." *Feminist Economics* 12 (1&2).

Angel-Urdinola, Diego F., and Arvo Kuddo. 2010. "Key Characteristics of Employment Regulation in the Middle East and North Africa." Social Protection Discussion Paper 1006, World Bank, Washington, DC.

Antón, Arturo. 2014. "The Effect of Payroll Taxes on Employment and Wages under High Labor Informality." *IZA Journal of Labor Development* 3 (20). https://doi.org/10.1186/2193-9020-3-20.

Bartelsman, Eric J., Pieter A. Gautier, and Joris de Wind. 2016. "Employment Protection, Technology Choice, and Worker Allocation." *International Economic Review* 57 (3): 787–826.

Bassanini, Andrea, Luca Nunziata, and Danielle Venn. 2009. "Job Protection and Productivity Growth in OECD Countries." *Economic Policy* 24 (58): 349–402.

Betcherman, Gordon. 2014. "Labor Market Regulations: What Do We Know about Their Impacts in Developing Countries?" Policy Research Working Paper 6819, World Bank, Washington, DC.

Botero, Juan C., Simeon Djankov, Rafael La Porta, Florencio Lopez-de-Silanes, and Andrei Shleifer. 2004. "The Regulation of Labor." *Quarterly Journal of Economics* 119 (4): 1339–82.

Bottasso, Anna, Maurizio Conti, and Giovanni Sulis. 2017. "Firm Dynamics and Employment Protection: Evidence from Sectoral Data." *Labour Economics* 48 (October): 35–53.

Brochu, Pierre, and David A. Green. 2011. "The Impact of Minimum Wages on Quit, Layoff and Hiring Rates." IFS Working Paper 06/11, Institute for Fiscal Studies, London.

Dauda, Seidu, Graciela Miralles Murciego, Georgiana Pop, and Azza Raslan. Forthcoming. "Restrictive Regulation as a Challenge for Competition, Productivity, and Jobs in the MENA Region: Closing the Gap." Background paper for *Jobs Undone: Reshaping the Role of Governments toward Markets and Workers in the Middle East and North Africa*. World Bank, Washington, DC.

Ebell, Monique, and Christian Haefke. 2003. "Product Market Deregulation and Labor Market Outcomes." Economics Working Paper, Department of Economics and Business, Universitat Pompeu Fabra, Barcelona.

Gatti, Roberta, Diego F. Angel-Urdinola, Joana Silva, and Andras Bodor, eds. 2014. *Striving for Better Jobs: The Challenge of Informality in the Middle East and North Africa*. Directions in Development: Human Development. Washington, DC: World Bank.

Griffith, Rachel, and Rupert Harrison. 2004. "The Link between Product Market Reform and Macro-economic Performance." Economic Paper 209, European Commission, Brussels.

Hallward-Driemeier, Mary, and Ousman Gajigo. 2015. "Strengthening Economic Rights and Women's Occupational Choice: The Impact of Reforming Ethiopia's Family Law." *World Development* 70: 260–73.

Harasty, Claire. 2004. "Successful Employment and Labour Market Policies in Europe and Asia and the Pacific." Employment Strategy Paper 2004/4, International Labour Organization, Geneva.

Hatayama, Maho. 2021. "Revisiting Labor Market Regulations in the Middle East and North Africa." Jobs Working Paper 64, World Bank, Washington, DC. https://openknowledge.worldbank.org/handle/10986/36887.

Hyland, Marie, Simeon Djankov, and Pinelopi Koujianou Goldberg. 2020. "Gendered Laws and Women in the Workforce." *American Economics Review: Insights* 2 (4): 475–490.

ILO (International Labour Organization). 1971. Minimum Wage Fixing Convention, 1971 (No. 131).

ILO (International Labour Organization). 2013a. "Labour Inspection and Employment Relationship." Working Document No. 28, ILO, Geneva.

ILO (International Labour Organization). 2013b. "The Situation of Workers of the Occupied Arab Territories." International Labour Conference, 102nd Session, 2013.

ILO (International Labour Organization). 2016a. *Non-standard Employment around the World: Understanding Challenges, Shaping Prospects*. Geneva: ILO.

ILO (International Labour Organization). 2016b. *Minimum Wage Policy Guide: Full Chapters*. Geneva: ILO.

ILO (International Labour Organization). 2020. Maternity Protection Convention, 2000 (No. 183).

Islam, Asif M., Silvia Muzi, and Mohammad Amin. 2019. "Unequal Laws and the Disempowerment of Women in the Labour Market: Evidence from Firm-Level Data." *Journal of Development Studies* 55 (5): 822–44.

ISSA (International Social Security Association). 2018. *Social Security Programs throughout the World: Europe, 2018*. Geneva: ISSA.

ISSA (International Social Security Association). 2019a. *Social Security Programs throughout the World: Africa, 2019*. Geneva: ISSA.

ISSA (International Social Security Association). 2019b. *Social Security Programs throughout the World: Asia and the Pacific, 2018*. Geneva: ISSA.

ISSA (International Social Security Association). 2020. *Social Security Programs throughout the World: The Americas, 2019*. Geneva: ISSA.

Kuddo, Arvo, David Robalino, and Michael Weber. 2015. *Balancing Regulations to Promote Jobs: From Employment Contracts to Unemployment Benefits*. Washington, DC: World Bank.

Kugler, Adriana, and Maurice Kugler. 2009. "Labor Market Effects of Payroll Taxes in Developing Countries: Evidence from Colombia." *Economic Development and Cultural Change* 57 (2): 335–58.

Kugler, Adriana, and Giovanni Pica. 2008. "Effects of Employment Protection on Worker and Job Flows: Evidence from the 1990 Italian Reform." *Labour Economics* 15 (1): 78–95.

Kugler, Adriana, and G. Saint-Paul. 2004. "How Do Firing Costs Affect Worker Flows in a World with Adverse Selection?" *Journal of Labor Economics* 22: 553–84.

Lehmann, Hartmut, and Alexander Muravyev. 2012. "Labor Market Institutions and Informality in Transition and Latin American Countries." IZA Discussion Paper 7035, Institute of Labor Economics, Bonn.

Mahmood, Syed Akhtar, and Meriem Ait Ali Slimane. 2018. *Privilege-Resistant Policies in the Middle East and North Africa: Measurement and Operational Implications*. MENA Development Report. Washington, DC: World Bank.

Maloney, William F., and Jairo Mendez. 2004. "Measuring the Impact of Minimum Wages: Evidence from Latin America." In *Law and Employment: Lessons from Latin America and the Caribbean*, edited by James J. Heckman and Carmen Pagés, 109–30. Cambridge, MA: National Bureau of Economic Research.

Nicoletti, Giuseppe, and Stefano Scarpetta. 2005. "Product Market Reforms and Employment in OECD Countries." OECD Economics Department Working Paper No. 472, OECD Publishing, Paris.

OECD (Organisation for Economic Co-operation and Development). 2012. *Towards New Arrangements for State Ownership in the Middle East and North Africa*. Paris: OECD Publishing.

Packard, Truman G., Ugo Gentilini, Margaret Grosh, Philip O'Keefe, Robert J. Palacios, David A. Robalino, and Indhira Santos. 2019. *Protecting All: Risk Sharing for a Diverse and Diversifying World of Work*. Human Development Perspectives. Washington, DC: World Bank.

Packard, Truman G., and Claudio Montenegro. 2017. "Labor Policy and Digital Technology Use: Indicative Evidence from Cross-Country Correlations." Policy Research Working Paper 8221, World Bank, Washington, DC.

Renahy, Emilie, Christine Mitchell, Agnes Molnar, Carles Muntaner, Edwin Ng, Farihah Ali, and Patricia O'Campo. 2018. "Connections between Unemployment Insurance, Poverty and Health: A Systematic Review." *European Journal of Public Health* 28 (2): 269–75.

World Bank. 2009. "Estimating the Impact of Labor Taxes on Employment and the Balances of the Social Insurance Funds in Turkey." World Bank, Washington, DC.

World Bank. 2013. *Jobs for Shared Prosperity: Time for Action in the Middle East and North Africa*. Washington, DC: World Bank.

World Bank. 2015. *Women, Business and the Law 2016: Getting to Equal*. Washington, DC: World Bank.

World Bank. 2019. *World Development Report 2019: The Changing Nature of Work*. Washington, DC: World Bank.

World Bank. 2020. *Morocco Infrastructure Review*. Washington, DC: World Bank.

World Bank. 2021. *Women, Business and the Law 2021*. Washington, DC: World Bank.

MOROCCO: A Safe Carpool Platform to Share Trip Costs

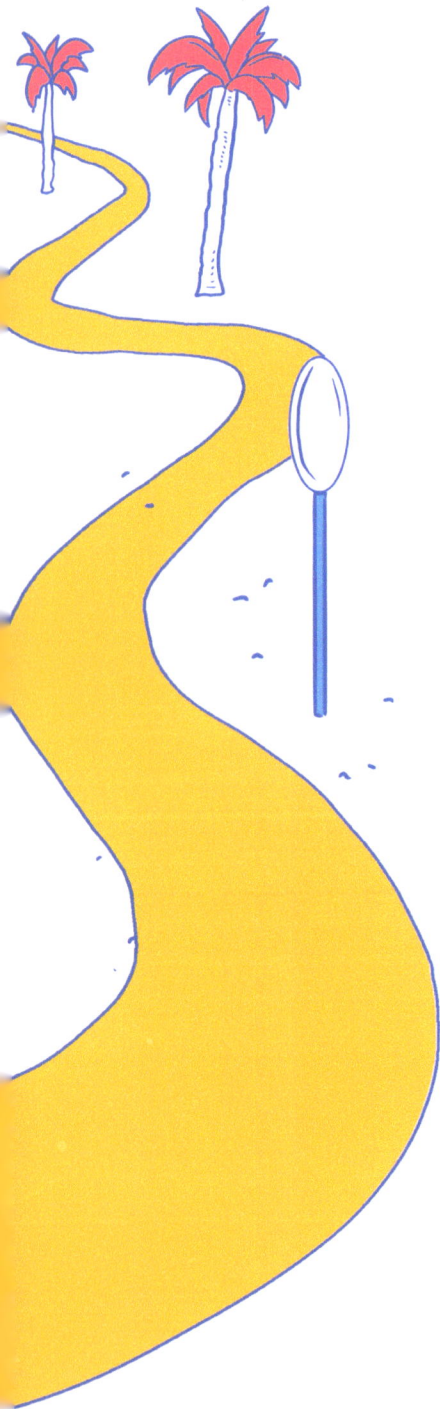

Hicham, a 31-year-old entrepreneur, is founder and chief executive officer (CEO) of a carpool platform that serves approximately 400,000 people across Morocco. Hicham lived in Kenitra and commuted every day to the capital, Rabat, for work. He realized that a carpool business between the city and the capital would facilitate travel back and forth and therefore would open employment opportunities. "I wanted to make people happy and serve their needs," Hicham explained. Hicham also wanted to provide women with a safe mode of transportation. One way he addressed this was by providing an option on the app for women to choose to share a ride with only other women.

Hicham's carpool platform is a creative social entrepreneurship venture built on the emerging share economy where passengers share the trip cost with drivers. Last year almost 10,000 drivers benefited from this service. It is an affordable and new transportation option increasingly available to many Moroccans. Through the company's app, passengers can find a driver who will take them to their destination and carpool with others going in the same direction, making their trip cheaper and better for the environment. The app's tracking software adds an element of safety to each passenger's journey whereby passengers can see on their app if they are on route or taking a potentially suspicious detour. The platform is much more affordable than traditional means of public transportation. For example, a trip from Fes to Casablanca could cost the equivalent of US$12 to US$28 by bus or train, which are the cheapest transportation options. However, making the trip through the platform would cost 50 percent to 75 percent less: between US$6 to US$9 per seat.

To foster trust between users, the app uses a rating system to encourage good driver and passenger behavior. Drivers are required to have their IDs verified before being able to drive others, and some personal information is listed on their profile in the app for extra reassurance. The company's website also recommends that passengers verify their ID on the app by providing their national identity card number (CIN) or a photo of their passport. This information is not shared with the driver. Instead, the company will check this information and then verify the passenger's account so the driver can be assured that they too are safe when they accept these passengers for a ride. Drivers usually prefer to take the ride with verified passengers. The firm currently has 10 full-time staff, but Hicham anticipates his employee numbers to rise by 50 percent each year in the next three years.

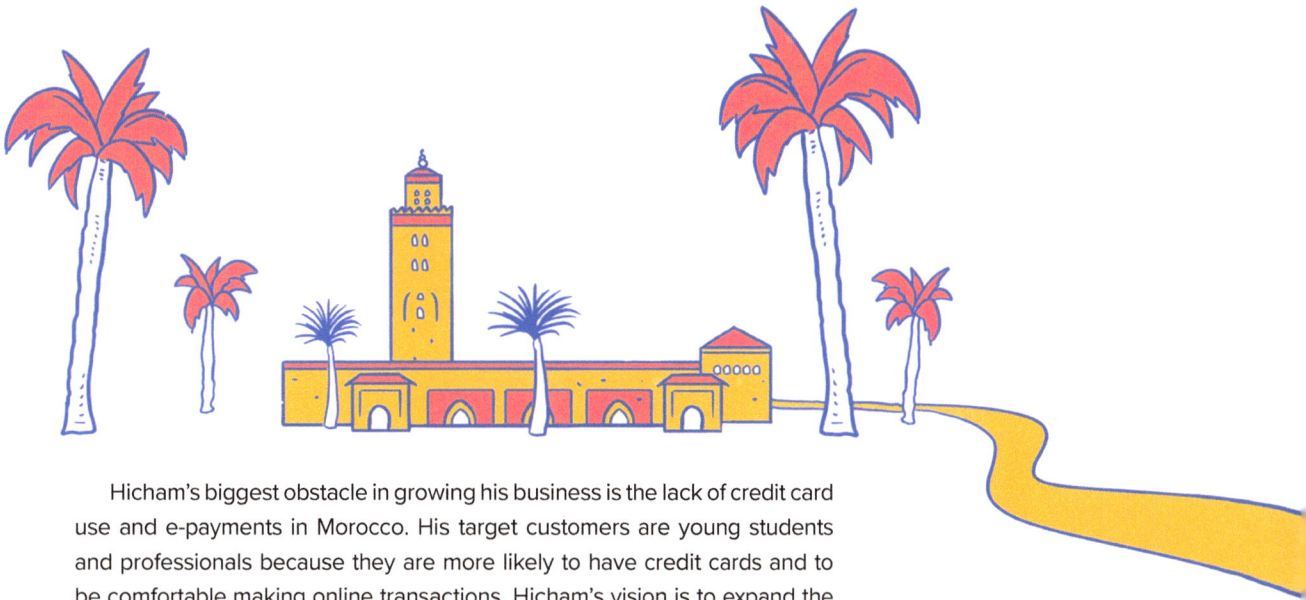

Hicham's biggest obstacle in growing his business is the lack of credit card use and e-payments in Morocco. His target customers are young students and professionals because they are more likely to have credit cards and to be comfortable making online transactions. Hicham's vision is to expand the service across the MENA region. He hopes to start expanding to other North African countries soon, especially Tunisia.

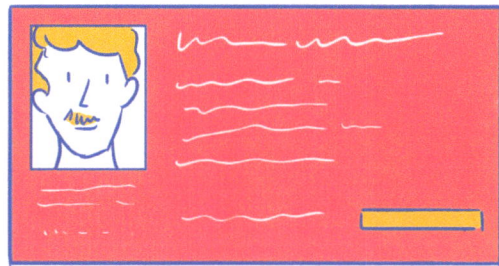

CHAPTER 5

Toward More Contestable Markets

INTRODUCTION

Chapters 2 and 3 illustrated some of the key challenges facing the labor market and the private sector that characterize most Middle East and North Africa (MENA) economies. The labor market potential of the young, the better educated, and women remains largely untapped. The labor force in the MENA region faces exclusion, unemployment, and informality. At the same time, the jobs of the region are emphatically not the jobs of the future. Meanwhile, MENA's private sector remains characterized by limited dynamism and job creation, is not gender inclusive, and does not invest much in its human and physical capital or in innovation. It also remains more politically connected than others around the world. The implications of these shortcomings for the region's macroeconomic performance are evident, with lower economic growth than peers, limited labor productivity growth—especially when it comes to structural change—and limited growth of capital per capita with a continuing large role of public investments. Whereas income peers around the world are catching up, many countries in the MENA region are stagnating.

The coronavirus (COVID-19) pandemic has undoubtedly worsened these outcomes. Output has contracted, and the poverty rate has increased significantly, exacerbated by job losses in an already anemic private sector that is riddled with informality. The ability of MENA governments to address these challenges has also been hampered by growing fiscal constraints.

The tremendous impact of the pandemic is likely to be long-lasting, paired with waves of young and increasingly educated populations that will continue to come into age and enter the labor force. It is time for the MENA region to shake the sclerotic labor market and private sector, and attain the economic potential of a growing, competent, and ambitious labor force. *If not now, when?*

To tackle this huge and urgent challenge, the report points to the need to focus on labor demand and the lack of market contestability, which influences job creation through several direct and indirect channels, while shifting the state's role from that of a competitor in the private sector to that of a guardian of equity and welfare. Despite the reforms that many countries in the region have made in the business environment over the past decade, including in some cases establishing competition laws and authorities, the state remains ever present in commercial activities, and this presence continues to hinder market contestability.

The road to contestability in the MENA region should be implemented through a multipronged approach along three key reform areas: (1) leveling the playing field in the product market given the high presence of the state; (2) reshaping the relationship between the government and workers; and (3) fostering women's inclusion in all economic spheres (see figure 5.1). Interventions on these three fronts would be essential pillars for a new social contract in MENA. At the same time, political considerations are pivotal in defining a feasible road to contestability in MENA countries (World Bank 2009). The challenging political economy landscape that characterizes the region may require a hybrid of reforms, combining the bold with those that are incremental and working at times along the margins. Last, but certainly not least, the road to contestability needs better data and transparency, which is lacking in most MENA countries, constraining both evidence-based policy making and effective implementation.

Figure 5.1 Toward a new social contract through contestable markets

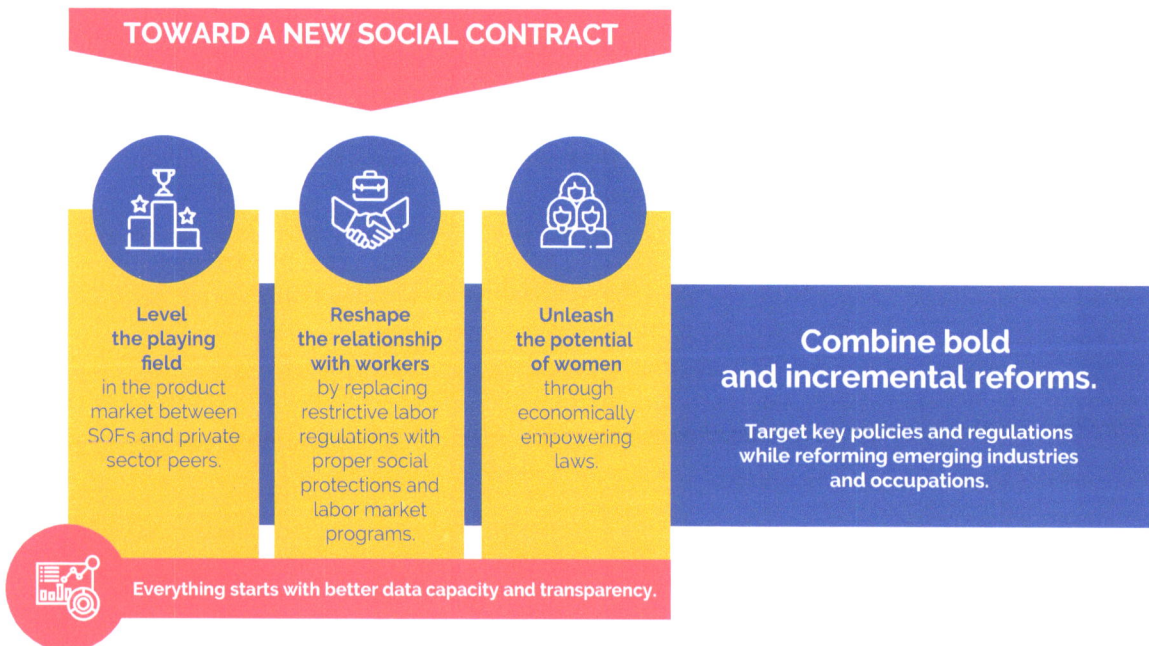

TOWARD A NEW SOCIAL CONTRACT

Level the playing field in the product market between SOEs and private sector peers.

Reshape the relationship with workers by replacing restrictive labor regulations with proper social protections and labor market programs.

Unleash the potential of women through economically empowering laws.

Combine bold and incremental reforms.

Target key policies and regulations while reforming emerging industries and occupations.

Everything starts with better data capacity and transparency.

Source: Flagship team elaboration.
Note: SOEs = state-owned enterprises.

LEVELING THE PLAYING FIELD IN THE PRODUCT MARKET

As chapter 4 showed, governments in the MENA region have a higher presence of state-owned enterprises (SOEs) in the market than comparable middle- and high-income countries. This presence is true even in sectors where there is not necessarily a clear economic rationale for public activity, and where private firms would likely generate better economic outcomes, such as manufacturing, accommodation, trade, repair, and construction. The findings also show little competitive neutrality that equates the treatment between all economic actors, and significant price controls for some goods and services.

According to the latest assessment available (OECD 2012), SOEs account for 30 percent of employment in the MENA region, compared to only 5 percent of employment worldwide. In terms of economic value added, SOEs in MENA account for 20 percent to 25 percent of GDP. The corresponding average for OECD economies and some African economies is 15 percent, and just 8 percent in Latin America.

This high presence of governments can stifle private sector development, especially in markets where competition is viable but SOEs do not compete on a level playing field. It can also hamper the economy and its ability to transform from lower value added activities to higher value added ones, ultimately creating more, better, and inclusive jobs. For countries where data are available, there is a negative correlation between the presence of SOEs in various sectors and the average growth of labor productivity in private sector firms (figure 5.2).

To improve market contestability, governments should reduce the presence of SOEs in economic sectors where the private sector could potentially thrive and where there are no obvious market failures justifying the government's presence. This could be corrected through a deliberate, gradual, and well-managed process of privatization of specific enterprises and activities—either partially or wholly. In designing a way forward, the region must learn from its own successes and its failures, especially from the large scale of privatizations in the region during the 1990s (World Bank 2015).

As the state gradually changes its presence in the market, it is important to level the playing field by fostering competitive neutrality between SOEs and the private sector. Reforms should focus on (1) promoting corporatization of SOEs and separating costs and revenues of their commercial and noncommercial activities; (2) fostering regulatory neutrality by eliminating exclusions and exceptions from laws applied to private operators, especially competition, procurement, and tax laws; and (3) limiting SOEs' preferential access to financial and nonfinancial support, including subsidies. Some countries in the region are already planning bold reforms in these areas (box 5.1).

Figure 5.2 **MENA's high presence of state-owned enterprises is associated with lower labor productivity growth compared to income peers**

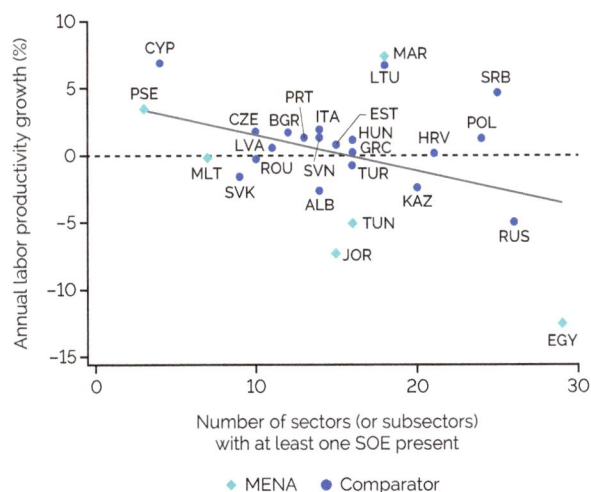

Sources: Flagship team elaboration. Annual labor productivity data are obtained from World Bank Enterprise Surveys for 26 economies surveyed in 2018–20. Data on SOE presence are obtained from the OECD and OECD-WBG Product Market Regulation (PMR) database, 2018–20.
Note: Middle East and North Africa economies surveyed are Egypt (EGY), Jordan (JOR), Malta (MLT), Morocco (MAR), Tunisia (TUN), and West Bank and Gaza (PSE). Labor productivity growth is captured between circa 2017 and 2019. Labor productivity is defined as sales per worker. OECD = Organisation for Economic Co-operation and Development; SOE = state-owned enterprise; WBG = World Bank Group.

Box 5.1 Iraq's proposed reforms to make its economy more dynamic and diversified

In 2020, the government of Iraq produced and adopted a White Paper that outlines some of the key reforms and initiatives that the government will undertake in the next three to five years. The aim of the White Paper is to "create a dynamic and diversified economy that gives citizens the opportunity for a dignified life."

The Paper recognizes first and foremost that one of the reasons behind the deterioration of the Iraqi economy has been the expansive role of the state, including nationalization policies in the 1970s, the war and conflict that it had seen since the 1980s, and the failure of the new political system since 2003 in creating tangible change for the people. The Paper remarkably recognizes the challenges that rising public employment has had on Iraq's fiscal space, and, more important, on the private sector.

Among the bold reforms that the Paper outlines is a reconsideration of the role of the state altogether in the economy, including the restructuring of state–owned enterprises (SOEs) (Axis 4). Proposed initiatives include: (1) entirely phasing out financial support provided by the state to these enterprises by the end of 2024; (2) privatizing the successful and profitable SOEs, either partially or completely, and restructuring the unprofitable ones; (3) increasing the number of SOEs that are listed in the stock exchange; and (4) restructuring employment within the enterprises and finding alternatives to the oversupply of employees. The Iraqi government's detailed reforms also extend to reducing subsidies in the economy and better targeting the poor and vulnerable through social assistance programs.

Sources: Government of Iraq, *Objectives and Axes of the White Paper for Iraq's Economic Reforms* (accessed June 2021), https://gds.gov.iq/ar/iraqs-white-paper-for-economic-reforms-vision-and-key-objectives/ and https://gds.gov.iq/ar/wp-content /uploads/2020/10/Iraq-white-paper-in-arabic-october-2020.pdf.

Governments should also reduce price controls. While regulating prices in natural monopolies might be necessary, in other markets price controls tend to have negative effects because restrictions to competition and innovation resulting from such policies outweigh their benefits. Retail price controls remain prevalent in the MENA region, especially on staples, liquified petroleum gas, gasoline, and medicine. This is done by far fewer governments in high-income countries and upper-middle-income countries. Instead of focusing on price controls, governments can focus on providing targeted assistance to the poor and vulnerable. Table 5.1 summarizes considerations for governments when assessing whether and how to implement price controls to help reduce negative effects.

Lastly, MENA countries should also enforce effective competition policies through systematized assessments of the potential for negative market impacts of laws and regulations. Systematized Regulatory Impact Assessments (RIAs) offer a critical filter to evaluate the costs and benefits of new regulations and policies. In the MENA region so far, only two countries (Morocco and the United Arab Emirates) have adopted general RIA frameworks.

Table 5.1 Economic considerations for the efficient design of price controls

Situations in which price controls may be warranted	Guidelines for setting and reviewing price controls
• Natural monopolies • Short-term issues in which competition cannot be relied on to determine market price (such as supply shocks)	• Set independently of producers • Analyze alternatives: targeted subsidies and analysis of potential restrictions to competition • Make price controls time bounded—they should not be indefinite • Review periodically to determine whether levels are optimal • Analyze impacts on nonprice competition

Source: World Bank Group and African Competition Forum 2016.

RESHAPING THE RELATIONSHIP BETWEEN THE GOVERNMENT AND WORKERS

This report has documented persistently suboptimal labor outcomes in the region. The workforce suffers from unemployment, idleness, and vulnerable informality, and transitions to more productive, formal jobs have been limited in many countries. As the public sector can no longer absorb all of the region's new and ambitious entrants, MENA governments must rethink their role in the labor market and their relationship with workers.

Chapter 4 presented evidence that some MENA economies have limiting labor regulations. A number of countries have relatively high severance pay, some middle-income countries have a considerably significant share of labor taxes in the larger tax obligations of firms and workers, others have limited use of fixed-term contracts, and coverage and updating of the minimum wage are limited. Moreover, reforms in labor market regulations have been limited in the region compared to others (figure 5.3). While in

Figure 5.3 MENA has implemented relatively few labor regulation reforms since 2006

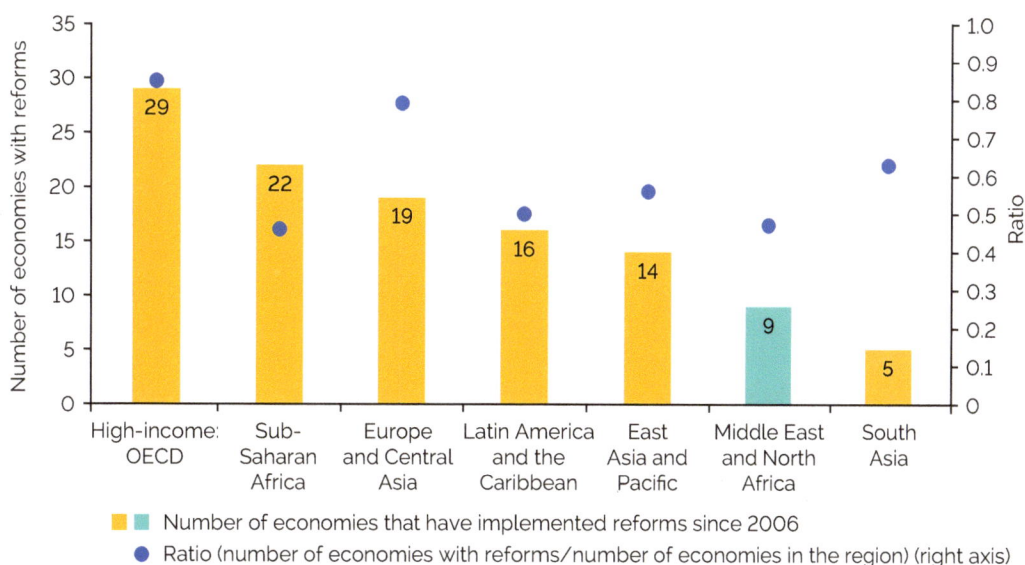

Number of economies that have implemented reforms since 2006

● Ratio (number of economies with reforms/number of economies in the region) (right axis)

Source: World Bank Employing Workers 2020 database.
Note: OECD = Organisation for Economic Co-operation and Development.

total 29 OECD countries have implemented reforms in labor regulations since 2006, only nine countries recorded reforms in the MENA region. Meanwhile, some MENA countries have made labor law more rigid and more costly to employers. Countries like Bahrain, Kuwait, and Saudi Arabia have added more provisions for redundancy and advanced notice requirements. The United Arab Emirates has reduced the duration of the single fixed-term contract from 48 to 24 months.

Strict regulations can unnecessarily reduce labor mobility and increase unemployment and informality. More important, they apply to the workers who work formally, who are a minority of workers in many countries in the region, especially when looking at private sector employment alone. They can also create a significant insider-outsider problem whereby informal workers remain outside the system, unable to influence policy decisions that might affect their chance of getting a better job (Lindbeck and Snower 1984).

Instead of focusing on labor regulation restrictions that protect the few, in lieu of these restrictions governments in the region should reconsider the role of social protection and active labor market programs. Social protection, which includes both noncontributory social assistance and contributory social insurance, can play an important role in transitioning workers and their households out of poverty and into sustainable livelihoods, as well as supporting them in the event of labor market shocks. Such policies have grown in importance as the MENA region has experienced the repercussions of COVID-19, which has affected all workers.

Moreover, transforming MENA economies toward more productive jobs necessitates effective labor market systems that improve people's human capital and align them with the shifting patterns of technological change. The 2019 *World Development Report* emphasizes that an effective modern system of social protection and labor market institutions requires three coordinated components: an anti-poverty safety net mechanism (with noncontributory social assistance at its core); universal social insurance to deal with long-term and short-term risks (with significant elements of fiscal financing); and modern labor market institutions that facilitate a dynamic private sector and better jobs (World Bank 2018b).

Compared to this paradigm, the social protection system in the MENA region is outdated and insufficient. Before the pandemic, less than half of the households in the poorest quintile were estimated to receive some form of social assistance. Spending on social assistance in the region was equivalent to only 1 percent of GDP, lower than the global average of 1.5 percent and lower than all other regions except for South Asia (World Bank 2018a). Instead, MENA countries spend little on targeted social assistance, and much more on universal and regressive subsidies (mainly for food and fuel), which have sat for many years at the heart of the region's social contract. However, things are starting to change in the face of fiscal constraints and the rise of some food prices, with some countries reducing subsidies of electricity and gas (Verme 2016), including some countries in the Gulf Cooperation Council (GCC), like Bahrain and Saudi Arabia, although to a lesser extent.

The COVID-19 pandemic has laid bare the inadequacies of the existing social protection systems, triggering a rapid response by many countries (box 5.2). For the majority of countries, including Algeria, the Arab Republic of Egypt, Iraq, Jordan, Lebanon, Morocco, and Tunisia, this rapid response has been in the form of temporary cash transfers to the vulnerable, mainly for households that rely on the informal sector for their livelihoods. Some GCC countries have also provided support to vulnerable households (Gentilini et al. 2021). However, except for countries where a targeted social assistance system already existed, such as Egypt, Jordan, and Tunisia, much of this support has not been targeted to the most in need. It has also been limited in terms of recipient households or has been temporary in nature. Some economies in the region have also provided some support to social insurance contributors (formal workers), such as subsidizing or suspending social insurance contributions for a period of time (such as Bahrain, the Islamic Republic of Iran, Jordan, Morocco, and West Bank and Gaza). Other countries have supported paid sick leave for workers affected by the virus. These measures, however, have also been generally marginal and temporary.

Box 5.2 MENA's social protection policy response to the COVID-19 pandemic

MENA has implemented several social protection interventions as a response to the pandemic (figure B5.2.1). Social assistance is the most widely used class of intervention, accounting for 181 measures. Among social assistance measures, waivers/reductions on utility and financial obligations, cash transfers, and in-kind support are major interventions. Among social insurance measures, social security contribution is the most commonly used measure by governments.

Figure B5.2.1 Composition of COVID-19–related measures for workers in MENA, by category

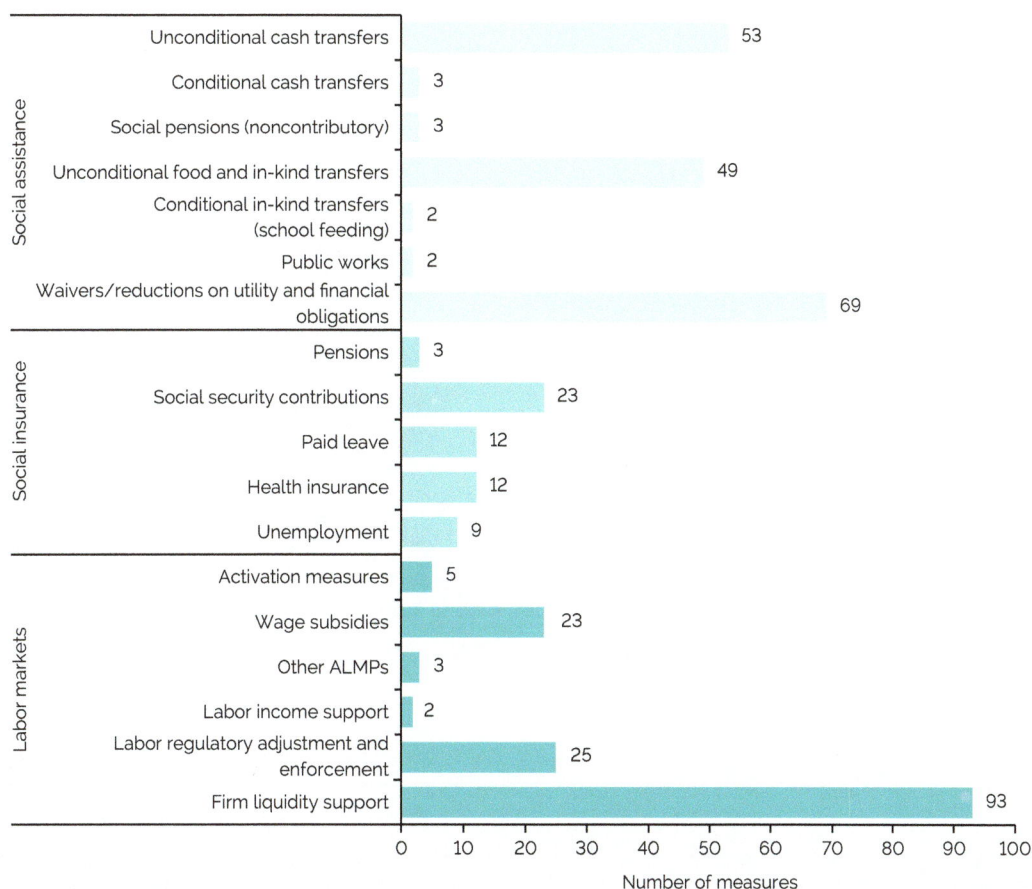

Source: De la Flor et al. 2021.
Note: ALMPs = active labor market policies.

Measures stimulating the labor markets account for 151 measures that have been introduced. For example, in Saudi Arabia, employers were entitled to request compensation payments from the General Organization for Social Insurance (GOSI) to cover 60 percent of the wages for their employees for three months (Gentilini et al. 2021). Jordan adjusted the regulation, and during the quarantine period, employers cannot count this period as annual leave or sick leave and

(box continues on next page)

Box 5.2 MENA's social protection policy response to the COVID-19 pandemic *(continued)*

cannot deduct it from their leave balance (Gentilini et al. 2021). About 98 percent of low- and middle-income countries implemented at least one labor market policy (that include public works, income tax reduction, training and placement assistance, unemployment benefits, wage subsidies, labor regulations, entrepreneur support, and firm liquidity) (de la Flor et al. 2021). The most prevalent measures have been firm liquidity support and labor regulation adjustments.[a]

a. See de la Flor et al. (2021); Gentilini et al. (2021). The labor market regulations include changes to severance payment obligations, hiring flexibility, dismissal procedures, modifications to working conditions, leave policies, and remuneration, as well as labor inspections.

Meanwhile, governments have provided little by way of labor-specific remedies, such as wage support and furloughs, which have been the central COVID-19 policy response in many European and Asian countries. Few MENA countries have effective unemployment insurance and unemployment assistance systems, so there was little to support workers who were laid off, or those whose paid working hours were reduced. In 2020, only nine countries in the region had an unemployment insurance scheme at all, and only four had noncontributory unemployment assistance programs, mostly targeted to new graduates or new labor market entrants.

Well-designed active labor market policies (ALMPs) can improve labor market outcomes, particularly in the long term (Romero and Kuddo 2019). However, in the MENA region, ALMPs were limited before the pandemic, meaning that programs such as wage subsidies could not be quickly deployed. Only two countries in the region—Egypt and Tunisia—offer a full set of employment services. While many economies have some vacancy databases, and some job placement services and training programs (figure 5.4), there is little evidence on their impact. Moreover, other key services that are crucial for labor market entrants, such as counseling and apprenticeship/internship programs and support for geographic mobility that ease work transitions, are uncommon. The region has ample scope to improve the quality and quantity of ALMPs.

As MENA countries consider options for reshaping the relationship between governments and workers, there is ample scope to modernize their labor regulations while strengthening their social protection and labor market support systems. Areas for labor regulatory reform include moving from severance pay to unemployment insurance as the central way to protect workers who have lost their jobs; making it easier for workers and employers to agree on fixed-term contracts; reducing labor taxes; and adopting and enforcing realistic minimum wages. This suite of reforms would help increase labor market dynamism, facilitate private sector job creation, and support workers' transitions between jobs.

However, since these reforms can also come at a potential cost to workers, three key reforms are also needed to improve the social protection system. First, social assistance to the poor in general needs to be improved to include more coverage, better targeting, and sufficient levels of payment. Second, more and better support is needed for informal workers, including expanding contributory social insurance coverage with innovative saving schemes.[1] Third, well-designed and well-targeted and well-evaluated labor market programs need to be put in place to build workers' human capital and facilitate their labor market transitions, especially for the young.

Figure 5.4 Active labor market programs are limited in the MENA region

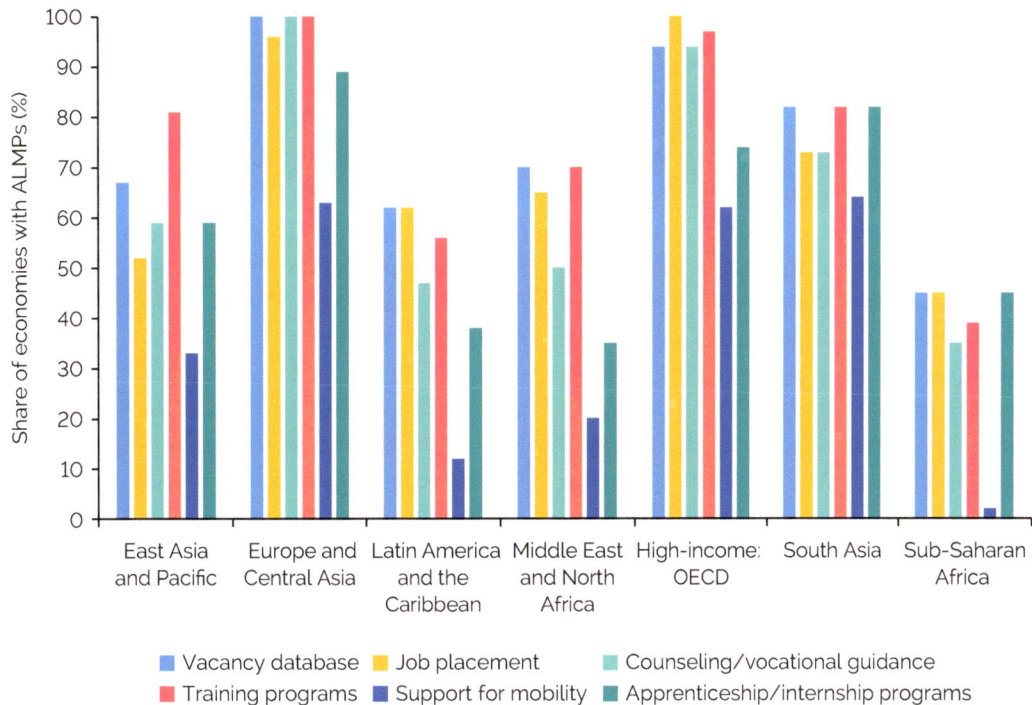

Source: Ulku and Georgieva 2021.
Note: Data are as of 2020. ALMPs = active labor market policies; OECD = Organisation for Economic Co-operation and Development.

FOSTERING WOMEN'S INCLUSION IN ALL ECONOMIC SPHERES

Chapters 2 and 3 showed that women are largely excluded from economic opportunities in the MENA region. Women's labor force participation is the lowest in the world, averaging about 20 percent in 2019. Younger women, who also happen to be better educated, have a higher aptitude for work. Yet, despite some improvements, the region's private sector is also not gender inclusive. Only 6 percent of firms in the MENA economies surveyed by the World Bank Enterprise Survey have a top woman manager, compared to an average of 23 percent for lower-middle-income countries, and 20 percent for upper-middle-income countries.

There are several explanations for the exclusion of women in the private sector. Social norms that assign women the role of caregiving or do not restrict harassment in public spheres may discourage women from participating in the private sector—or outside the home in general. Lack of market contestability may also hurt women by reducing available job opportunities (Elson 1999; Hellerstein, Neumark, and Troske 2002; Heyman, Svaleryd, and Vlachos 2013; Weichselbaumer and Winter-Ebmer 2007). Finally, legal restrictions erect barriers for women working (Islam, Muzi, and Amin 2019).

There is ample scope to reform the laws that affect women's relationship to market activities, as highlighted in chapter 4. As a result of the multiple layers of legal restrictions that women face, the region stands at the bottom of the Women, Business and the Law (WBL) index of legal equality. Women are restricted from working in some industries, or in night shifts, and are burdened with obtaining spousal permission to get jobs or suffer some legal ramifications should there be marital conflict. Once in a job, they face additional restrictions in the workplace, such as limited working hours for women who are not pregnant or nursing. They also face unequal pay compared to men. For example, in Egypt, Jordan, and Tunisia the gender pay gap ranges between approximately 13 percent and 28 percent (ILO 2019).

Globally, the removal of legal restrictions is positively correlated with the share of women in managerial positions. The same pattern is apparent within MENA: countries with fewer legal restrictions for women have a larger share of firms with women entrepreneurs (figure 5.5).

However, there are positive signs. Findings from the World Bank Enterprise Surveys analyzed for this report show that the few firms led by women in the private sector perform relatively well. They invest more in physical capital, in training their workers, and in research and development. Firms that are managed by women had higher employment growth over the past few years than their male counterparts and are more likely to employ women. Moreover, they are more likely to be digitally connected than firms led by men, presenting the potential and opportunity that the region can leverage for change.

Recent years have also witnessed legal reforms that remove several barriers for women. In fact, some countries in the region now appear as top reformers in the WBL index. There are signs that these efforts are bearing fruit. For instance, Saudi Arabia has implemented bold reforms, and its female labor force participation rose from 17 percent in 2007 to 27 percent in 2019.

However, on the downside, the COVID-19 pandemic is threatening to undo some of these gains. Many women have left their jobs to assume the burden of family care. In the private sector, small and medium enterprises (SMEs)—where most women work—have been hit hardest. Even more troubling, domestic violence has been on the rise, as people shelter in place (Agüero 2021; Leslie and Wilson 2020). It is crucial that governments and international organizations act urgently to protect recent gains and give a renewed impetus to including women in the labor market and taking advantage of the huge asset that female human capital represents in MENA.

Figure 5.5 In MENA and around the world, economies with fewer legal restrictions for women have a larger share of firms with women entrepreneurs

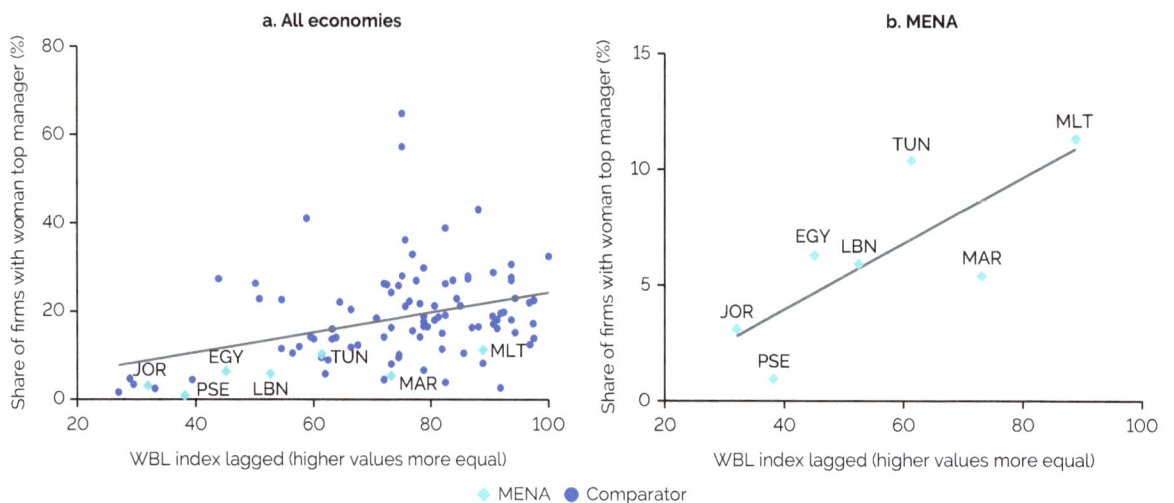

Sources: World Bank Enterprise Surveys; Women, Business and the Law (WBL) database.
Note: Economies marked by green diamonds are within the Middle East and North Africa region: Egypt (EGY), Jordan (JOR), Lebanon (LBN), Malta (MLT), Morocco (MAR), Tunisia (TUN), and West Bank and Gaza (PSE).

WORKING "AT THE MARGINS" TO FIND FEASIBLE REFORM PATHS

As in many parts of the world, the political economy of reform in MENA is challenging. Past evidence shows that it remains difficult to implement structural competition-oriented reforms, for example, due to political economy challenges, despite the likely medium- and long-term benefits of these reforms (Mahmood and Slimane 2018).

Unfortunately, as mentioned in chapter 3, increased market contestability does not necessarily generate better short-term outcomes for powerful incumbents and stakeholders who gain from the existing rigidities. For example, existing employment protection norms (which rely on severance pay) shift risks toward firms, favoring firms with better financial access or with government funds to cover them. Firms could also seek protection from competition to offset the costs imposed by the labor code. On the worker side, when it is difficult for workers to enter the market and difficult to cope in case of being fired, especially given nonexistent unemployment benefits, they will justifiably want to be protected from job losses through more labor code rigidities. This may imply resistance for structural reforms that aim at enhancing market dynamism.

This makes it important to carefully sequence reforms to promote greater market contestability and sometimes to adopt an incremental approach, as has been done in the MENA region in the telecommunications sector, moving gradually to increase competition. There are alternative points of entry. One approach is first to reform the law to establish an independent regulator, which can then gradually encourage more contestability (box 5.3). But other countries have first promoted a role for private firms in the sector before establishing a regulatory authority (Cambini, Ezzat, and Staropoli 2018).

The successful market contestability reforms implemented in Sweden in the 1990s started by lowering barriers to new firms, especially early adopters of new technologies and users of skilled labor. Sweden also introduced wage flexibility and mobility-friendly labor market policies. Finally, it allowed foreign ownership in existing large firms and loosened their linkages with the government (Heyman, Norbäck, and Persson 2018).

Box 5.3 Telecommunications liberalization in Bahrain

In 2002, Bahrain established the Telecommunications Regulatory Authority (TRA) through the adoption of the Telecommunications Law of 2002. In the same year, the government created the first Telecommunications National Plan to outline liberalization intentions and goals. Before this authority was established, the telecommunications sector was dominated by Batelco (Bahrain Telecommunications Company), first set up in 1982 and owned to this day by various government entities. In 2003, the first competitor, Zain, entered the mobile market, followed in 2009 by what is now STC Bahrain. Full fixed–line liberalization was introduced in 2004, and eventually in 2011 the Authority allowed phone number mobility between operators. The Authority continued to update its national plans, gradually licensing new technologies to upgrade the services of the sector. It communicates its legal instruments online to both operators and consumers and publishes annual reports and key market indicators periodically.

Sources: ITU 2014 and the TRA's online website.

Another possible approach to finding a politically feasible path to reform is to focus first on emerging sectors where there are few incumbents and interest groups have less power. This can facilitate the emergence of new occupations, so the disruption for existing workers is less evident—and the new activities can even be complementary, rather than replacing existing jobs.

The COVID-19 pandemic has brought to the fore the potential of the digital economy as a rapidly emerging new sector. Digital platform businesses can "grow the pie" rather than slicing it thinner by opening new links and increasing the efficiency of traditional product and service markets, both locally and globally. Low-cost digital technology reduces set-up costs, fosters networking and outsourcing, and shares information better than the personal networks that often characterize informal markets.

A good example is the emergence of ride-hailing services in MENA. Although they compete with the incumbents that run traditional taxi services, they also help to compensate for bad public transportation services, effectively amplifying routes and improving frequency, thus increasing access to remote areas. In some cases, they also allow women to choose female drivers (such as the Uber option in Saudi Arabia, and Lady Go taxi in Iraq). These are new markets that increase total demand.

The entrepreneurs highlighted in this volume's case studies (Voices) provide other good examples of expanding the digital economy through new technologies—for example, a digital platform in Egypt that connects pharmaceuticals demand and supply and enables home delivery; a software company in Lebanon that helps restaurants operate more effectively; and an e-commerce delivery service firm in Saudi Arabia that helps people complete errands. Careful studies suggest that the potential upside of the digital economy is massive: it could increase MENA's GDP per capita by more than 40 percent (Cusolito et al. 2021).

Regulatory reform to encourage the digital economy thus emerges as an exciting way forward. In the product market, infrastructure improvements are key, as are regulatory changes to support services. In the digital labor market, reforms to facilitate shorter-term contracts and other flexible arrangements and promote efficient modern social protection schemes would make eminent sense.

Another sector where incremental reforms might set in motion structural transformations is the green economy, where transitions can dynamize new industries, benefit workers, and protect the environment all at the same time. This is especially important for the region's oil-importing countries, but also for the GCC countries, which are well-endowed with renewable resources, such as for solar energy generation. Expanding these sectors is an opportunity that should not be missed. Beyond energy, there is ample potential for other green sectors such as sustainable farming and agriculture and ecotourism. Facilitating these sectors with modern regulations could support economic development and create new types of jobs such as environmental engineers, lawyers, and marine biologists.

New regulations and policies are also needed to encourage adoption of green practices by the private sector. New World Bank Enterprise Survey data show that only 20 percent of MENA firms have adopted any energy-efficiency measures, dropping to 16 percent if Malta is excluded. Few firms monitor energy consumption (38 percent), set energy consumption targets (16 percent), or monitor water usage (16 percent). Only 10 percent of firms have adopted air pollution control measures, 12 percent have engaged in climate-friendly on-site generation of energy, 11 percent have adopted water management measures, and 23 percent have adopted energy management measures. The European Bank for Reconstruction and Development's 2019–20 *Transition Report* provides an aggregate score of average quality of green management. Apart from Malta, the rest of the MENA economies covered by the data—Jordan, Lebanon, and West Bank and Gaza—score in the bottom 7 of the 37 economies (EBRD 2019). In short, there is ample scope for governments to promote the greening of MENA's private sector.

Incremental reforms and the promotion of new sectors and occupations do not negate the importance of reforms to encourage contestability more broadly to unleash the potential of the private sector in the region and expand job creation. But they can help to establish credible models and legitimize the strategy.

DATA FOR REFORMS

Improving the availability and transparency of data is crucial to enhancing trust in government in MENA (Arezki et al. 2020). This has become even more important as the region faces the dual shocks of the COVID-19 pandemic and the collapse in oil prices.

There are several ways that the quality of the data ecosystem can support economic development (Islam and Lederman 2020; World Bank 2021). First, good data are the basis for successful policy making. Data also provide benchmarks on other countries' experiences and global lessons. Second, widening data access can generate better policies. Sophisticated users can expand the knowledge frontier, developing policies that are more likely to work in the country's context. Richer economies are researched more than poorer economies and capitalize on this analysis to improve policies. Poorer economies are hampered by a lack of data accessibility and limited research.

Third, without good data, there can be a gap between perceptions and reality. Reform proposals may not find support when there are insufficient data to track the resulting gains. That may foster frustration and social unrest. Similarly, poor-quality data will undermine public confidence and contribute to a lack of trust between citizens and their governments. And once a government starts down the path of limited data access as a mechanism for political management, it can be hard to turn back.

MENA is particularly data deprived and lagging in statistical capacity. Even when data exist, many governments have shied away from sharing them with the research community, or even between government institutions. Although concerns for data privacy are not unfounded, little attention has been afforded to the costs of inadequate data and information in silos that exclude the best minds from working to improve policy making. MENA has the lowest statistical capacity of all regions around the world. Even worse, MENA's data capacity declined between 2005 and 2020 (figure 5.6).

The preparation of this report has been greatly constrained by the lack of up-to-date data. For example, there are insufficient data on the size of SOEs in terms of employment and value added. Labor force surveys are essential to understanding livelihoods and informing policies. But labor force and

Figure 5.6 MENA has low and deteriorating statistical capacity

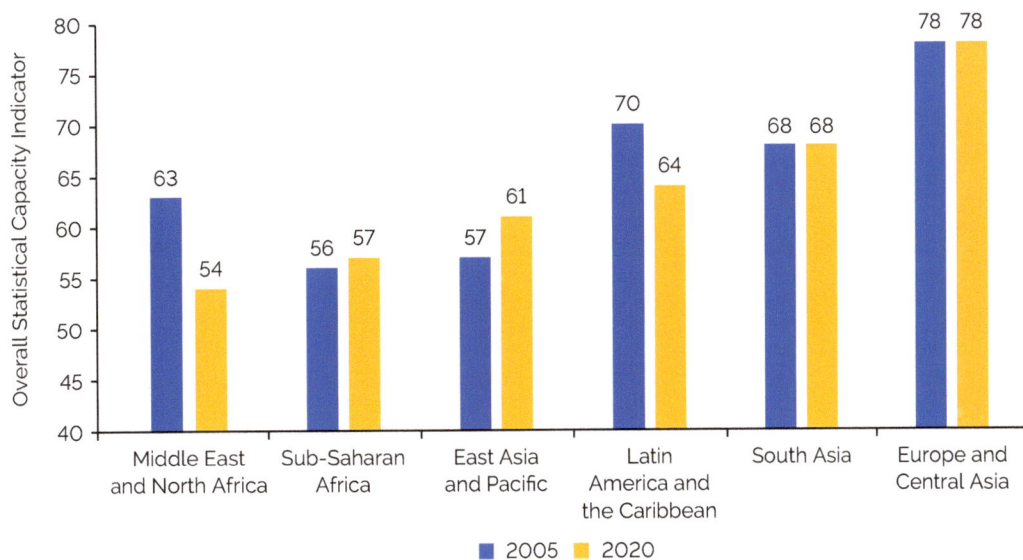

Source: World Bank Statistical Capacity Indicator, https://datatopics.worldbank.org/statisticalcapacity/.

household surveys are unavailable, inaccessible, or outdated in several countries. In several countries, labor force data have not been collected for many years (including conflict countries such as Libya and the Syrian Arab Republic); are simply not gathered at all (Bahrain and Iraq); or the microdata are not accessible for researchers (most GCC countries as well as Morocco).

The region also suffers from limited firm-level census and survey data, which are needed to analyze firm dynamism and estimate capital and labor misallocation and develop policy proposals to support firm creation and expansion. The firm-level findings in this report were restricted to manufacturing and a few service sectors that are captured in the World Bank Enterprise Surveys. Although some countries have such surveys, such as Saudi Arabia's Small and Medium-Sized Establishments Survey, access beyond selected aggregate indicators is not possible. There is also little data on informal enterprises (with the exception of Morocco's two waves of informal businesses surveys), limiting understanding of this important sector.

Although this report presents new data on product market regulations, the full set of indicators needed to calculate the overall index was available only for Egypt. The report was unable to quantify the extent of the economic role of SOEs in the economy in terms of employment, value added, and even productivity.

In short, every section in this report has faced major data challenges. Improving data capacity, collection, and transparency in MENA is long overdue. Good data are essential for economies to prosper. Transparency and openness are the key elements in the process and are needed to address all the challenges and proposed areas of reforms highlighted in this report. To address data challenges, the *World Development Report 2021* (World Bank 2021) recommends the forging of a new social contract for data to create economic and social value, while ensuring equitable access and fostering trust. Implementation of the social contract for data calls for an integrated national data system (INDS). A well-functioning INDS explicitly builds data production, protection, exchange, and use into planning and decision-making and actively integrates the various stakeholders into the data life cycle and into the governance structures of the system.

NOTE

1. An upcoming regional report on the future of social protection in the MENA region, to be published in 2022, will delve into these issues more elaborately.

REFERENCES

Agüero, Jorge M. 2021. "COVID-19 and the Rise of Intimate Partner Violence." *World Development* 137: 105217. https://doi.org/10.1016/j.worlddev.2020.105217.

Arezki, Rabah, Daniel Lederman, Amani Abou Harb, Nelly El-Mallakh, Rachel Yuting Fan, Asif Islam, Ha Nguyen, and Marwane Zouaidi. 2020. "How Transparency Can Help the Middle East and North Africa." *Middle East and North Africa Economic Update* (April). World Bank, Washington, DC.

Cambini, Carlo, Riham Ezzat, and Carine Staropoli. 2018. "Do Reforms Sequences Matter for Telecom Sector Performance? Evidence from MENA Countries." *Revue d'economie politique* 128 (5): 713–43.

Cusolito, Ana Paula, Clément Gévaudan, Daniel Lederman, and Christina A. Wood. 2021. *The Upside of Digital in the Middle East and North Africa: How Digital Technology Adoption Can Accelerate Growth and Create Jobs*. Washington, DC: World Bank.

de la Flor, Luciana, Ingrid Mujica, Maria Belén Fonteñez, David Newhouse, Claudia Rodriguez Alas, Gayatri Sabharwal, and Michael Weber. 2021. "Taking Stock of COVID-19 Labor Policy Responses in

Developing Countries." *Jobs Watch COVID-19*. World Bank, Washington, DC. https://openknowledge
.worldbank.org/handle/10986/35331.

EBRD (European Bank for Reconstruction and Development). 2019. *Transition Report 2019–20*. London: EBRD.

Elson, Diane. 1999. "Labour Markets as Gendered Institutions: Equality, Efficiency and Empowerment Issues."
World Development 27 (3): 611–27.

Gentilini, Ugo, Mohamed Almenfi, John Blomquist, Pamela Dale, Luciana de la Flor Giuffra, Vyjajanti Desai, Maria
Belén Fonteñez, Rabadan Galicia, Veronica Lopez, Georgina Marin, Ingrid Mujica, Harish Natarajan, David
Newhouse, Robert J. Palacios, Ana Patricia Quiroz, Claudia Rodriguez Alas, Gayatri Sabharwal, and Michael
Weber. 2021. "Social Protection and Jobs Responses to COVID-19: A Real-Time Review of Country
Measures." Living Paper Version 15 (May 14, 2021). World Bank, Washington, DC.

Hellerstein, Judith K., David Neumark, and Kenneth R. Troske. 2002. "Market Forces and Sex Discrimination."
Journal of Human Resources 37 (2): 353–80.

Heyman, Fredrik, Petr-Johan Norbäck, and Lars Persson. 2018. "Who Creates Jobs and Who Creates Productivity?
Small versus Large versus Young versus Old." *Economics Letters* 164 (C): 50–57.

Heyman, Fredrik, Helena Svaleryd, and Jonas Vlachos. 2013. "Competition, Takeovers, and Gender Discrimination."
ILR Review 66 (2): 409–32.

ILO (International Labour Organization). 2019. *Global Wage Report 2018/19*. Geneva: ILO.

Islam, Asif M., and Daniel Lederman. 2020. "Data Transparency and Long-Run Growth." Policy Research Working
Paper 9493, World Bank, Washington, DC.

Islam, Asif, Silvia Muzi, and Mohammad Amin. 2019. "Unequal Laws and the Disempowerment of Women in the
Labour Market: Evidence from Firm-Level Data." *Journal of Development Studies* 55 (5): 822–44.

ITU (International Telecommunication Union). 2014. *Trends in Telecommunications Reform Special Edition.
4th Generation Regulations: Driving Digital Communications Ahead*. Geneva: ITU.

Leslie, Emily, and Riley Wilson. 2020. "Sheltering in Place and Domestic Violence: Evidence from Calls for
Service during COVID-19." *Journal of Public Economics* 189: 104241. https://doi.org/10.1016/j
.jpubeco.2020.104241.

Lindbeck, Assar, and Dennis J. Snower. 1984. "Involuntary Unemployment as an Insider-Outsider Dilemma."
Seminar Paper No. 309, Institute for International Economic Studies, University of Stockholm, Sweden.

Mahmood, Syed Akhtar, and Meriem Ait Ali Slimane. 2018. *Privilege-Resistant Policies in the Middle East and
North Africa: Measurement and Operational Implications*. MENA Development Report. Washington, DC:
World Bank.

OECD (Organisation for Economic Co-operation and Development). 2012. *Towards New Arrangements for State
Ownership in the Middle East and North Africa*. Paris: OECD Publishing.

Romero, Jose Manuel, and Arvo Kuddo. 2019. "Moving Forward with ALMPs: Active Labor Policy and the Changing
Nature of Labor Markets." Social Protection and Jobs Discussion Paper 1936, World Bank, Washington, DC.

Ulku, Hulya, and Dorina Georgieva. 2021. "Unemployment Benefits, Active Labor Market Policies, and Economic
Outcomes: Evidence from New Global Data." World Bank, Washington, DC.

Verme, Paolo. 2016. "Subsidy Reforms in the Middle East and North Africa Region: A Review." Policy Research
Working Paper 7754, World Bank, Washington, DC.

Weichselbaumer, Doris, and Rudolf Winter-Ebmer. 2007. "The Effects of Competition and Equal Treatment Laws on
Gender Wage Differentials." *Economic Policy* 22 (50): 235–87.

World Bank. 2009. *From Privilege to Competition: Unlocking Private-Led Growth in the Middle East and North
Africa*. MENA Development Report. Washington, DC: World Bank.

World Bank. 2015. *Jobs or Privileges: Unleashing the Employment Potential of the Middle East and North Africa*. Washington, DC: World Bank.

World Bank. 2018a. *The State of Social Safety Nets 2018*. Washington, DC: World Bank.

World Bank. 2018b. *World Development Report 2019: The Changing Nature of Work*. Washington, DC: World Bank.

World Bank. 2021. *World Development Report 2021: Data for Better Lives*. Washington, DC: World Bank.

World Bank Group and African Competition Forum. 2016. *Breaking Down Barriers: Unlocking Africa's Potential to Vigorous Competition Policies*. Nairobi: World Bank.

ARAB REPUBLIC OF EGYPT: A Platform to Deliver Pharmacy Services

Doaa is the founder and chief executive officer (CEO) of an online pharmacy platform based in Cairo. She has a degree in agricultural engineering from the University of Tanta.

Doaa started her career at multinational and national digital marketing firms. Her entrepreneurship journey originated from a personal health crisis. During her treatment, Doaa was able to access a lot of things she needed online except for medicine. She struggled to get her medications nearby. She met other patients at local hospitals and clinics who shared this frustration.

Doaa's platform serves hundreds of thousands of customers across Egypt, allowing them to order medicine and have it delivered directly to their homes by the pharmacy. Through the app, customers can locate medicine in nearby pharmacies by using a search engine. The app then churns out information regarding the whereabouts and affordability of products that fit their needs. The website also provides free information regarding medicine, allergies, diseases, vitamins, and supplements. In addition to enabling online pharmaceutical orders and deliveries, the platform is becoming a source of learning and community for millions of customers trying to manage their chronic diseases by connecting them to one another to share knowledge. Customers do not pay fees for ordering services through the platform. Instead, the pharmacy whose products they purchase is charged a monthly fee of 5 percent of the total medicine sales executed, and 10 percent of their sales on beauty care products. The app sends monthly statements to each pharmacy and collects payments electronically. Doaa had only 91 clients when the app first launched. As of January 2020, approximately 200,000 customers had received medical services through the platform. Annual revenue from the platform grew by 30 percent between 2018 and 2019, and by 300 percent in 2020 due to the government-mandated COVID-19 lockdown. Currently, the platform employs 54 full-time staff, 60 percent of whom are female. The number of staff grew from 16 to 54 in just two years.

Several factors helped Doaa launch her business. Importantly, she did extensive research at the very beginning. She studied similar businesses overseas and then customized her business ideas to fit the local Egyptian context. Accessing finance was difficult. She applied to and was accepted at Flat6labs, a start-up accelerator in Cairo. Through this accelerator, she received US$17,000 in cash as a seed fund in April 2018. Flat6labs provided not only seed money but also strategic advice, business training, and networking resources. She had to navigate confusing business laws.

A cultural barrier observed by Doaa is parental pressure to work for an established, "safe" company. According to Doaa, there is a misconception that start-ups are not real businesses, so parents push for their children to get "safe" jobs. Doaa's message to women in the MENA region is: "If you have an idea, act on it."

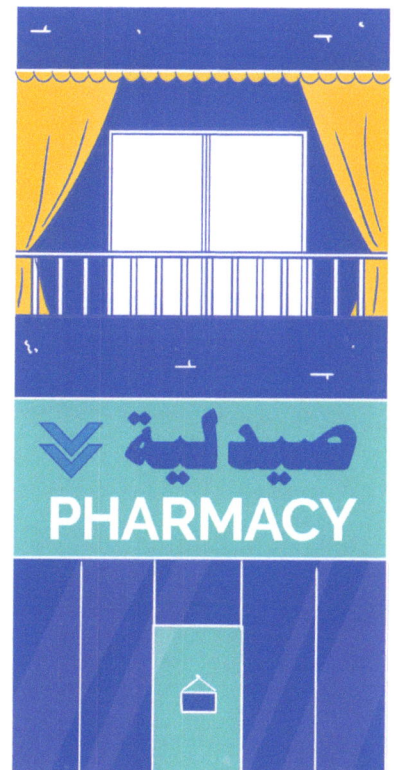

LEBANON: A Platform with Global Appeal to Help Restaurants Personalize Guests' Dining Experience

Sarah is an entrepreneur from Beirut who cofounded a software company that provides a platform for restaurants to personalize their guests' experience and maximize revenue per seat. Sarah graduated from the Lebanese American University with a bachelor's degree in business and marketing and then completed her MBA. She started her career at a management consulting firm, where she worked for five years as a senior research consultant in the technology and telecommunications sector. Although she had no intention of starting a business, she gravitated toward entrepreneurship when she discovered a problem that no one was addressing and won a start-up competition based on the identified opportunity.

The restaurant integrated reservation system tracks guest data with a centralized database and allows restaurants to understand their guests' dining preferences and habits to make better decisions and create campaigns that increase guest returns, visits, and overall spending.

The COVID-19 pandemic has hurt the hospitality sector considerably. Sarah and her team have been innovating their services to help restaurants open safely and give guests comfort about dining out. Her company developed a product, the contactless digital menu, that allows customers to view and order from a menu that can be accessed via QR code scanned by smartphones or before the reservation. In addition, they release payments where restaurants can charge a guest in advance to lower last-minute cancellations and no-shows. Since its launch in 2016, the company grew to employ 30+ staff between its office in Beirut and the regional and main office in Dubai, which was opened in 2017. The firm now serves thousands of clients in the MENA region (Bahrain, Egypt, Lebanon, Malta, Qatar, Saudi Arabia, and the United Arab Emirates), as well as in Europe (Austria, Belgium, and the Netherlands) and Asia (India and Singapore). While Sarah hopes to expand further into the European market in the coming years, she notes that such expansion requires significant capital investment.

Lebanon presents unique and unexpected challenges and obstacles for entrepreneurs. Lebanon's commercial law is outdated, highly bureaucratic, and opaque. Navigating through these laws requires a lot of patience and time. Moreover, the crumbling infrastructure coupled with the economic and

geopolitical instability has made it hard for entrepreneurs. Despite this, Sarah built a product with global appeal. Sarah believes in creating a competitive business to fuel economic growth and offer jobs that can better serve people and companies at competitive prices. She also believes that women in the MENA region should take bold steps to create companies that they believe serve a purpose and that they are passionate about, especially those that could add to the digital economy. Sarah notes that although "the learning curve is quite steep, there is immense value in creating a start-up company where you are continuously learning and growing."

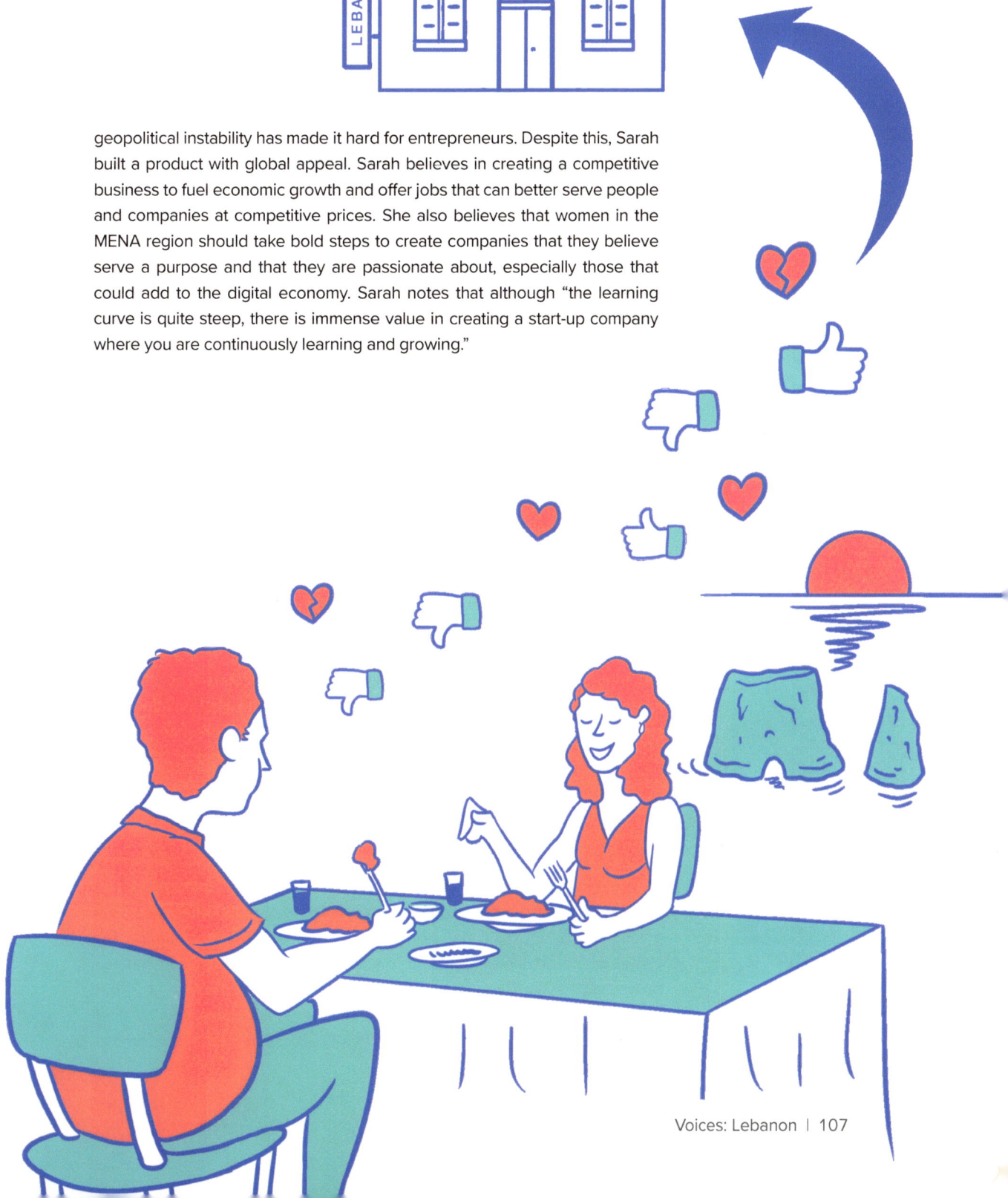

SAUDI ARABIA: A Platform to Help Women and Other Customers Run Errands

Naif is the cofounder and chief executive officer (CEO) of a delivery service firm in the e-commerce sector that assists families and individuals in completing their day-to-day errands. Naif has an engineering degree in architecture and urban design from King Saud University. In 2015, when Naif launched his app, women faced mobility restrictions in Saudi Arabia—a law since repealed. Naif often received requests from family to run errands, interrupting his work schedule. Thus, he created an app to address the widespread societal need for inexpensive and accessible errand runners. Many well-off families hire migrant drivers (mainly from Southeast Asia) to run their household errands. However, for most families, hiring a migrant driver is costly and inconvenient due to visa requirements. Naif says his app is like Uber except that it focuses on completing household tasks and delivering household items as opposed to providing transportation services. Naif's app and website give clients the power to manage, monitor, and evaluate the services they receive and rate the quality of services and drivers' performance. This enforces good behavior and gives the client the power to choose between different drivers and monitor services as they are occurring—an aspect that is significant in such a conservative society.

Naif's app was one of the first movers in the e-commerce industry introducing a creative household delivery service through a user-friendly app. The company eventually became a hub for testing new technology, including artificial intelligence, to analyze consumers' preferences and build an effective logistical system to better utilize drivers' time. Naif's platform has served about 8 million customers in Saudi Arabia. Annual revenue grew by 300 percent from 2016 to 2019 and jumped to 400 percent in 2020. The number of full-time staff with benefits has grown 30 percent per year over three years.

It is Naif's belief that the main obstacle in Saudi Arabia's entrepreneurial ecosystem for information technology (IT) companies is that the government has not been able to keep up with digital transformations. Furthermore, Naif feels the business registration process needs to be smoother, especially given the need for rapid start-up development in the IT sector. Funding is a challenge. In 2016, Naif applied to the Badir Accelerator in Riyadh and was accepted. "Having Badir as a resource was invaluable. We were provided a physical office and basic business training, most notably how to pitch the business idea to investors in the Kingdom of Saudi Arabia and abroad,

including in Europe. This was very useful to reduce our fears of being in front of an investor." However, Naif is pessimistic about expanding his platform in the MENA region due to the limited IT infrastructure and varied rules and regulations in each country. Even so, he feels strongly about youth in entrepreneurship: "We must encourage Saudi youth to enter the entrepreneurial market and compete." The more motivated youths there are, the better, as "they feel stronger when they operate as a community. They can learn from one another. This is the soul of innovation in Silicon Valley, for instance." He adds that "youth don't just need money . . . they need 'smart money,' like when angel investors and venture capital companies become their strategic partners, not only investors."

Appendix A | Product Market Regulations

The analysis in this report is based on a simplified version of the Organisation for Economic Co-operation and Development (OECD) Product Market Regulation (PMR) questionnaire that focuses on those aspects most relevant for less developed economies and emerging markets and does not capture implementation. Data based on the simplified methodology were collected as of December 2020 for eight Middle East and North Africa (MENA) economies: the Arab Republic of Egypt, Jordan, Kuwait, Morocco, Saudi Arabia, Tunisia, the United Arab Emirates, and West Bank and Gaza. In addition, PMR data for Egypt collected in 2017, for Kuwait in 2018, and for Tunisia in 2017 were used in the analysis.[1] The sample represents a diverse group of economies including high- and middle-income; resource-rich and poor; and labor-abundant and scarce.[2] The simplified version of the PMR data is used to compare qualitative dimensions of policies and regulations in the selected MENA economies against two sets of comparators included in the 2018 PMR database: 37 high-income countries and 14 upper-middle-income countries.[3] Figure A.1 provides additional details on the methodology.

Figure A.1 Economywide and sector PMR methodology

a. PMR economywide components

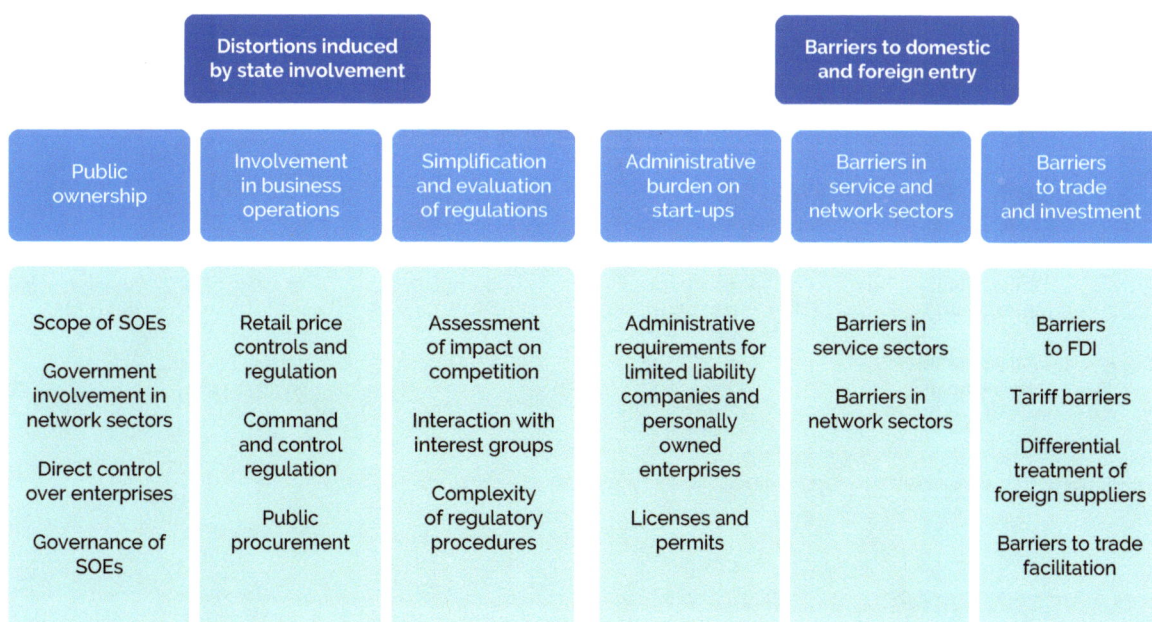

(figure continues on next page)

Figure A.1 Economywide and sector PMR methodology *(continued)*

b. PMR network sectors covered

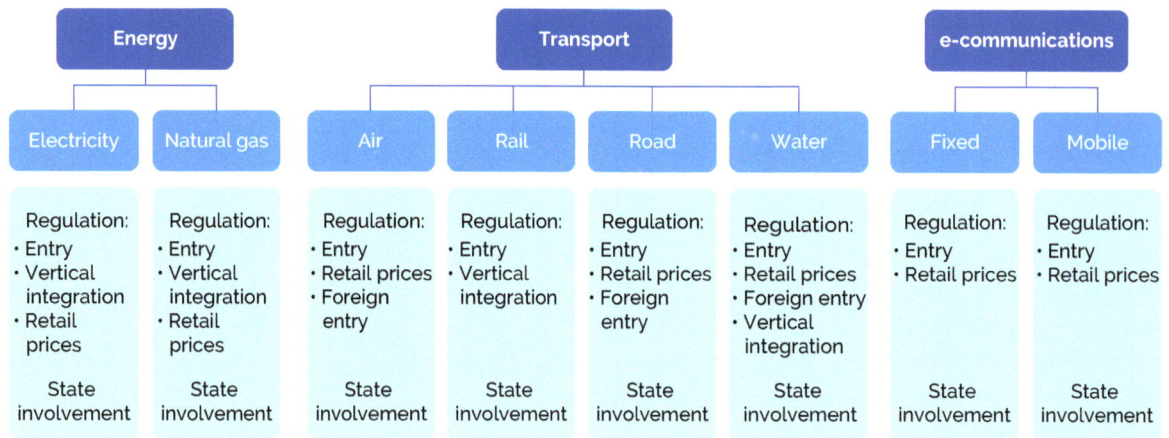

Energy			Transport				e-communications	
Electricity	Natural gas	Air	Rail	Road	Water		Fixed	Mobile
Regulation: • Entry • Vertical integration • Retail prices	Regulation: • Entry • Vertical integration • Retail prices	Regulation: • Entry • Retail prices • Foreign entry	Regulation: • Entry • Vertical integration	Regulation: • Entry • Retail prices • Foreign entry	Regulation: • Entry • Retail prices • Foreign entry • Vertical integration		Regulation: • Entry • Retail prices	Regulation: • Entry • Retail prices
State involvement	State involvement	State involvement	State involvement	State involvement	State involvement		State involvement	State involvement

c. PMR professional services covered

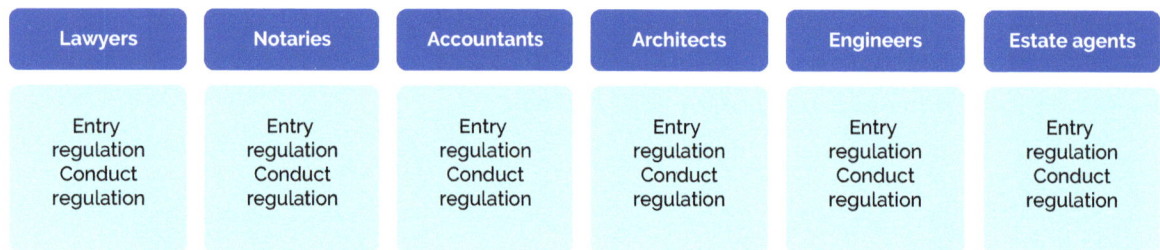

Lawyers	Notaries	Accountants	Architects	Engineers	Estate agents
Entry regulation Conduct regulation	Entry regulation Conduct regulation	Entry regulation Conduct regulation	Entry regulation Conduct regulation	Entry regulation Conduct regulation	Entry regulation Conduct regulation

d. PMR retail services covered

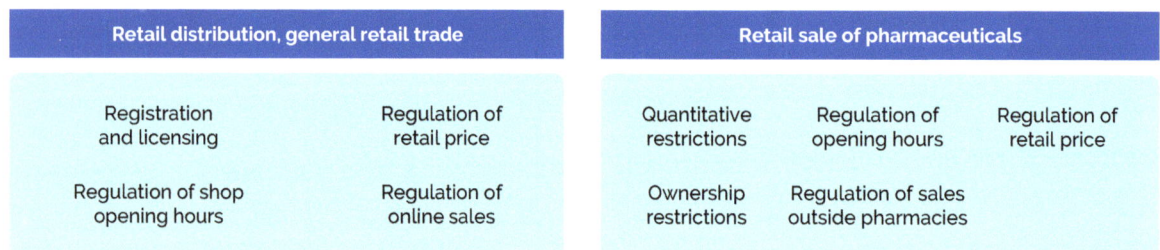

Retail distribution, general retail trade		Retail sale of pharmaceuticals		
Registration and licensing	Regulation of retail price	Quantitative restrictions	Regulation of opening hours	Regulation of retail price
Regulation of shop opening hours	Regulation of online sales	Ownership restrictions	Regulation of sales outside pharmacies	

Source: Flagship team elaboration, based on Vitale et al. (2020).
Note: FDI = foreign direct investment; PMR = product market regulation; SOEs = state-owned enterprises.

PMR COUNTRY/ECONOMY TABLES

The tables that follow (tables A.1–A.13) report the results for each of the eight countries/economies (Egypt, Jordan, Kuwait, Morocco, Saudi Arabia, Tunisia, the United Arab Emirates, and West Bank and Gaza) for which data were collected with the simplified methodology. Three main topics are covered: (1) state-induced distortions; (2) barriers to trade and investment; and (3) barriers in network industries and professional services.

State-Induced Distortions

Table A.1 Scope, public ownership, and control of SOEs: Equity

Question	Egypt, Arab Rep.	Jordan	Kuwait	Morocco	Saudi Arabia	Tunisia	United Arab Emirates	West Bank and Gaza
Do national, state, or provincial governments hold equity stakes in the largest firm in the sector?								
ELECTRICITY								
Electricity generation	Y	Y	Y	Y	Y	Y	Y	Y
Electricity transmission	Y	Y	Y	Y	Y	Y	Y	Y
Electricity distribution	Y	Y	Y	Y	Y	Y	Y	Y
GAS								
Gas generation	Y	Y	Y	Y	Y	Y	Y	N
Gas transmission	Y	Y	Y	Y	Y	Y	Y	N
Gas distribution	Y	N	Y	N	Y	Y	Y	N
TELECOMMUNICATIONS								
Telecommunications	Y	Y	Y	Y	Y	Y	Y	Y

Sources: Flagship team elaboration, based on OECD and OECD-WBG Product Market Regulation (PMR) database 2018–2020. PMR data for Egypt were collected in 2017, for Kuwait in 2018, and for Tunisia in 2017. Data for the other five Middle East and North Africa (MENA) economies were collected by the flagship team using a simplified version of the 2018 OECD PMR methodology, and they reflect the situation in the economy as of December 2020.
Note: Most questions are Yes/No questions, unless indicated otherwise. Y = Yes and N = No. OECD = Organisation for Economic Co-operation and Development; SOEs = state-owned enterprises; WBG = World Bank Group.

Table A.2 Scope, public ownership, and control of SOEs: Control

Question	Egypt, Arab Rep.	Jordan	Kuwait	Morocco	Saudi Arabia	Tunisia	United Arab Emirates	West Bank and Gaza
Do national, state, or provincial governments control at least one firm in the sector?								
ELECTRICITY								
Electricity generation	Y	Y	Y	Y	Y	Y	Y	N
Electricity transmission	Y	Y	Y	Y	Y	Y	Y	Y
Electricity distribution	Y	N	Y	Y	Y	Y	Y	Y
GAS								
Gas generation	Y	Y	Y	N	Y	Y	Y	N
Gas transmission	Y	Y	Y	Y	Y	Y	Y	N
Gas distribution	Y	N	Y	Y	Y	Y	Y	N

(table continues on next page)

Table A.2 Scope, public ownership, and control of SOEs: Control *(continued)*

Question	Egypt, Arab Rep.	Jordan	Kuwait	Morocco	Saudi Arabia	Tunisia	United Arab Emirates	West Bank and Gaza
Do national, state, or provincial governments control at least one firm in the sector? *(continued)*								
TRANSPORT								
Railways—Passenger transport	Y	Y	N	Y	Y	Y	Y	N
Railways—Freight transport	Y	Y	N	Y	Y	Y	Y	N
Railways—Operation of railroad infrastructure	Y	Y	N	Y	Y	Y	Y	N
Sea, coastal, and inland passenger water transport	Y	Y	Y	N	Y	Y	Y	N
Sea, coastal, and inland freight water transport	Y	Y	Y	N	Y	Y	N	N
Operation of terminal facilities (such as harbors and piers)	Y	Y	Y	Y	Y	Y	Y	N
Air transport—Domestic passenger transport	Y	Y	Y	Y	Y	Y[a]	Y	N
Air transport—International passenger transport	Y	Y	Y	Y	Y	Y[a]	Y	N
Air transport—Operation of airports	Y	Y	Y	Y	Y	Y[b]	Y	N
Road transport—Freight transport by road (ISIC Rev. 4.0 4923)	Y	Y	N	N	Y	Y[c]	N	N
Road transport—Operation of road infrastructure (ISIC Rev. 4.0 part of 5221)	Y	Y	N	Y	Y	Y[d]	Y	N
Water collection, treatment and supply (ISIC Rev. 4.0 X)	Y	Y	Y	Y	Y	Y	Y	Y
OTHER SECTORS								
Manufacture of tobacco products (ISIC Rev. 4.0 12)	Y	N	N	N	N	Y	N	N
Manufacture of refined petroleum products (ISIC Rev. 4.0 192)	Y	Y	Y	Y	Y	Y	Y	N
Manufacture of basic metals (ISIC Rev. 4.0 24)	Y	N	N	Y	Y	Y	Y	N
Manufacture of fabricated metal products, machinery, and equipment (ISIC Rev. 4.0 25)	Y	N	N	N	Y	N	Y	N
Building and repairing of ships and boats (ISIC Rev. 4.0 301)	Y	N	Y	Y	Y	N	Y	N
Manufacture of railway and tramway locomotives and rolling stock (ISIC Rev. 4.0 302)	Y	N	N	N	N	—[e]	N	N
Manufacture of aircraft and spacecraft (ISIC Rev. 4.0 303)	Y	N	N	Y	Y	—[f]	Y	N
Construction (ISIC Rev. 4.0 41, 42, 43)	Y	N	N	Y	Y	N	Y	N
Wholesale trade, incl. of motor vehicles (ISIC Rev. 4.0 46, part of 45)	Y	Y	Y	Y	Y	Y	Y	N

(table continues on next page)

Table A.2 Scope, public ownership, and control of SOEs: Control *(continued)*

Question	Egypt, Arab Rep.	Jordan	Kuwait	Morocco	Saudi Arabia	Tunisia	United Arab Emirates	West Bank and Gaza
Do national, state, or provincial governments control at least one firm in the sector? *(continued)*								
OTHER SECTORS *(continued)*								
Retail trade, incl. of motor vehicles (ISIC Rev. 4.0 47, part of 45)	Y	Y	Y	Y	Y	Y	Y	N
Accommodation, food and beverage service activities (ISIC Rev. 4.0 55, 56)	Y	Y	Y	Y	Y	N	Y	N
Other urban, suburban, and interurban passenger transport (ISIC Rev. 4.0 4921, 4922)	Y	Y	Y	Y	Y	Y	Y	N
Financial service activities, except central banking, insurance, and pension funding (6419, 642, 643, 649, 661, part of 663)	Y	N	Y	Y	Y	Y	Y	Y
Insurance, reinsurance, and pension funding (ISIC Rev. 4.0 65, 662, part of 663)	Y	Y	Y	Y	Y	Y	Y	Y
Other business activities (ISIC Rev. 4.0 70, 71, 73, 74, 78, 80, 812, 82, 855)	Y	Y	Y	—g	Y	—	N	N
Human health activities (ISIC Rev. 4.0 86)	Y	Y	Y	Y	Y	Y	Y	Y
Motion picture distribution and projection (ISIC Rev. 4.0 59)	Y	N	N	N	Y	N	Y	N
Manufacture of pharmaceuticals, medicinal chemical and botanical products	Y	N	N	N	N	Y	N	N
Manufacture of chemicals and chemical products	Y	Y	N	Y	Y	N	Y	N
Manufacture of computer, electronic, and optical products	Y	N	N	N	N	N	N	N
Manufacture of motor vehicles and their parts and accessories	Y	N	N	N	N	N	N	N
Gambling and betting activities	Y	N	N	N	N	N	N	N

Sources: Flagship team elaboration, based on OECD and OECD-WBG Product Market Regulation (PMR) database 2018–2020. PMR data for Egypt were collected in 2017, for Kuwait in 2018, and for Tunisia in 2017. Data for the other five Middle East and North Africa (MENA) economies were collected by the flagship team using a simplified version of the 2018 OECD PMR methodology, and they reflect the situation in the economy as of December 2020.

Note: Most questions are Yes/No questions, unless indicated otherwise. Y = Yes and N = No. — = not available; an answer was not provided for the specific question/ economy. OECD = Organisation for Economic Co-operation and Development; SOEs = state-owned enterprises; WBG = World Bank Group.

a. No value (answer) was provided, but the comment section mentions that the state controls the company Tunisair.

b. No value (answer) was provided, but the comment section mentions that the state controls the company Office National de l'Aviation Civile.

c. No value (answer) was provided, but the comment section mentions that the state controls the company Office National de Transports Inter-urbain.

d. No value (answer) was provided, but the comment section mentions that the state controls the company Tunisie Autoroute.

e. There is no railway or tramway locomotives manufacturing in Tunisia.

f. There is no aircraft or spacecraft manufacturing in Tunisia.

g. Not found in the Ministry of Finance (MoF) report.

Table A.3 Scope, public ownership, and control of SOEs: Market shares and structure

Question	Egypt, Arab Rep.	Jordan	Kuwait	Morocco	Saudi Arabia	Tunisia	United Arab Emirates	West Bank and Gaza
What is the market share of the largest firm/the incumbent in each of the following sectors?[a]								
ELECTRICITY								
Electricity generation	50%–90%	< 50%	> 90%	< 50%	> 90%	> 90%	> 90%	< 50%
Electricity transmission	> 90%	> 90%	> 90%	> 90%	> 90%	> 90%	> 90%	> 90%
Electricity distribution	> 90%	50%–90%	> 90%	50%–90%	> 90%	> 90%	> 90%	50%–90%
GAS								
Gas generation	—[b]	> 90%	> 90%	—[c]	> 90%	> 90%	> 90%	—[d]
Gas transmission	—	> 90%	> 90%	> 90%	> 90%	> 90%	> 90%	—
Gas distribution	—	< 50%	> 90%	50%–90%	> 90%	> 90%	> 90%	—
TELECOMMUNICATIONS								
What is the market share of the incumbent in the provision of retail fixed line services (voice, video, and data)?	> 90%	> 90%	> 90%	50%–90%	50%–90%	> 90%	50%–90%	50%–90%
TRANSPORT								
How many firms compete in the same market in the following sectors?[e]								
Railways—Passenger transport (ISIC Rev. 4.0 4911)	1	1	—[f]	1	1	1	1	3
Railways—Freight transport (ISIC Rev. 4.0 4912)	1	1	—	1	1	1	1	3

Sources: Flagship team elaboration, based on OECD and OECD-WBG Product Market Regulation (PMR) database 2018–2020. PMR data for Egypt were collected in 2017, for Kuwait in 2018, and for Tunisia in 2017. Data for the other five Middle East and North Africa (MENA) economies were collected by the flagship team using a simplified version of the 2018 OECD PMR methodology, and they reflect the situation in the economy as of December 2020.

Note: — = not available; an answer was not provided for the specific question/economy. OECD = Organisation for Economic Co-operation and Development; SOEs = state-owned enterprises; WBG = World Bank Group.

a. Options provided are: (1) greater than 90%; (2) between 50% and 90%; or (3) smaller than 50%.

b. No information on market shares for any of the market segments, but a list of SOE affiliate companies in each sector.

c. No information on market share, but the flagship team understands that production in Morocco is performed by two private operators along with the National Office of Hydrocarbons and Mines (ONHYM) using concessions/licenses as per Law 21-90, which stipulates that the state must retain up to a 25 percent interest.

d. According to the General Petroleum Authority, GPA does not work on developing gas generation but imports all its gas from Israel and has signed a monopoly agreement with two Israeli petroleum companies, one for West Bank and one for Gaza.

e. The answer is open-ended.

f. There is no railway in Kuwait.

Table A.4 SOE governance: Decision-making

Question	Egypt, Arab Rep.	Jordan	Kuwait	Morocco	Saudi Arabia	Tunisia	United Arab Emirates	West Bank and Gaza
Who exercises the ownership rights in the SOEs?[a]	Line ministries	Specialized agency NOT at arm's length from government	Specialized agency NOT at arm's length from government	Treasury/ Ministry of Finance/ Ministry of Economy	Specialized agency NOT at arm's length from government	Treasury/ Ministry of Finance/ Ministry of Economy	Specialized agency NOT at arm's length from government	Line ministries
Who appoints the Chief Executive Officer (CEO) in SOEs?[b]	Public authorities	Public authorities	Combination of board and public authorities	Public authorities	Board of the firm	Public authorities	Combination of board and public authorities	Board of the firm

Sources: Flagship team elaboration, based on OECD and OECD-WBG Product Market Regulation (PMR) database 2018–2020. PMR data for Egypt were collected in 2017, for Kuwait in 2018, and for Tunisia in 2017. Data for the other five Middle East and North Africa (MENA) economies were collected by the flagship team using a simplified version of the 2018 OECD PMR methodology, and they reflect the situation in the economy as of December 2020.

Note: OECD = Organisation for Economic Co-operation and Development; SOEs = state-owned enterprises; WBG = World Bank Group.

a. Options provided are: (1) specialized agency at arm's length from government; (2) specialized agency NOT at arm's length from government; (3) Treasury/Ministry of Finance/Ministry of Economy; (4) line ministries coordinated by a specialized agency; (5) line ministries.

b. Options provided are: (1) board of the firm; (2) combination of board and public authorities; or (3) public authorities.

Table A.5 Competitive neutrality

Question	Egypt, Arab Rep.	Jordan	Kuwait	Morocco	Saudi Arabia	Tunisia	United Arab Emirates	West Bank and Gaza
Are there any SOEs which are not incorporated into limited liability companies?	Yes	Yes	Yes	Yes	Yes	Yes	Yes	No
If you have answered yes to the question above, are these SOEs subject to private company law?[a]	No	No (but statutes that set them up impose constraints similar to private company law)	No	No (but statutes that set them up impose constraints similar to private company law)	No (but statutes that set them up impose constraints similar to private company law)	No	No (but statutes that set them up impose constraints similar to private company law)	—
Can SOEs have access to finance at conditions that are better than those available to private firms?[b]	Yes (in all sectors)	No	Yes	Yes (only in some sectors)	No	Yes	Yes (in all sectors)	No
If an SOE performs one or more non-competitive activities and one or more potentially competitive activities, is there a requirement for this firm to separate the noncompetitive activities from the potentially competitive ones?	No	No	No	No	No	—	No	No
Do mergers, equity issues, and/or restructuring plans of any SOEs have to be reviewed or cleared in advance by national, state, regional, or provincial governments?	Yes	No	Yes	Yes	Yes	Yes	Yes	No

(table continues on next page)

Table A.5 Competitive neutrality *(continued)*

Question	Egypt, Arab Rep.	Jordan	Kuwait	Morocco	Saudi Arabia	Tunisia	United Arab Emirates	West Bank and Gaza
Is there a rule that excludes or exempts from competition law conduct that is required or authorised by another government authority (in addition to exclusions that might apply to complete sectors)?	Yes	Yes	No	Yes	Yes	Yes	Yes	No
Are SOEs subject to an exclusion/exemption, either complete or partial, from the application of the competition law in specific sectors (from which privately owned firms do not benefit) when performing commercial activities in competition or potentially in competition with private firms?[c]	Yes (in all sectors)	No	Yes (in all sectors)	No	No	Yes (in all sectors)	Yes (in all sectors)	No
Are SOEs exempt from the application of at least some specific laws and regulations (excluding competition law) which apply to private firms?[d]	Yes (only in some sectors)	Yes (only in some sectors)	Yes (only in some sectors)	Yes (only in some sectors)	No	No	Yes (in all sectors)	No
Can SOEs benefit from other favorable treatments that are not available to private firms?[d]	Yes (only in some sectors)	Yes (only in some sectors)	Yes (only in some sectors)	Yes (only in some sectors)	Yes (only in some sectors)	Yes (only in some sectors)	Yes (only in some sectors)	No
If an SOE performs one or more non-competitive activities and one or more potentially competitive activities, is there a requirement for this firm to separate the noncompetitive activities from the potentially competitive ones?[e]	No	No	No	No	No	No	No	No

Sources: Flagship team elaboration, based on OECD and OECD-WBG Product Market Regulation (PMR) database 2018–2020. PMR data for Egypt were collected in 2017, for Kuwait in 2018, and for Tunisia in 2017. Data for the other five Middle East and North Africa (MENA) economies were collected by the flagship team using a simplified version of the 2018 OECD PMR methodology, and they reflect the situation in the economy as of December 2020.

Note: Most questions are Yes/No questions, unless indicated otherwise. — = not available; an answer was not provided for the specific question/economy. OECD = Organisation for Economic Co-operation and Development; SOEs = state-owned enterprises; WBG = World Bank Group.

a. Options provided are: (1) Yes; (2) No (but statutes that set them up impose constraints similar to private company law); or (3) No.
b. Options provided are: (1) Yes (in all sectors); (2) Yes (only in some sectors); or (3) No. Note that for Kuwait and Tunisia the answers are Yes.
c. Options provided are: (1) Yes (in all sectors); (2) Yes (only in some sectors); or (3) No.
d. Options provided are: (1) Yes (in all sectors); (2) Yes (only in some sectors); or (3) No.
e. Options provided are the same as in note "a" above.

Table A.6 Public procurement

Question	Egypt, Arab Rep.	Jordan	Kuwait	Morocco	Saudi Arabia	Tunisia	United Arab Emirates	West Bank and Gaza
Does the following apply to public procurement tenders for construction services?								
There is explicit access discrimination in favour of local firms.	Y	Y	N	N	Y	Y	Y	Y
Domestic content of personnel and/or goods is required.	Y	Y	Y	Y	Y	Y	Y	Y
Technical specifications affect the conditions of competition in favour of local providers.	N	N	N	N	N	Y	N	N
Qualification processes and procedures are discriminatory.	N	N	N	N	N	N	N	N
Contracts are awarded on the basis of nonobjective/discriminatory criteria.	N	N	N	Y	N	N	N	N
Procurement laws, regulations, and procedures are transparent.	Y	Y	Y	Y	Y	Y	Y	Y
Foreign suppliers are provided the opportunity to challenge the consistency of the conduct of a procurement with the laws and regulations.	Y	Y	Y	Y	Y	Y	Y	N
Does the following apply to public tenders for public works?								
There is explicit access discrimination in favour of local firms.	Y	Y	N	N	Y	Y	Y	Y
Domestic content of personnel and/or goods is required.	Y	Y	Y	Y	Y	Y	Y	Y
Technical specifications affect the conditions of competition in favour of local providers.	N	N	N	N	N	Y	N	N
Qualification processes and procedures are discriminatory.	N	N	N	N	Y	N	N	N
Contracts are awarded on the basis of nonobjective/discriminatory criteria that favour domestic firms over foreign ones.	N	N	N	Y	N	N	N	N
Procurement laws, regulations, and procedures are not transparent.	Y	Y	Y	Y	Y	Y	N	N
Foreign suppliers are not provided with the opportunity to challenge the consistency of the conduct of a tender with the laws and regulations.	N	N	N	N	N	N	N	Y
When a tender is run, does the contracting authority provide a reference price in the tender documentation for the goods and services it requires?[a]	No (but not explicitly prohibited)	No (but not explicitly prohibited)	No (but not explicitly prohibited)	Yes (it is required to provide a reference price)	No (but not explicitly prohibited)	No (but not explicitly prohibited)	No (but not explicitly prohibited)	Yes (it is required to provide a reference price)

(table continues on next page)

Table A.6 **Public procurement** *(continued)*

Question	Egypt, Arab Rep.	Jordan	Kuwait	Morocco	Saudi Arabia	Tunisia	United Arab Emirates	West Bank and Gaza
Does the public procurement regulatory framework of your country require that a certain share of the public procurement of goods and services is reserved to specific categories of firms (such as small and medium enterprises and/or socially responsible firms)?[b]	Yes (in all or most sectors)	Yes (in all or most sectors)	Yes (in all or most sectors)	Yes (in all or most sectors)	No	Yes (in all or most sectors)	Yes (in all or most sectors)	No
When a tender is run, does the tendering authority provide in the tender documentation a reference price for the public works it requires?[a]	No (but not explicitly prohibited)	No (but not explicitly prohibited)	No (but not explicitly prohibited)	Yes (it is required to provide a reference price)	No (but not explicitly prohibited)	No (but not explicitly prohibited)	No (but not explicitly prohibited)	Yes (it is required to provide a reference price)
Does the public procurement regulatory framework of your country require that a certain share of the public procurement of public works is reserved to specific categories of firms (such as small and medium enterprises and/or socially responsible firms)?[b]	Yes (in all or most sectors)	Yes (in all or most sectors)	Yes (in all or most sectors)	Yes (in all or most sectors)	Yes (in all or most sectors)	Yes (in all or most sectors)	Yes (in all or most sectors)	No
Does the public procurement regulatory framework of your country require or permit that a percentage of the contract is reserved to domestic firms in public tenders for the provision of goods and services?[b]	Yes (in all or most sectors)	No	Yes (in all or most sectors)	No	No	Yes (in all or most sectors)	No	Yes (only in few sectors)
Does the public procurement regulatory framework in your country require suppliers to use domestic content, at least partially, when performing a contract for the provision of goods and services?[b]	Yes (in all or most sectors)	No	Yes (in all or most sectors)	No	Yes (in all or most sectors)	Yes (in all or most sectors)	Yes (in all or most sectors)	Yes (only in few sectors)
Does the public procurement regulatory framework in your country require suppliers to use domestic content, at least partially, when undertaking public works?[b]	Yes (in all or most sectors)	No	Yes (in all or most sectors)	No	Yes (in all or most sectors)	Yes (in all or most sectors)	Yes (in all or most sectors)	Yes (only in few sectors)
Does the public procurement regulatory framework of your country require or permit that a percentage of the contract is reserved to domestic firms in public tenders for undertaking public works?[b]	Yes (in all or most sectors)	No	Yes (in all or most sectors)	No	Yes (in all or most sectors)	Yes (in all or most sectors)	No	Yes (only in few sectors)

Sources: Flagship team elaboration, based on OECD and OECD-WBG Product Market Regulation (PMR) database 2018–2020. PMR data for Egypt were collected in 2017, for Kuwait in 2018, and for Tunisia in 2017. Data for the other five Middle East and North Africa (MENA) economies were collected by the flagship team using a simplified version of the 2018 OECD PMR methodology, and they reflect the situation in the economy as of December 2020.

Note: Most questions are Yes/No questions, unless indicated otherwise. Y = Yes and N = No. OECD = Organisation for Economic Co-operation and Development; WBG = World Bank Group.

a. Options provided are: (1) No (it is not prohibited); (2) No (but not explicitly prohibited); (3) Yes (it provides a reference price but only in some sectors/cases); (4) Yes (it usually provides a reference price); or (5) Yes (it is required to provide a reference price).

b. Options provided are: (1) Yes (in all or most sectors); (2) Yes (only in few sectors); or (3) No.

Table A.7 Price regulation: Retail distribution

Question	Egypt, Arab Rep.	Jordan	Kuwait	Morocco	Saudi Arabia	Tunisia	United Arab Emirates	West Bank and Gaza
Are the retail prices of certain products subject to price controls/regulation?								
Staple goods (e.g., milk, bread, corn)	Y	Y	Y	Y	Y	Y	Y	Y
Gasoline	Y	Y	Y	N	Y	Y	Y	Y
Tobacco	Y	N	N	Y	N	Y	Y	N
Alcohol	N	N	N	N	N	N	N	N
All nonprescription medicines	Y	Y	Y	Y	Y	Y	Y	N
A subset of nonprescription medicines	Y	Y	Y	Y	Y	Y	Y	N
Prescription medicines	Y	Y	Y	Y	Y	Y	Y	N
Cellular communication (except international roaming)	N	Y	Y	N	Y	Y	Y	Y
Internet services	N	Y	Y	N	Y	N	Y	Y
Pre-booked taxi rides	N	Y	N	Y	Y	N	Y	N
Taxi rides hailed in the street	N	Y	N	Y	Y	N	Y	Y
Books	N	N	N	Y	N	N	N	N
CDs	N	N	N	N	N	N	N	N
LPG (liquefied petroleum gas)	Y	Y	Y	Y	Y	Y	Y	Y
Are there any special regulations prohibiting or restricting sales below costs beyond a prohibition of predatory pricing by dominant firms?	N	N	Y	Y	N	Y	N	N
Are retail tariffs for all mobile services (voice, data, and video) or a subset of them (e.g., only voice) regulated or approved by the government, ministry, regulator, or other public body?[a]	No	Yes (for all consumers, households, and business)	Yes	No	Yes (for all consumers, households, and business)	Yes	Yes (for all consumers, households, and business)	Yes (for all consumers, households, and business)

Sources: Flagship team elaboration, based on OECD and OECD-WBG Product Market Regulation (PMR) database 2018–2020. PMR data for Egypt were collected in 2017, for Kuwait in 2018, and for Tunisia in 2017. Data for the other five Middle East and North Africa (MENA) economies were collected by the flagship team using a simplified version of the 2018 OECD PMR methodology, and they reflect the situation in the economy as of December 2020.

Note: Most questions are Yes/No questions, unless indicated otherwise. Y = Yes and N = No. CDs = compact disks; OECD = Organisation for Economic Co-operation and Development; WBG = World Bank Group.

a. Options provided are: (1) Yes (for all consumers, households, and business); (2) Yes (only for household and small business); (3) Yes (only for vulnerable consumers); or (4) No. Answers for Kuwait and Tunisia are "Yes."

Table A.8 Price regulation: Price controls in network industries and regulated professions

Question	Egypt, Arab Rep.	Jordan	Kuwait	Morocco	Saudi Arabia	Tunisia	United Arab Emirates	West Bank and Gaza
Are electricity retail tariffs regulated or approved by the government, ministry, regulator, or other public body for any of these categories of consumers?[a]	Yes (for all domestic and non-domestic consumers)	Yes (for all domestic and non-domestic consumers)	Yes (for all domestic and non-domestic consumers)	Yes (for all domestic and non-domestic consumers)	Yes (for all domestic and non-domestic consumers)	Yes (for all domestic and nondomestic consumers)	Yes (for all domestic and nondomestic consumers)	Yes (for all domestic and nondomestic consumers)
If electricity retail tariffs are regulated, are there measures in place which require that the regulated retail tariffs are based on the tariffs or costs of the most efficient supplier?	N	Y	N	N	N	N	N	Y
Are gas retail tariffs regulated or approved by the government, ministry, regulator, or other public body for any of these categories of consumers?[b]	Yes (for all domestic and non-domestic consumers)	Yes (for all domestic and non-domestic consumers)	Yes (for all domestic and non-domestic consumers)	Yes (for domestic and small and medium non-domestic consumers)	Yes (for all domestic and non-domestic consumers)	Yes (for all domestic and nondomestic consumers)	Yes (for all domestic and non-domestic consumers)	No
If gas retail tariffs are regulated, are there measures in place which require that the regulated retail tariffs are based on the tariffs or costs of the most efficient supplier?	N	Y	N	N	N	N	N	N
Are the fees/tariffs that professionals and/or professional firms in the accountancy profession charge for their services regulated by government, parliament, or by the profession itself?	N	N	N	N	N	Y	N	N
If fees/prices are regulated or self-regulated, what is the nature of these regulations?[c]	—	—	—	—	—	Nonbinding recommended fees/tariffs for some activities	—	—
Are the fees/tariffs that professionals and/or professional firms in the legal profession charge for their services regulated by government, parliament, or by the profession itself?	N	N	N	N	N	Y	N	Y
If fees/prices are regulated or self-regulated, what is the nature of these regulations?[c]	—	—	—	—	—	Nonbinding recommended fees/tariffs for some activities	—	Nonbinding recommended fees/tariffs for some activities

(table continues on next page)

Table A.8 Price regulation: Price controls in network industries and regulated professions *(continued)*

Question	Egypt, Arab Rep.	Jordan	Kuwait	Morocco	Saudi Arabia	Tunisia	United Arab Emirates	West Bank and Gaza
Are the fees/tariffs that professionals and/or professional firms in the engineering profession charge for their services regulated by government, parliament, or by the profession itself?	N	N	N	N	N	Y[d]	N	Y
If fees/prices are regulated or self-regulated, what is the nature of these regulations?[c]	—	—	—	—	—	Binding maximum fees/tariffs for some activities	—	Binding minimum or fixed fees/tariffs for some activities
Are the fees/tariffs that professionals and/or professional firms in the architecture profession charge for their services regulated by government, parliament, or by the profession itself?	N	N	N	N	N	Y[d]	—	Y
If fees/prices are regulated or self-regulated, what is the nature of these regulations?[c]	—	—	—	—	—	Binding maximum fees/tariffs for some activities	—	Binding minimum or fixed fees/tariffs for some activities

Sources: Flagship team elaboration, based on OECD and OECD-WBG Product Market Regulation (PMR) database 2018–2020. PMR data for Egypt were collected in 2017, for Kuwait in 2018, and for Tunisia in 2017. Data for the other five Middle East and North Africa (MENA) economies were collected by the flagship team using a simplified version of the 2018 OECD PMR methodology, and they reflect the situation in the economy as of December 2020.

Note: Most questions are Yes/No questions, unless indicated otherwise. Y = Yes and N = No. — = not available; an answer was not provided for the specific question/economy. OECD = Organisation for Economic Co-operation and Development; WBG = World Bank Group.

a. Options provided are: (1) No, tariffs are not regulated; (2) Yes, but only for vulnerable consumers; (3) Yes, for domestic and small nondomestic consumers; (4) Yes, for domestic and small and medium nondomestic consumers; or (5) Yes, for all domestic and nondomestic consumers.

b. Options provided are the same as in note "a" above. Answer for Kuwait is "Yes."

c. Options provided are: (1) Nonbinding recommended fees/tariffs for some activities; (2) Nonbinding recommended fees/tariffs for all activities; (3) Binding maximum fees/tariffs for some activities; (4) Binding maximum fees/tariffs for all activities; (5) Binding minimum or fixed fees/tariffs for some activities; (6) Binding minimum or fixed fees/tariffs for all activities; or (7) Other (please describe).

d. Self-regulated except for civil buildings. Binding maximum prices for some services for civil buildings. Nonbinding recommended prices for all services.

Table A.9 Design regulations: Assessment of impact on competition

Question	Egypt, Arab Rep.	Jordan	Kuwait	Morocco	Saudi Arabia	Tunisia	United Arab Emirates	West Bank and Gaza
Is there a requirement to conduct a Regulatory Impact Assessment to inform the development of new primary laws?	N	N	N	Y	N	N	Y	N
When developing a Regulatory Impact Assessment are regulators required to include the assessment of the impact (i.e., costs and benefits) of a new primary law on competition?	N	N	N	N	N	N	N	N
Is there an independent body in your jurisdiction that can advocate competition at central and local government level?	Y	N	Y	Y	Y	Y	N	N

Sources: Flagship team elaboration, based on OECD and OECD-WBG Product Market Regulation (PMR) database 2018–2020. PMR data for Egypt were collected in 2017, for Kuwait in 2018, and for Tunisia in 2017. Data for the other five Middle East and North Africa (MENA) economies were collected by the flagship team using a simplified version of the 2018 OECD PMR methodology, and they reflect the situation in the economy as of December 2020.

Note: Most questions are Yes/No questions, unless indicated otherwise. Y = Yes and N = No. OECD = Organisation for Economic Co-operation and Development; WBG = World Bank Group.

Barriers to Trade and Investment

Table A.10 Barriers to domestic market entry

Question	Egypt, Arab Rep.	Jordan	Kuwait	Morocco	Saudi Arabia	Tunisia	United Arab Emirates	West Bank and Gaza
Is there an explicit program to reduce the compliance costs and administrative burdens imposed by the national government on enterprises?	Y	Y	Y	Y	Y	Y	Y	N
Is there a program underway to review and reduce the number of permits and licenses required by the national government?	Y	Y	Y	Y	Y	Y	Y	N
Is it a standard procedure to use the "silence is consent" rule for issuing licenses required to open up a business?	N	N	N	Y	N	N	N	N

Sources: Flagship team elaboration, based on OECD and OECD-WBG Product Market Regulation (PMR) database 2018–2020. PMR data for Egypt were collected in 2017, for Kuwait in 2018, and for Tunisia in 2017. Data for the other five Middle East and North Africa (MENA) economies were collected by the flagship team using a simplified version of the 2018 OECD PMR methodology, and they reflect the situation in the economy as of December 2020.
Note: Most questions are Yes/No questions, unless indicated otherwise. Y = Yes and N = No. OECD = Organisation for Economic Co-operation and Development; WBG = World Bank Group.

Table A.11 Restrictions on foreign entry

Question	Egypt, Arab Rep.	Jordan	Kuwait	Morocco	Saudi Arabia	Tunisia	United Arab Emirates	West Bank and Gaza
Is foreign ownership constrained by allowing only joint ventures in at least one sector?	Y	Y	Y	Y	Y	Y	Y	N
Is foreign ownership constrained by restricting mergers and acquisitions in at least one sector?	N	Y	Y	Y	Y	Y	Y	N
Are foreign suppliers of computer services discriminated in the application of financial or technical criteria when participating in public procurement tenders?	N	N	N	N	N	Y	N	N
Are foreign professionals prohibited from supplying their services to the government or are preferences given to local suppliers in the following professions?								
Accountancy profession	Y	Y	N	Y	Y	Y	N	N
Legal profession	Y	Y	N	Y	Y	Y	N	N
Engineering profession	Y	Y	N	Y	Y	Y	N	Y
Architecture profession	Y	Y	N	Y	Y	Y	N	Y
Are foreign telecommunication firms discriminated in the application of financial or technical criteria when participating in public procurement tenders?	N	N	N	Y	N	—	N	N

Sources: Flagship team elaboration, based on OECD and OECD-WBG Product Market Regulation (PMR) database 2018–2020. PMR data for Egypt were collected in 2017, for Kuwait in 2018, and for Tunisia in 2017. Data for the other five Middle East and North Africa (MENA) economies were collected by the flagship team using a simplified version of the 2018 OECD PMR methodology, and they reflect the situation in the economy as of December 2020.
Note: Most questions are Yes/No questions, unless indicated otherwise. Y = Yes and N = No. — = not available; an answer was not provided for the specific question/ economy. OECD = Organisation for Economic Co-operation and Development; WBG = World Bank Group.

Barriers in Network Industries and Professional Services

Table A.12 Structural separation and access regulation in network industries

Question	Egypt, Arab Rep.	Jordan	Kuwait	Morocco	Saudi Arabia	Tunisia	United Arab Emirates	West Bank and Gaza
What is the nature of vertical separation of the following sectors from electricity transmission?[a]								
Electricity generation	Legal separation	Legal separation	No separation	No separation	No separation	No separation	Legal separation	Ownership separation
Electricity retail supply	Legal separation	Ownership separation[b]	No separation	No separation	No separation	No separation	Legal separation	Ownership separation
What is the nature of vertical separation of the following other sectors from gas transmission?[a]								
Gas generation	Legal separation	Legal separation	Legal separation	No separation	No separation	No separation	Legal separation	Ownership separation
Gas retail supply	Legal separation	Ownership separation	Legal separation	No separation	No separation	No separation	Legal separation	Ownership separation
How are the terms and conditions of third-party access (TPA) to the electricity distribution networks determined?[c]	TPA is regulated	No TPA	No TPA	TPA is negotiated	No TPA	No TPA	No TPA	TPA is regulated
Is there a liberalised wholesale market for electricity (such as a bilateral market or a pool)?	N	N	N	N	N	N	N	N
How are the terms and conditions of third-party access (TPA) to the gas distribution networks determined?[c]	No TPA	No TPA	No TPA	TPA is regulated	No TPA	No TPA	No TPA	No TPA
Is there a liberalised wholesale market for gas (such as a bilateral market or a pool)?	N	N	N	Y	N	N	N	N
If there is an operator (or group of operators) that has significant/substantial market power, is this operator (or group of operators) required to provide at least one of the following?								
Access to a wholesale product (such as Bit stream or VULA)	Y	Y	N	Y	Y	—	Y	Y
Access to an unbundled product (such as unbundled local loops)	Y	Y	N	Y	Y	Y	Y	Y
Is mobile phone interconnection mandated?	Y	Y	Y	Y	Y	Y	Y	Y
Is fixed number portability mandated?	N	N	N	Y	Y	Y	Y	Y
Is mobile number portability mandated?	Y	Y	N	Y	Y	Y	Y	Y
Are the prices of the interconnection tariffs regulated directly or indirectly where one operator has significant market power?								
Access to a wholesale product (such as Bit stream or VULA)	N	Y	—	N	Y	—	Y	Y
Access to an unbundled product (such as unbundled local loops)	N	Y	Y	N	Y	Y	Y	Y
Access to infrastructure (such as ducts and poles)	N	Y	—	N	Y	—	Y	Y

(table continues on next page)

Table A.12 Structural separation and access regulation in network industries *(continued)*

Question	Egypt, Arab Rep.	Jordan	Kuwait	Morocco	Saudi Arabia	Tunisia	United Arab Emirates	West Bank and Gaza
Are mobile phone interconnection prices regulated?	N	Y	Y	Y	Y	Y	Y	Y
Are international wholesale roaming rates regulated?	N	Y	Y	N	Y	Y	Y	N
Are international retail roaming rates regulated?	N	Y	Y	N	Y	Y	Y	N

Sources: Flagship team elaboration, based on OECD-WBG Product Market Regulation (PMR) database 2018–2020. PMR data for Egypt were collected in 2017, for Kuwait in 2018, and for Tunisia in 2017. Data for the other five Middle East and North Africa (MENA) economies were collected by the flagship team using a simplified version of the 2018 OECD PMR methodology, and they reflect the situation in the economy as of December 2020.

Note: Most questions are Yes/No questions, unless indicated otherwise. Y = Yes and N = No. — = not available; an answer was not provided for the specific question/economy. OECD = Organisation for Economic Co-operation and Development; TPA = third-party access; VULA = virtual unbundling of local access; WBG = World Bank Group.

a. Options provided are: (1) No separation; (2) Accounting separation; (3) Legal separation; or (4) Ownership separation. Note that answers in the 2018 PMR are slightly different: (1) No separation; (2) Accounting/Operational separation; (3) Legal separation/Operational separation/A combination of the two; (4) Ownership separation.

b. Answer selected based on no information on government control over the Jordan Electric Power Company (JEPCO) found in this regard.

c. Options provided are: (1) TPA is regulated; (2) TPA is negotiated; or (3) No TPA.

Table A.13 Command and control (conduct) regulations in professional services

Question	Egypt, Arab Rep.	Jordan	Kuwait	Morocco	Saudi Arabia	Tunisia	United Arab Emirates	West Bank and Gaza
Are there restrictions on the legal form of business (whether imposed by law or self-regulation by professional bodies, or a combination of the two) in:[a]								
Accounting profession	Only sole proprietorship/personally owned enterprise is allowed	Only sole proprietorship/personally owned enterprise is allowed	Incorporation allowed (but not the trading of shares on stock market)	Other	No restrictions on legal form	Incorporation allowed (but not the trading of shares on stock market)	Other	Other
Legal profession	Other	Only sole proprietorship/personally owned enterprise is allowed	Incorporation allowed (but not the trading of shares on stock market)	Only sole proprietorship/personally owned enterprise is allowed	No restrictions on legal form	Incorporation allowed (but not the trading of shares on stock market)	Other	Other
Engineering profession	Only sole proprietorship/personally owned enterprise is allowed	No restrictions on legal form	Incorporation allowed (but not the trading of shares on stock market)	Other	No restrictions on legal form	Only sole proprietorship/personally owned enterprise is allowed	Other	Other
Architecture profession	Only sole proprietorship/personally owned enterprise is allowed	No restrictions on legal form	Incorporation allowed (but not the trading of shares on stock market)	Only sole proprietorship/personally owned enterprise is allowed	No restrictions on legal form	Other	Other	Other

(table continues on next page)

Table A.13 Command and control (conduct) regulations in professional services *(continued)*

Question	Egypt, Arab Rep.	Jordan	Kuwait	Morocco	Saudi Arabia	Tunisia	United Arab Emirates	West Bank and Gaza
Are there restrictions on advertising and marketing by professionals?								
Accounting profession	Y	Y	—[b]	Y	Y	Y	N	Y
Legal profession	Y	Y	Y	Y	Y	Y	Y	Y
Engineering profession	Y	Y	N	Y	N	N	N	Y
Architecture profession	Y	Y	N	N	N	Y	N	N
Provided advertising is neither false, misleading, or deceptive, are there restrictions on advertising and marketing by professionals and/or professional firms (whether imposed by law or self-regulation by professional bodies, or a combination of the two)?[c]								
Accounting profession	Yes (all forms of advertising and marketing are prohibited)	Yes (some forms of advertising and marketing are prohibited)	Yes (some forms of advertising and marketing are prohibited)	No (all forms of advertising and marketing are allowed)	No (all forms of advertising and marketing are allowed)	No (all forms of advertising and marketing are allowed)	Yes (all forms of advertising and marketing are prohibited)	Yes (all forms of advertising and marketing are prohibited)
Legal profession	Yes (all forms of advertising and marketing are prohibited)	Yes (all forms of advertising and marketing are prohibited)	Yes (all forms of advertising and marketing are prohibited)	Yes (all forms of advertising and marketing are prohibited)	No (all forms of advertising and marketing are allowed)	Yes (some forms of advertising and marketing are prohibited)	Yes (all forms of advertising and marketing are prohibited)	Yes (all forms of advertising and marketing are prohibited)
Engineering profession	Yes (some forms of advertising and marketing are prohibited)	Yes (some forms of advertising and marketing are prohibited)	Yes (all forms of advertising and marketing are prohibited)	Yes (all forms of advertising and marketing are prohibited)	No (all forms of advertising and marketing are allowed)	No (all forms of advertising and marketing are allowed)	Yes (some forms of advertising and marketing are prohibited)	No (all forms of advertising and marketing are allowed)
Architecture profession	Yes (some forms of advertising and marketing are prohibited)	Yes (some forms of advertising and marketing are prohibited)	Yes (all forms of advertising and marketing are prohibited)	Yes (all forms of advertising and marketing are prohibited)	No (all forms of advertising and marketing are allowed)	No (all forms of advertising and marketing are allowed)	Yes (some forms of advertising and marketing are prohibited)	No (all forms of advertising and marketing are allowed)

Sources: Flagship team elaboration, based on OECD-WBG Product Market Regulation (PMR) database 2018–2020. PMR data for Egypt were collected in 2017, for Kuwait in 2018, and for Tunisia in 2017. Data for the other five Middle East and North Africa (MENA) economies were collected by the flagship team using a simplified version of the 2018 OECD PMR methodology, and they reflect the situation in the economy as of December 2020.

Note: Most questions are Yes/No questions, unless indicated otherwise. Y = Yes and N = No. — = not available; an answer was not provided for the specific question/economy. OECD = Organisation for Economic Co-operation and Development; WBG = World Bank Group.

a. Options provided are: (1) No restrictions on legal form; (2) Incorporation allowed (but not the trading of shares on stock market); (3) Limited liability allowed (but not incorporation); (4) No limited liability is allowed; (5) Only sole proprietorship/personally owned enterprise is allowed; or (6) Other (please provide details in the Comments).

b. No value (answer) was provided, but a comment mentions advertising/marketing prohibited under Article of 20 (d) of Law 5 of 1981 regarding Auditors' Profession.

c. Options provided are: (1) No (all forms of advertising and marketing are allowed); (2) Yes (some forms of advertising and marketing are prohibited); or (3) Yes (all forms of advertising and marketing are prohibited).

NOTES

1. An earlier PMR methodology (2013–17) was applied to three countries in MENA to identify anticompetitive regulations: Egypt (2017), Kuwait (2018), and Tunisia (2017). For Tunisia, data collected have not been verified by the Tunisian government.

2. See World Bank, Country Grouping Classifications, Natural Resource Abundance, Growth, and Diversification in the Middle East and North Africa (September 2012), available at https://elibrary.worldbank.org/action/showCitFormats?doi=10.1596%2F9780821395912_App (last accessed March 8, 2021). The study classifies MENA countries based on resources into resource-poor labor-abundant; resource-rich labor-abundant; or resource-rich labor-importing.

3. Data used and collected for these comparator countries are based on the 2018 PMR methodology. This section uses the following income categorization: High-income countries consist of Australia, Austria, Belgium, Canada, Chile, Croatia, Cyprus, the Czech Republic, Denmark, Estonia, Finland, France, Germany, Greece, Hungary, Iceland, Ireland, Israel, Italy, Japan, the Republic of Korea, Latvia, Lithuania, Luxembourg, Malta, the Netherlands, New Zealand, Norway, Poland, Portugal, Romania, the Slovak Republic, Slovenia, Spain, Sweden, Switzerland, and the United Kingdom. Upper-middle-income countries consist of Albania, Argentina, Brazil, Bulgaria, Colombia, Costa Rica, Indonesia, Kazakhstan, Mexico, Peru, the Russian Federation, Serbia, South Africa, and Turkey. The classifications for MENA economies are high-income (Kuwait, Saudi Arabia, and the United Arab Emirates); upper-middle-income (Egypt, Jordan, Morocco, and Tunisia); and lower-middle-income (West Bank and Gaza).

REFERENCE

Vitale, Cristiana, Rosamaria Bietett, Isabelle Wanner, Eszter Danitz, and Carlotta Moiso. 2020. "The 2018 Edition of the OECD PMR Indicators and Database: Methodological Improvements and Policy Insights." OECD Economics Department Working Paper 1604, Organisation for Economic Co-operation and Development Publishing, Paris.

Appendix B | Labor Market Regulations

The main data sources about labor regulations are the World Bank Employing Workers 2020 data set, the World Bank Paying Taxes 2020 data set, International Social Security Association (ISSA) 2018–19 data, and the International Labour Organization (ILO) data bank. Data in Employing Workers 2020 and Paying Taxes 2020 are as of May 2019. To make the data comparable across countries, they are based on case assumptions about workers and employers. Therefore, some analysis reflects only a subpopulation and needs to be interpreted in light of such assumptions. For example, the Employing Workers study focuses on the regulations and laws that apply to workers in the formal private sector in the retail sector but does not cover informal or casual workers or workers in other sectors.

Table B.1 summarizes the key characteristics of labor market regulations in the Middle East and North Africa (MENA) region. MENA in this analysis includes 19 economies: Algeria, Bahrain, Djibouti, the Arab Republic of Egypt, the Islamic Republic of Iran, Iraq, Jordan, Kuwait, Lebanon, Libya, Morocco, Oman, Qatar, Saudi Arabia, the Syrian Arab Republic, Tunisia, the United Arab Emirates, West Bank and Gaza, and the Republic of Yemen.

Table B.1 Summary of labor market regulations in the MENA region

	Regulation	Algeria	Bahrain	Djibouti	Egypt, Arab Rep.	Iran, Islamic Rep.	Iraq	Jordan	Kuwait	Lebanon
Hiring rules	FTCs prohibited for permanent work	Yes	No	Yes	No	No	Yes	No	No	No
	Restrictions on night shifts	Yes	No	No	No	No	Yes	Yes	No	No
	Restrictions on overtime	No	No	Yes	No	No	No	Yes	Yes	Yes
	Restrictions on weekly rest days	No	No	No	No	No	No	No	Yes	No
Minimum wages	Minimum wage for a full-time worker (US$/month)	149.40	0.00	198.40	0.00	371.20	256.80	308.90	216.00	431.20
	Ratio of minimum wage to value added per worker	0.3	0.0	0.7	0.0	0.6	0.3	0.5	0.1	0.5
Redundancy rules	Notification requirements for the dismissal of one or a group of workers	Yes	Yes	Yes	Yes	Yes	Yes	Yes	No	Yes
	Approval requirements for the dismissal of one or a group of workers	No	No	No	Yes	Yes	Yes	Yes	No	No
	Retraining or reassignment obligation before redundancy dismissal	Yes	No	No	No	No	No	No	No	No
	Priority rules requirements for redundancy and reemployment	No	No	No	No	No	No	No	No	Yes
	Notice period for redundancy dismissal (average for workers with 1, 5, and 10 years of tenure, in weeks of salary)	4.3	4.3	4.3	10.1	0.0	0.0	4.3	13.0	8.7
	Severance pay for redundancy dismissal (average for workers with 1, 5, and 10 years of tenure, in weeks of salary)	13.0	9.3	0.0	26.7	23.1	10.7	0.0	15.1	0.0
	Availability of unemployment insurance	Yes	Yes	No	Yes	Yes	No	Yes	Yes	No
Labor tax	Statutory social security contributions (%)	34.0	20.0	14.7	40.0	22.0	0.0	21.8	18.5	14.5
	Labor tax and contributions (% of profit)	31.1	13.5	17.7	25.5	25.9	13.5	16.1	13.0	24.9
	Total tax and contribution rate (% of profit)	66.1	13.8	37.9	44.4	44.7	30.8	28.6	13.0	32.2

(table continues on next page)

Regulation		Libya	Morocco	Oman	Qatar	Saudi Arabia	Syrian Arab Republic	Tunisia	United Arab Emirates	West Bank and Gaza	Yemen, Rep.
Hiring rules	FTCs prohibited for permanent work	No	Yes	No	No	No	No	No	No	No	No
	Restrictions on night shifts	No	No	Yes	Yes	No	No	No	No	Yes	No
	Restrictions on overtime	No	No	Yes	Yes	No	No	No	No	No	No
	Restrictions on weekly rest days	No	Yes	No	No	Yes	Yes	No	Yes	Yes	No
Minimum wages	Minimum wage for a full-time worker (US$/month)	284.50	266.40	781.90	0.00	0.00	37.10	251.90	0.00	403.80	38.20
	Ratio of minimum wage to value added per worker	0.4	0.7	0.5	0.0	0.0	0.3	0.6	0.0	0.8	0.3
Redundancy rules	Notification requirements for the dismissal of one or a group of workers	Yes	Yes	No	No	No	Yes	Yes	No	Yes	Yes
	Approval requirements for the dismissal of one or a group of workers	No	Yes	No	No	No	Yes	Yes	No	No	No
	Retraining or reassignment obligation before redundancy dismissal	No	Yes	No	No	No	No	Yes	No	No	No
	Priority rules requirements for redundancy and reemployment	No	Yes	No	No	No	No	Yes	No	No	No
	Notice period for redundancy dismissal (average for workers with 1, 5, and 10 years of tenure, in weeks of salary)	4.3	7.2	0.0	7.2	8.6	8.7	4.3	4.3	4.3	4.3
	Severance pay for redundancy dismissal (average for workers with 1, 5, and 10 years of tenure, in weeks of salary)	15.2	13.5	0.0	16.0	15.2	0.0	17.2	0.0	23.1	23.1
	Availability of unemployment insurance	No	Yes	No	No	Yes	No	Yes	No	No	No
Labor tax	Statutory social security contributions (%)	14.25	19.86	18.5	15.0	22.0	24.1	24.65	0.0	0.0	16.0
	Labor tax and contributions (% of profit)	10.3	23.3	13.0	11.3	13.5	19.3	25.3	14.1	0.0	11.3
	Total tax and contribution rate (% of profit)	32.6	45.8	27.4	11.3	15.7	42.7	60.7	15.9	15.3	26.6

Sources: World Bank, Employing Workers 2020; World Bank, Paying Taxes 2020; International Social Security Association (ISSA) 2018–19 data.
Note: FTCs = fixed-term contracts.

Appendix C | Gendered Laws in the MENA Region

To demonstrate where laws facilitate or hinder women's economic participation, the Women, Business and the Law database presents an index structured around the life cycle of a working woman. To ensure comparability across each economy, the woman in question is assumed to reside in the main business city of her economy and to be employed in the formal sector. Eight indicators constructed around women's interactions with the law as they begin, progress through, and end their careers are used to align different areas of the law with the economic decisions women make at various stages of their lives. The eight indicators are mobility, workplace, pay, marriage, parenthood, entrepreneurship, assets, and pension.

The Women, Business and the Law data set is constructed using laws and regulations that are currently in force. Unless they are codified, religious and customary laws are not considered. Because the indicators serve as a basis for legal equality of opportunity, implementation of laws is also not measured. In total, 35 questions are scored across the eight indicators. Overall scores are then calculated by taking the average of each indicator, with 100 representing the highest possible score. The resulting data set allows the index to function as an easily replicable way to benchmark the regulatory environment for women as entrepreneurs and employees.

Table C.1 summarizes the results from the Women, Business and the Law Survey of 19 economies in the Middle East and North Africa (MENA) region for the year 2020. The 20 MENA economies are Algeria, Bahrain, Djibouti, the Arab Republic of Egypt, the Islamic Republic of Iran, Iraq, Jordan, Kuwait, Lebanon, Libya, Morocco, Oman, Qatar, Saudi Arabia, the Syrian Arab Republic, Tunisia, the United Arab Emirates, West Bank and Gaza, and the Republic of Yemen.

Table C.1 Results from the Women, Business and the Law Survey for the MENA region, 2020

Indicator	Question		Trend (% of economies)		
Mobility	Can a woman choose where to live in the same way as a man?	Yes	50	50	No
	Can a woman travel outside her home in the same way as a man?	Yes	45	55	No
	Can a woman apply for a passport in the same way as a man?	Yes	70	30	No
	Can a woman travel outside the country in the same way as a man?	Yes	65	35	No
Workplace	Can a woman get a job in the same way as a man?	Yes	55	45	No
	Does the law prohibit discrimination in employment based on gender?	Yes	70	30	No
	Is there legislation on sexual harassment in employment?	Yes	55	45	No
	Are there criminal penalties or civil remedies for sexual harassment in employment?	Yes	55	45	No
Pay	Does the law mandate equal remuneration for work of equal value?	Yes	45	55	No
	Can a woman work at night in the same way as a man?	Yes	50	50	No
	Can a woman work in a job deemed dangerous in the same way as a man?	Yes	35	65	No
	Can a woman work in an industrial job in the same way as a man?	Yes	45	55	No
Marriage	Is there no legal provision that requires a married woman to obey her husband?	Yes	50	50	No
	Can a woman be head of household in the same way as a man?	Yes	55	45	No
	Is there legislation specifically addressing domestic violence?	Yes	55	45	No
	Can a woman obtain a judgment of divorce in the same way as a man?	Yes	10	90	No
	Does a woman have the same rights to remarry as a man?	Yes	5	95	No
Parenthood	Is paid leave of at least 14 weeks available to mothers?	Yes	40	60	No
	Does the government pay 100% of maternity leave benefits?	Yes	25	75	No
	Is paid leave available to fathers?	Yes	50	50	No
	Is there paid parental leave?	Yes	5	95	No
	Is dismissal of pregnant workers prohibited?	Yes	50	50	No
Entrepreneur-ship	Does the law prohibit discrimination in access to credit based on gender?	Yes	35	65	No
	Can a woman sign a contract in the same way as a man?	Yes	100	0	No
	Can a woman register a business in the same way as a man?	Yes	100	0	No
	Can a woman open a bank account in the same way as a man?	Yes	100	0	No
Assets	Do men and women have equal ownership rights to immovable property?	Yes	100	0	No
	Do sons and daughters have equal rights to inherit assets from their parents?	Yes	5	95	No
	Do female and male surviving spouses have equal rights to inherit assets?	Yes	5	95	No
	Does the law grant spouses equal administrative authority over assets during marriage?	Yes	100	0	No
	Does the law provide for the valuation of nonmonetary contributions?	Yes	5	95	No
Pension	Is the age at which men and women can retire with full pension benefits the same?	Yes	30	70	No
	Is the age at which men and women can retire with partial pension benefits the same?	Yes	70	30	No
	Is the mandatory retirement age for men and women the same?	Yes	80	20	No
	Are periods of absence due to childcare accounted for in pension benefits?	Yes	45	55	No

Source: World Bank, Women, Business and the Law 2021.

www.ingramcontent.com/pod-product-compliance
Lightning Source LLC
Chambersburg PA
CBHW050907210326
41597CB00002B/57